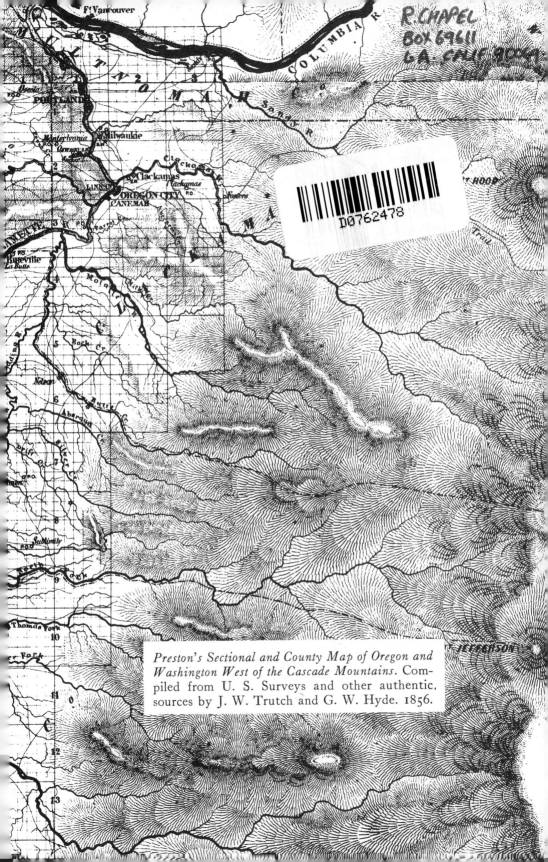

Preston's Sectional and County Map of Oregon and Washington West of the Cascade Mountains. Compiled from U. S. Surveys and other authentic. sources by J. W. Trutch and G. W. Hyde. 1856.

Views on cover and title page show celebrations at Champoeg landing and monument site on Willamette River. Near here was heart of early Oregon grain and agricultural development, as well as location of 1843 meeting to form Oregon's Provisional Government. Cover view (1905) shows *Pomona*, one of three steamboats which brought excursionists. *Ruth* and *Oregona* (shown here) came in 1907. and others in many following years. Champoeg meeting site (1843) was determined by Governor T. T. Geer, George H. Himes (Asst. Sec. of Oregon Historical Society) and participant F. X. Matthieu, in 1900. Later park development added much in area and enjoyable dimensions to site (OHS Cols.).

WILLAMETTE LANDINGS

Ghost Towns of the River

by

Howard McKinley Corning

SECOND EDITION
OREGON HISTORICAL SOCIETY
PORTLAND, OREGON

1973

INTRODUCTION

WHEN the settlers along the Atlantic coast had disposed of the soldiers of George III, and forced a peace, and set up a nation to be known as the "United States of America," they promptly forgot about the Old World, so far as they could. They turned with all possible dispatch to home affairs. They thought, in particular, of the untold and virtually unknown riches to the westward, beyond Cumberland Gap, the headwaters of the Ohio and the other passes of the Alleghenies leading to the interior of the continent. And, since thought was the equivalent of action with these pioneer Americans, they promptly departed, by whatever means they could manage, through the mountain passes into the continent.

And this is something which we tend to forget, since so much intervenes to obscure our picture of that old migration: They did not fan out across plains and through forests when they made that crossing. There were no roads. There were no railways. And, coming from the seacoasts and the coastal rivers, they were used to water traffic. So they followed down the reaches of the Ohio and the reaches of the Tennessee, and followed up the tributaries of these and other rivers. They settled as close as possible to the banks, and once settled they used the network of rivers and streams for highways. This method of settlement and this way of life were so striking that in the final decades of the Eighteenth century and the first decades of the Nineteenth century, the men of the migration into the interior of the continent were known as the "Men of the Western Waters."

First there were the flatboats, or scows, and the many varieties of rowboats and canoes. Sail was used at times. Then steam power. And the river flourished into greater and greater importance.

It was toward the end of this period of river greatness— but still in that period—that the westernmost of the pioneers began moving from the Mississippi Valley to the Pacific Coast; specifically, so far as most of the farmers were concerned, to the Willamette Valley in Oregon. During the 1840's, their wagon wheels dug the ruts of the Oregon Trail.

In the latter years of that decade there was the California gold rush to deepen those ruts. And all through the 1850's, and after, the wagons rolled on and the ruts worked farther into the hard plain and the harder mountains.

But these travelers were still the "Men of the Western Waters." They had not yet accepted the plain. Entering the valley of the Willamette, they did as they had been accustomed to do. The first of them established their farms on the banks of the Willamette. The next followed up the tributaries. Those a little later, and so excluded from these choicer sites, nevertheless crowded as close as possible. And all promptly began using the stream for the transport of their crops to market, for their journeys to town, and for their visits in the neighborhood. This was particularly necessary because of the sogginess of the land in the rainy season. Steam-use was logical, and, besides, romance just then surrounded the steamboat. So scores of landings were built along the Willamette, and many more along tributaries that today look unnavigable.

It is this story of development that is told in *Willamette Landings*. Here is the record of the boisterous and yet bucolic years of river traffic. And of course the story ends with the construction of railways and roads, over which produce and people could move swiftly and more directly. And so the old landings were left to fall into decay or to be carried away by the freshets.

The historian always finds it an adventure to come upon a good study, such as this, in some comparatively new field. But this book is more than just a good study. It has been done with due regard for the romance and the drama involved, and in admirable literary style. The layman will get as much pleasure as the historian in the reading of this book.

PHILIP H. PARRISH

1947

REPRISE

RESEARCH for this book was begun by the WPA Oregon Writers' project in 1936, under the general supervision of Dean Alfred Powers of the State System of Higher Education. Seven or eight persons worked on it until 1938 when Howard McKinley Corning was assigned to assemble all earlier work and write the final draft. This he did, using the considerable body of able research and the partial writing of others; he concluded the manuscript in 1939. At the time the Writers' Project was terminated in 1942, the manuscript had not been published, and was sent with other material to the Oregon State Library. In 1945 the manuscript was released to the Oregon Historical Society, where much of the research had originally been done, and was again turned over to the writer, who prepared the copy published in the original edition of 1947.

In this study, the reality of actual scene, together with a compounding of human events and natural occurrences, guided the author's endeavors toward evolving something of the warm storylike manner of Oregon living in earlier, simpler times. History is not facts only, but is pulse and breath, a human record—just as also it is a narrative of recollection, retold years later and drawn from many lives, all conditioned by individual, sometimes unique circumstances. Above all, facts must be honored, but legend too is history.

Special acknowledgment must be made to the good work done by the book's first editor, Verne Bright, and to staff members Charles Oluf Olsen, Joseph R. McLoughlin, Curtis Merrick, Leland Gilbert, Andrew Sherbert and Robert Wilmot. Credit also is due to Claire Warner Churchill, under whose direct supervision the work was carried on during 1936-39.

For this second edition the book has been reviewed for accuracy of fact and historical emphasis, and a few nominal warranted adjustments have been made. Finally, a third of a century after its writing, the author has added a new chapter, looking at the Willamette and its changing life over recent times and as it exists today. In reconsidered instances some old facts wear new perspectives, more recent facts provide new concerns. For added understanding, a selection of maps, early and more recent, have been provided, those of original land survey being furnished by the U. S. Bureau of Land Management. Descriptive interest has been aided significantly by an assortment of photographs, some picturing old communities and river-life activities, including also many photos of the boats that plied the Willamette, gathered from OHS files. A handful of present-day photos view the river as we see it.

For helpful aid in field and map work, and some good editorial counsel in preparation of the additional chapter, the author's appreciation is extended to Richard H. Corning, his son. Many photo sources also warrant his thanks. And again, Mrs. Lewis A. McArthur has read the material with the eye and knowledge of the long-conversant Oregon historian. *Willamette Landings* is republished under the sponsorship of the Oregon Historical Society, as originally, and with the aid of its Western Imprints Fund and the Louis and Maud Hill Family Foundation. Finally, my special gratitude and thanks to Tom Vaughan, Priscilla Knuth and photographer Maurice Hodge of the Oregon Historical Society for their exceptional contributions to this new publication.

HOWARD MCKINLEY CORNING

1973

CONTENTS

Passenger steamboat going down Willamette.
Portland, Oregon, 1900.
(Seufert Col., OHS)

ILLUSTRATIONS

MAPS AND PLATS

WILLAMETTE LANDINGS

Oregon City (note Imperial Mills), with steamboats above and below the Falls, photo by Watkins, 1867. (OHS Cols.)

THE WILLAMETTE is one of the few American rivers of any volume flowing north. It is the largest river contained wholly within the state of Oregon.

"Lying like a cupped leaf dropped on the map of Oregon, with its veins the tributaries and its stem the main artery," wrote Verne Bright, the Oregon poet, in 1941, "the Willamette drains twelve thousand square miles of territory. Precisely confined by the snow-tipped Cascade Range, the ancient Calapooyas, and the newer elevations of the Coast Range, it gathers moisture from the east, south and west, and in one tremendous north-flowing stream, pours it toward the Columbia. From the stem of the leaf where the Willamette enters the Columbia to the distant tip where the least faint stream fades in a mountain-side trickle, the veins are numerous and varied. Some, like the Tualatin, the Pudding, and the Long Tom are deceptively sluggish much of the year. . . Other branches, like the Clackamas, the Santiam, the Molalla, and the McKenzie are as unruly as the sound of their names. . ."

From the mountainous region at the head of the valley, the Willamette emerges as three forks. The Coast Fork bubbles from a mountain spring in a deeply forested wilderness. The Middle Fork flows from the base of Emigrant Butte, which towers over the pioneer road that threads through the Calapooyas. These two streams join in the valley's upper reaches. At a second point, not many miles below and to the north, the third fork, the McKenzie, joins the other two. To this fountain-head stream, in 1812, came Donald McKenzie, of Astor's Pacific Fur Company, exploring the river's possibilities as a source of beaver skins; but not for at least fifteen years more was it given his name. The courageous Scotsman did not guess the origin of the swift waters, though he must have glimpsed the white crests of the Three Sisters, from whose base they rise, to the eastward in the Cascades.

The Willamette River had not one, but several discoverers, for no single man first saw more than a portion of its

190-mile length. Peering through the haze of late October, 1792, the English navigator, Lieutenant William R. Broughton, was first of all white men to sight the river's mouth. A member of the British maritime expedition of Captain George Vancouver, he had sailed up the "River of the West," the Columbia, beyond reach of his master's heavier-burdened vessel, and so entered the Willamette and its history.

Thirteen years passed before Captains Meriwether Lewis and William Clark, overland trail-breakers to the unknown West, entered the Oregon Country. They and their men were destined to pass unknowingly the mouth of the river Willamette, both on the journey to and from the Pacific. Returning, their eyes intently eastward, they ascended the Columbia River as far as the mouth of the Sandy before they were aware of their oversight. On April 2, 1806, Captain Clark, he of the red thatch and the nimble but poor-spelling pen, was informed by visiting Indians of a "river which discharges itself into the Columbia on its south side some miles below us," and "runs a considerable distance to the south between the Mountains." Clark thereupon took a small party and returned. He wrote in his *Journal:* "I entered this river . . . called Multnomah . . . from a nation who reside on Wappato Island, a little below the enterence. . ."

The following day, the record shows, he proceeded a few miles upstream, but the mist over the gray waters was so thick he could see but a short distance up the bending river. Yet when he left he was "perfectly satisfied of the size of the magnitude of this great river which must water that vast tract of Country between the Western range of mountains and those on the sea coast as far S. as the waters of California."

After the passing of Lewis and Clark over the curve of the continent, the name of the little-known river changed from Multnomah to Willamette—but sometimes with devious spellings; for so the stream was called by the trader-travelers, Gabriel Franchere, Alexander Ross and Ross Cox, all of whom left reputable records.

For the first dwellers along the Willamette—the native races—the river had no name. Instead, areas of the green-banked waterway were known after the tribes dwelling within them. Multnomah, as the lower river was first called, was the name of the resident Indian tribe, dwellers on Wappato Island and in scattered camps along the west bank of the river southward to *Hyas Tyee Tumwater*, or "the falls," twenty-five miles inland. In like fashion the red inhabitants dwelling along the stream known as the Clackamas and which debouched from the east just below the falls, were of that tribal name. Above this area of brawling waters lived the Clough-we-wallahs, along the Willamette's eastern shore; but no geographical feature retains their name.

Spreading over the wide Tualatin Plains, westward of the Willamette waters, wandered the Tuality Indians, or the Atfaliti Tribe, giving their name to the meandering river that drains this beautiful expanse, and sharing, not too willingly, their "good hunting" with visiting Klickitats and Snakes from east of the Cascades.

Southward in the valley dwelt other tribes, the Molallas and Santiams to the east, the Yamhills to the west, and centrally throughout the wide prairies and into the foothills and mountains of the south, dwelt the wandering Calapooyas. All of these tribes had central camps by principal streams. Thus, from native tribes, most of the river tributaries of the Willamette acquired names, usually of white bestowal but of red origin.

Of the name Willamette itself, at least one historian of an early day claims that the term was first used to designate a place on the river's west bank—"green waters"—just below the falls. Probably no tribe bore the name. Undergoing various spellings, it crystallized into the present accepted form with the visit in 1841 of Lieutenant Charles Wilkes of the United States Exploring Expedition.

The native dwellers of the Willamette were greatly dwindled in numbers when the white settlers came. Historians attribute their rapid decline during the last of the eighteenth and the early nineteenth centuries to epidemics directly or indirectly traceable to maritime traders into the Columbia, to smallpox and scarlet fever and other foreign ailments, and to the natives' usually fatal methods of combating illness by means of sweat-baths followed by cold plunges. Thus, with the advent of white homeseekers, the aborigines were already releasing, unwittingly and tragically, the land of their forebears. More than eighty per cent of their once large numbers had perished. As a consequence, the Indians put up little resistance to white occupation.

Along the tributaries, in the evergreen wilderness from which the Willamette emerges, are occasional waterfalls. But on the main river there is only the one great overleap, known as Willamette Falls. As early as 1838, in his *Journal of an Exploring Tour Beyond the Rocky Mountains*, the Rev. Samuel Parker wrote in somewhat romantic vein of this geographic feature:

"The river above spreads out into a wide, deep basin, and runs slowly and smoothly until within a half mile of the falls, when its velocity increases, its width diminishes, eddies are formed in which the water turns back as if loath to make the plunge; but it is forced forward by the water in the rear, and when still nearer it breaks upon the volcanic rocks scattered across the channel, and then as if resigned to its fate, smooths its agitated surges, and precipitates down an almost perpendicular . . . presenting a somewhat whitened column . . . The rising mist formed in the rays of the sun a beautiful bow. . ."

Of the extensive Willamette country, much of a descriptive nature appears in the accounts of early day travelers through the region. Joel Palmer, settler, mill owner and early Indian agent, in his *Journal of Travels over the Rocky Mountains, 1845–46*, makes this observation: "The Willamette valley, including the first plateaus of the Cascade and Coast ranges, may be said to average a width of about sixty, and a length of about two hundred miles. It is beautifully diversified with timber and prairie."

Of this diversity, Lieutenant Wilkes wrote in his *Narrative of the United States Exploring Expedition* into the Oregon country in 1841: "The prairies are at least one-third greater in extent than the forest; they were again seen carpeted with the most luxuriant growth of flowers, of the richest tints of red, yellow and blue, extending in places a distance of fifteen to twenty miles."

"Many of the prairies . . .," remarked J. Quinn Thornton, Oregon settler of 1846, "are several miles in extent. But the smaller ones . . . where the woodland and plain alternate frequently, are the most beautiful, although the prospect is more confined. . . The space between these small prairies is covered with an open forest of tall, straight evergreens. . . The clusters of trees are so beautifully arranged, the openings so gracefully curved, the grounds so open and clean, that it seems to be the work of art; and these beautiful avenues are calculated to cheat the imagination into the belief that they lead to some farmhouse or pleasant village."

There were, however, noticeable differences in the extreme lower and upper valley. The lower Willamette, from its mouth to the falls, was darkly covered with evergreens and had few openings. Only the cottonwoods and alders held their yellow torches against the autumn sky. Mountains stood closer. Of the upper valley, "the narrowing toward its head," observed Frances Fuller Victor, Oregon historian, in 1872, in *All Over Oregon and Washington*, "brings mountains, plains, and groves within the sweep of unassisted vision, and the whole resembles a grand picture. We have not here the heavy forests of the Columbia River region, nor even the frequently recurring fir-groves of the Middle Wallamet. The foothills of the mountains approach within a few miles of either side, but those nearest the valley are rounded, grassy knolls, over which are scattered groups of firs, pines, or oaks, while the river-bottom is bordered with tall cottonwoods, and studded rather closely with pines of a lofty height and noble form."

Settlement in the beautiful valley began about 1829–30, when released Hudson's Bay Company trappers, principally French -Canadians, located farms on the rich prairies above the falls. Soon thereafter came the first American settlers, a mere handful. In 1834, a group of Methodist missionaries, headed by the Rev. Jason Lee, arrived, building a mission station on the southern fringe of French Prairie. Father F. N. Blanchet and other Catholic priests came in 1838 and established a mission on the prairie. George Ebbert, Joseph Meek, Robert Newell, Caleb Wilkins, and other American "mountain men" out of the Rockies, entered

the region with their Indian wives and half-breed children
to make homes. By 1840 there were a few hundred settlers
established in the area between the Willamette Falls and the
Jason Lee mission on the central Willamette bottoms and
across the river on the Tuality Plains to the northwest.

Joseph Drayton's 1841 sketch of Indians fishing at Willamette Falls.
(Original at OHS, A. N. Morgan Collection.)

THE LOWER WILLAMETTE AND THE TOWNS THAT GREW

CULTIVATION of the land, not the founding of towns, was the primary purpose of the pioneers. Many an immigrant, his last dollar spent to reach the fertile land of promise, could only turn to the soil for livelihood.

Most of them selected claims convenient to waterways which would furnish routes of travel not only on social and political errands but, most important of all, on trips to and from the centers of trade.

The earliest points of commerce were the Hudson's Bay Company stores at Vancouver, on the Columbia, and the fur station at Champoeg, a small supply depot operated almost exclusively for trappers of the company and ex-trappers turned farmers.

With the American invasion of the Pacific Northwest, Dr. John McLoughlin, Chief Factor of the Hudson's Bay Company, foresaw the early decline of the fur trade and the rise of agriculture and industry. Modifying the company's usual policy of non-assistance to settlers, the "White-Headed Eagle" of the Columbia district shared with some of the more needy the resources of the great fur company. Through that assistance many Americans were enabled to obtain and maintain a foothold in the new country.

Although there were a few exceptions, early Oregon settlements tended to be communal in character. There was the group of French-Canadian trapper-settlers on French Prairie, with Champoeg as its center; and the teaching unit of the Methodist Church to the south where the missionaries had established a school primarily to teach the Indian children—an event that actually stimulated the occupation of the Oregon Country. But town-founding was not a motive of either group.

A few individuals, however, did envision towns in the wilderness. The first of those forest municipalities was a mere figment of fancy platted on paper in 1832 by Hall J. Kelley, a Boston schoolmaster. The "city" he proposed sprawled over the moist, sometimes flooded lowland penin-

sula that thrusts like a wet thumb between the Columbia
River and the upper mouth of the Willamette. For several
years Kelley made urgent appeal to East Coast dwellers,
seeking to enlist west-bound settlers who would bring to
reality his dream of an Oregon empire. This appeal served
to fire the imagination of one Easterner, Nathaniel J. Wyeth,
also of Boston, who in 1832 and again in 1834 led expedi-
tions across the continent to set himself up in business as a
trader in the new country.

Ignoring Kelley's townsite, Wyeth built Fort William
(around which he hoped to establish a town) on the west
side of Sauvie or Wappato Island. But circumstances moved
against him and he retraced his way eastward, never to return.

In 1829, Dr. John McLoughlin, anticipating needs not to
be supplied by the soil or wilderness bounty, laid claim to
the area immediately adjacent to the east shore of the river
at "the Falls." Because of settlement on French Prairie,
where wheat-raising was begun, a flour mill was needed. To
make the operation of one feasible, the Hudson's Bay Company, in 1832, blasted out sufficient rock from the fall's
eastern fringe to clear a narrow but free-flowing mill-race.
A flour mill and sawmill were soon in operation. In the
middle 'thirties three log cabins were erected and a field
planted to potatoes. McLoughlin, in 1840, found it expedi-
ent to establish a trading station there, for the receipt of
furs and the issuing of supplies to the Hudson's Bay Company trappers.

Strategically situated on the main water artery up the
Willamette Valley, the Falls soon became the principal
trading point and overnight stop for travelers. Portage of
boats and supplies around the falls was necessary; usually
one night was spent in rest. There Jason Lee, and his companion missionaries, tarried for sleep on trips up and down
the river in 1834 and after. There evangelizing members
later returned to establish a mission.

In 1841 Lieutenant Wilkes wrote in his report: "We
reached the falls about noon where we found the missionary
station under charge of Rev. Mr. Waller. The Hudson's Bay
Company have a trading post there and are packing fish
which the Indians catch in great quantities."

In the same year the Island Milling Company built saw- and gristmills on an island in mid-stream at the falls. George Abernethy, a Methodist Mission settler of 1840, opened a Mission store and in competition with the Hudson's Bay Company bought wheat from the settlers and salmon from the Indians, and shipped these products to Honolulu to be traded for sugar, molasses and other needed commodities. A boat transported passengers from Clackamas Rapids, three miles below the Mission community, to the foot of the falls.

In 1842 a small overland migration of 137 persons under Dr. Elijah White arrived and began to build houses for winter shelter. That same year, too, Dr. McLoughlin, who from the first claimed the entire falls property but gener- ously shared its advantages for settlement, hired Sidney Walter Moss to survey a townsite at the water's edge. He thereupon called the location Oregon City. It was the first townsite south of the Columbia River.

In 1843, following preliminary steps toward the formation of provisional government in the Pacific Northwest, Oregon City became the first seat of government. In 1844 the first legislature met there. In that year the town was replatted, the first brick house built—by Abernethy—and the first furniture factory opened. In 1846 the first issue of the *Oregon Spectator* was pulled from a hand-press operated by William G. T'Vault.

From the very beginning the town had a significant life. There all civil and military action affecting the well-being of the new country was taken. There the majority of settlers rested after the long westward journey and there they re- outfitted for the final miles of travel to permanent homesites in the Willamette and adjacent valleys. A few remained, however, to build the town. "As settlers advanced," wrote Eva Emery Dye in a sketch of Oregon City published in Joseph H. Gaston's *Portland, Its History and Builders*, in 1911, "the Indians moved their camps to the first bench, the second, and finally to the third . . . sixty feet back under the rocks the Indians used to lie in wet weather and look down upon the building of the settlement."

The Cayuse War east of the Cascade Range, in the late

'forties, and the capture and hanging in 1850 of the Marcus Whitman murderers, created great excitement in local life. Late in 1847, to avenge the deaths of the missionary, his wife Narcissa, and twelve others, the "Oregon Rifles" was organized at Oregon City. That was the second military force organized for the protection of Oregon Country settlers.

In 1849 the Mounted Rifle Regiment crossed the plains to Oregon, to provide Federal protection for the newly created Oregon Territory. This regiment was stationed at Oregon City for more than a year.

The 'fifties were years of growth. A female seminary was opened in the town, and the Willamette Iron Works began the manufacture of sawmill parts. Oregon City found itself in competition with Linn City, a companion town with industrial ambitions, across the river. "Gold rush" money from California and from the southern Oregon mines stimulated commercial development. Finally, in 1864 Oregon's first woolen mill utilized the power of the falls. Soon afterward a paper mill, the first on the Pacific Coast, began the manufacture of paper.

Down river, another small town was bidding for growth. Linnton, situated on the west bank of the Willamette just above Sauvie Island, was platted in 1844 by M. M. McCarver and Peter H. Burnett, immigrants of the previous year. McCarver had dreams of a city that would stand at this point near the Willamette's mouth and where his only conceivable handicap lay in not securing nails soon enough to build his city before some other enterprising individual built one of promise elsewhere. But growing impatient, he departed for the Puget Sound country where he later founded Tacoma. Linnton, however, was not doomed, but struggled on as a shipping point through the decades and into another century, eventually to become a small lumber-mill town.

Of Linnton townsite, and another greater city to be, Jesse A. Applegate, son of Lindsay Applegate, wrote in *Recollections of My Boyhood:*

"Not long after passing Linnton we landed on the west shore, and went into camp on the high bank where there was little underbrush among the pine trees. No one lived there and the place had no name; there was nothing to show that the place had ever been visited except a small log hut near the river, and a broken mast of a ship leaning against the high bank. There were chips hewn from timber, showing that probably a new mast had been made there. We were at this place a day or two and were visited by two men from the prairie country up the river, then known as the 'plains.' "

"Where we should locate was the all-absorbing topic of conversation at this camp in the woods. It seemed to be difficult to decide where to settle down in such a vast unappropriated wilderness. We were then actually encamped on the site of the city of Portland, but there was no prophet with us to tell of the beautiful city that was to take the place of that gloomy forest."

Every townsite founder on the lower Willamette believed he had indisputable reasons why his chosen location would become the great city of Oregon. First, the lower river was the natural gateway to the expansive upper country. Along the Willamette must pass much of the valley trade and from its mouth must go the deep-sea commerce of the entire region. Where then would the future great city stand? Surely at the head of navigation. And where was the feasible head of navigation? At the foot of Willamette Falls? Just below the rock-strewn mouth of the Clackamas River? Was Swan Island an obstacle in the channel? Was there any reason why ships should sail farther inland than the head of Sauvie Island where the Willamette divided its channel? Each town founder of the 'forties and early 'fifties, claimed the advantages of his location and invited public settlement.

"The situation of Portland," reported the British officers Henry J. Warre, and M. Vavasour, visiting the country in 1845, "is superior to that of Linnton, and the back country easier of access." That the site faced deep water added to its promise as a port. Conscious of these factors, A. L. Lovejoy and Francis W. Pettygrove surveyed the Portland townsite in 1844-45. The property had been obtained by them from William Overton, a destitute Tennessean, who late in 1843 landed there from an Indian canoe. Lacking the filing fee required by enactment of the provisional government, Overton interested Lovejoy and Pettygrove in the property, offering them one-half ownership if they would secure the title. The quick eye of Lovejoy saw the advantages of this spot where Indians sometimes camped, and the three men soon completed the transaction. But before improvement could be made, Overton became restless and sold his interest to Pettygrove for fifty dollars.

Lovejoy, a native of Massachusetts, had read the glowing literature circulated in the East by Kelley, and under its influence emigrated to Oregon in 1842 with the Elijah White party. *En route* he was detained by Marcus Whitman at Waiilatpu, and with him made a return ride in the dead of winter. The following spring he joined the "Great Migration" and again set out for Oregon. This time he reached "the settlements." That same year of 1843, Pettygrove, a native of Maine, entered the Columbia River aboard the bark *Victoria*. With him came his family and a stock of merchandise. The latter he exchanged at Oregon City for a quantity of French Prairie wheat, which he then shipped abroad. With money thus obtained he built the first log cabin on his Portland claim.

A few lots sold before the town had any name. That name was ceremoniously chosen—not at Portland but at Oregon City—by the flipping of a coin. Lovejoy wished the new town to be named Boston, while Pettygrove wanted it to be called Portland. Two of three tosses fell in Pettygrove's favor, and Portland became the name of the new town among the fir stumps.

Growth started slowly. For nearly three years the majority of emigrants paused there only briefly, then passed on to settle in the ample Tualatin Plains or around Oregon City, or on the broad prairies higher up the Willamette.

One of the first to linger was James Terwilliger, who erected a blacksmith shop. Pettygrove put up a store but for a time had little business. Sailing vessels, with growing frequency anchored in the river and enjoyed more trade exchanging imported cargo for furs and wheat, than did Pettygrove as a merchant. On an adjacent claim Daniel H. Lownsdale started a tannery. Presently a road mounted westward out of town.

Next, John Waymire came to build the first double log cabin and did also a small hauling business with a pair of oxen. He also started a sawmill with an overhead whipsaw brought from Missouri. In operating it the man beneath received a face full of sawdust each time he pulled the blade down.

The products of a shingle mill, begun about that time by William Bennett, were sold to the incoming settlers; among them were Col. William King, the town's first politician, and Dr. Ralph Wilcox, a physician, who, besides tending the local ill, became Portland's first school teacher. Another merchant, J. L. Morrison, dealt in flour, feed and shingles.

Meanwhile, a rival town was growing nearby. A few miles up the Willamette on the opposite shore, Lot Whitcomb had platted Milwaukie in 1848. Whitcomb claimed loudly that his wharves stood at the all-time head of navigation. The towns above, he vigorously pointed out, were cut off from that advantage by the gravel bar which the inflowing Clackamas had dumped into the Willamette channel. Only a few deep-sea vessels had then ever negotiated that obstruction. The fall's towns hotly protested Whitcomb's claim, although finally acknowledged the "sand-bagging." Consequently, as a port, Milwaukie prospered for several years.

But there were shoals lying a few miles downstream, and with Portland harbor so readily accessible, Milwaukie was, in the early 1850s, abandoned by sea-going commerce. Thereafter her livelihood was maintained by riverboats and by her sawmills. In later years she became a town of moderate size, largely detached from river life.

Discovery of gold in California in 1848 brought increased business to Portland. Although many men left to seek their fortunes, enough remained to handle the extensive trade with the distant gold-fields. More and more vessels put in for cargo, with lumber the chief commodity for shipment. Gold dust augmented grain and peltry as mediums of exchange.

The arrival of Captains John H. Couch and George H. Flanders in 1849 gave Portland great impetus as a seaport. Couch was interested in several vessels, and was soon doing a large buying and selling trade with the back-country ranchers who hauled produce to Portland docks for ocean shipment, principally to the Sandwich Islands. He also induced other craft to tie up in Portland harbor. Nathaniel Crosby who earlier had founded a "paper" town he named Milton, on Multnomah Channel, engaged in similar commerce, and built Portland's first commodious residence. New settlers staked claims and felled timbers. The town's perspectives widened.

In 1850–51 Portland townsite owners—her founders had been replaced by Stephen Coffin, William W. Chapman, and Daniel H. Lownsdale—began negotiations that led to the purchase in California of the sidewheel steamer *Goldhunter*. At Milwaukie, Lot Whitcomb, builder of the riverboat that bore his name, also acted as agent for a line of ocean vessels.

Portland was incorporated in 1851, and in the same year three brick buildings were erected. The advent of steam craft on the river added greatly to the town's prosperity. And as population increased, river commerce grew. Imports destined for distribution inland were unloaded at Portland wharves and transferred to riverboats. The Rev. Ezra Fisher of Oregon City, visiting the growing town in January, 1853, described it in unemotional but promising terms: "Portland is the principal port in Oregon. The present population is estimated at seven hundred souls. It contains thirty-five wholesale and retail stores, two tin shops, four public taverns, two steam sawmills, one steam flouring mill, with two runs of stones, six or eight drinking shops and billiard tables, one wine and spirit manufactory, a variety of mechanic shops and from eight to fifteen merchant vessels are always lying at anchor in the river or at the wharves... This is the place where nearly all the immigrants by water land and from which they will go to their various points of destination."

In 1854 Portland became the seat of government of the new Multnomah County, created out of parts of Washington and Clackamas counties. The assessed valuation of property in 1855 was $1,196,034; the population was 1,209. Added settlement constantly expanded the town's boundaries. Covered wharves, privately owned, were built along the waterfront, and a public levee was constructed. Many merchants who became active in the municipality in those years rose to leadership in commercial and civic life. Henry W. Corbett, William S. Ladd, Josiah and Henry Failing, Cicero H. Lewis, John C. Ainsworth and others in time became sustaining pillars in the industrial structure. The *Oregonian*, begun in 1850, became a lusty mouthpiece for the growing commonwealth. Its successive editors, Thomas Dryer, Simeon Francis, and Harvey W. Scott were widely known.

The discovery of gold in Idaho and eastern Oregon in the early 1860's, brought a second boom to Portland's commercial life. Freight and passengers for the upper Columbia and many Snake River points, were taken aboard steamers at Portland's wharves. Rates of shipment, often exorbitant, were usually paid with little protest. Customarily, an empty wagon shipped aboard a riverboat was measured from tongue-tip to end-gate and assessed for the square feet it thus occupied; the tongue was then removed, placed under the wagon, and the wagon-bed piled full of a miscellaneous freight being paid for by another shipper. During that era the few villages east of the Cascades and on the route of the Oregon Trail assumed the aspect of towns, with much of their staple goods and building commodities coming from Portland merchants.

Oregon's first railroad—other than a few short portage lines—crept southward out of Portland in 1869, with the first locomotive laboring into Oregon City on Christmas Day and continuing to Parrott Creek. From there it slowly continued up the valley. This quicker route to market for Willamette Valley produce was destined to reshape the economic order of the towns located upon it. Increased prosperity came to Portland, although for some years yet the riverboats contributed greatly to the town's commercial leadership of the Oregon country.

"As we approach Portland," wrote Mrs. Victor in 1872, on a trip by boat up the river, "we observe its new, yet thrifty, appearance; the evidence of forests sacrificed to the growth of a town; and the increasing good taste and costliness of its buildings going up or recently built in the newest

portions of the city. A low, level margin of ground, beautifully ornamented with majestic oaks, intervenes between us
and the higher ground on which the town is built. Passing
by this and the first few blocks and warehouses, with their
ugly rears toward the river, we haul up alongside a handsome, commodious wharf, and begin to look about.

"Portland is, we find, a cheerful-looking town of about
9,000 inhabitants; well paved, with handsome public buildings, and comfortable, home-like dwellings. It is at the head
of ocean steam navigation, and owes its prominence as the
commercial town of Oregon to the fact. Here the smaller
steamers which ply on the Wallamet River have hitherto
brought the produce of the valley to exchange for imported
goods, or to be shipped on sailing vessels to foreign ports;
and here have centered the commercial wealth and political
influence of the State.

"The river in front of Portland is about one-fourth of a
mile wide, with water enough for large vessels to lie in; and
the rise and fall of the tide amounts to a couple of feet.
During the winter flood in the Wallamet, which is occasioned
by heavy rains, the water rises about eight feet. For this
reason the wharves are all built in two stories—one for low,
and one for high water. The great flood of 1861–62 and that
of 1870, brought the water over the wharves and even over
Front street, which is twenty-five feet above low-water mark.
The summer floods in the Columbia, occasioned by the melting of snow in the mountains where it has its source, back
the water up in the Wallamet as far as Oregon City, which
makes its necessary to abandon the lower wharves. These
two rises keep the Wallamet supplied with water through the
greater portion of the year. . ."

Portland was connected with the eastern states by transcontinental railroad, the Northern Pacific, in 1883. Henry
Villard, leading spirit of this enterprise, feted the town in
celebration of the achievement. Thereafter business increased and trade volume grew; heavy manufacturing established itself with an eye to the future in a town where the
sputtering oil street lamps had already given way to sputtering gas jets. Before the 1880's closed, street railways—
that in 1872 had begun as a single horse-drawn line along

Looking north from Pine along Front St., Portland, "high water" of 1876. (OHS Collections)

First Street—had fanned out, with tracks on Morrison Street and connecting laterals, all operating with electric equipment. Portland's first bridge spanned the Willamette in 1887, and the first California through-train arrived in town.

Portland's Stark Street Ferry, above, began operation in 1855, providing across-the-river service for man, vehicle and livestock, until Morrison Bridge construction in 1887. Craft pictured here in later 1860s is steam-driven, with paddle wheels on sides; earlier ferry was horse-propelled, by treadmill. (David L. Stearns Col., OHS) View below is of Portland harbor, 1876, with doubledecker docks, viewed from east side over railroad tracks of yet uncompleted transcontinental.

Portland harbor in 1900, about 7 a.m. (Shaver
Transportation Co., Bates Col., OHS)

THE first vessel of record to enter the Willamette River was the *Owyhee*, a Boston trading ship that in 1829 ascended the river to within a mile of the falls. After her, in 1836, the Hudson's Bay Company supply boat *Beaver*, first steam vessel in Pacific waters, made brief excursions into the lower "Wallamut." Other trading vessels, now lost to record, cruising cautiously under reduced sail, may have ascended the river by one or the other of its two mouths. In 1840 the brig *Maryland* ventured the full distance to Willamette Falls. She was in command of the doughty Yankee, Captain John H. Couch, who made a return voyage two years later in the *Chenamus*. The *Chenamus* went as far as Clackamas Rapids; thence her cargo was transferred by flatboat to the "falls settlements." Thereafter other sail-driven craft were on the Willamette, a few from the Sandwich Islands; but most, like those of Couch, from the trade ports of the north Atlantic Coast.

These all were foreign vessels trading off the new country. The first ocean-going vessel constructed on the Willamette was the *Star of Oregon*, built because of the desperate need of the settlers for livestock. The Hudson's Bay Company, owning nearly all the domestic cattle in the country, refused, prior to 1843, to sell stock to incoming homeseekers. A band of Spanish cattle driven north from California in 1837 by Ewing Young, who put them to grazing in the Chehalem Hills, proved to be such untamable creatures that few ranchers cared to own them. Stock less wild than this could be obtained for a price in California. With such a purchase in view, Joseph Gale was engaged by a group of valley settlers to build a ship that could be sailed to the port of Yerba Buena (San Francisco), there to be traded for the much needed cattle.

The keel of the *Star of Oregon* was laid in the fall of 1840 on the wooded east shore of Swan Island. Beneath the yellowing cottonwoods of the dying year and the rains of one long gray winter, Gale and eight or ten assistants fashioned the small sailing craft, using tools borrowed from Lee's Mission. Cordage and other articles indispensable in ship construction were obtained from Fort Vancouver, at the request of Lieutenant Wilkes. Wilkes further gave Gale papers necessary for ocean navigation, a set of instruments and—equally important to his enterprise—an American flag.

The *Star of Oregon*, clinker-built, of Baltimore clipper model, 53 feet 6 inches long, 10 feet 9 inches at her widest, and drawing 4 feet 6 inches of water in ballast, was launched from Swan Island on May 19, 1841. Her frame was of white oak, her knees of red cedar, and she was planked with cedar to the waterways. After further refitting on Oak (Ross) Island, the *Star* set sail on August 27, 1842, proceeding cautiously down the Willamette, and two days later dropped anchor before Fort Vancouver. Hoisting her colors, she proudly declared that Uncle Sam, as well as John Bull, had a vessel in Oregon waters. A few days later, far down the Columbia, she dipped her colors before Fort George. She remained in the Columbia estuary for two weeks, while Gale, who alone knew anything of navigation, instructed his novices in seamanship.

Thus on September 12, the *Star of Oregon*, her sails confidently set, slipped across the Columbia bar on her thousand-mile journey to California. Despite the fact that Gale's crew of five men and a ten-year-old Indian boy were seasick almost all the way, the hazardous voyage was safely made in five days. On September 17 the vessel sailed through the Golden Gate.

At Yerba Buena, Gale disposed of his young vessel to a French sea-captain, obtaining in an advantageous deal 350 head of desirable cattle. These Gale and his men grazed locally until spring, when they herded their half-tame cattle over the mountains into the Willamette Valley.

Transportation by flatboat on the Willamette was first undertaken commercially in the summer of 1844. Aaron Cook, an Englishman, believed there was profit to be made from a craft that would operate regularly up and down the river, replacing the numerous Indian canoes and settlers' rafts. He built the *Callapooiah*, thirty-five tons burden, a cross between a scow and a schooner. Jack Warner, a young Scotsman with a good education and some practical knowledge of the sailor's craft, did much of the caulking and rigging. One day while pitching the hull of the *Callapooiah* with a kettle of hot pitch and a long-handled comb, he was accosted by an "uncouth Missourian" who had evidently never seen anything of the kind before, and asked Jack what he was about. "I am a landscape painter by profession," the replay came in broad accents, "and I am doing a wee bit of adornment for Captain Cook's schooner!"

Rigged for sails, the *Callapooiah* was launched in August and left down-river for Astoria. She reached there in four days. Thereafter she ran between Willamette and Columbia River points, on a frequent and more or less regular schedule. But twenty-one months after launching, Cook offered the *Callapooiah* for sale. By that time the competition of similar though smaller craft had become so keen that lowered transportation rates yielded small profit. One of these crude vessels, running between Oregon City and Astoria in 1847, charged a point-to-point fare of $20, provided the passenger boarded himself and helped pull the boat! Operated by B. C. Kindred, the *Callapooiah* made regular stops at the river-side landing called Portland, but contemptuously referred to by non-residents as "Little Stumptown."

Meanwhile, other men built and operated similar flatboats above the falls. There the *Mogul* and *Ben Franklin* were in use as early as 1846, running between "the falls" and Champoeg, center of trade on the middle river. The distance was eighteen miles, and transit time of those Indian-powered, paddle-driven craft was from seven to ten hours. It was claimed that they had "good sailing and pulling qualities." The passenger fare was fifty cents and trips were made twice-weekly. Business grew so rapidly that in May of that year a third flatboat, the *Great Western*, went into operation. Principal owner of the three boats was Robert, more familiarly called "Doc" Newell, Rocky mountain trapper.

A few ocean-going vessels, some of note, entered the river in those years. Among them was the bark *Whiton* from New York, in 1847. The following year came the brig *Sequin*, which, returning in 1849, brought the first United States mail sacks to Portland from San Francisco and inaugurated regular mail service.

Late in July 1848 the schooner *Honolulu* put into Portland

harbor. Captain Newell (not the mountain man) immediately set about gathering all the picks, crowbars and hardware obtainable, and as much clothing and provisions as local storekeepers had on hand—presumably for the use of California coal miners employed in getting out coal for the steam vessels that were now beginning to appear in western waters. Only when an ample cargo had been secured did he announce that gold had been discovered on the Sacramento River. As evidence, he paid for his purchases in gold dust.

Portland and the scattered riverside hamlets went wild. In the excitement that followed, nearly two-thirds of Oregon's able-bodied men left by water and by land for the heralded Eldorado.

The Rev. George H. Atkinson, tending his small Congregational flock at Oregon City, in September, 1848, wrote in his diary: "8, Friday. It has been a week of excitement in town. Most of our men, mechanics, loafers, farmers, merchants, &c. have been preparing to leave for California to make their fortunes digging gold this winter. It is astonishing. Men from the sanctifying influences of the camp meeting, from the communion table, from the comforts of home, from the bosom of their families are leaving every comfort to camp in the woods, or on the plains in snow and rain for months with no provisions but flour to obtain the gold. They go in thousands and leave good business, sacrifice property, pay high for goods, venture health, all for gold. Boys go. Morals will suffer with industry, habits, minds, bodies, friends. The last company & last probably this fall will leave tomorrow. The elder of our chh. goes, also all our physicians 4 in no., 3 or 4 ministers go, 2 merchants. At one store $500. in goods has been sold for successive days."

Those who resisted the great exodus and remained at home hastened to increase agricultural production to supply as much of the miners' needs as possible, not neglecting to charge them all the market would stand.

As early as the spring of 1849, the raw gold of the south was flowing into Oregon in a steady stream. Sawmills and flour mills ran full blast; wages rose and prices advanced. Old debts were paid and new obligations were optimistically incurred. The medium of exchange became gold, where before it had been wheat. A new age began in the Oregon Country.

In 1849, many sailing vessels entered the Willamette. Joseph Kellogg, Lot Whitcomb, and William Terrance, men soon to become prominent in local marine history, built the 22-ton schooner *Milwaukie*, loaded her with provisions and sent her to San Francisco, where sale of ship and cargo yielded sufficient to enable her builders to purchase the brig *Forrest*. Their newly-acquired vessel they ran regularly between San Francisco and Milwaukie.

The bark *John W. Cater* likewise covered that route. In August the bark *Madonna*, under Captain Couch, earlier of the *Chenamus*, arrived at Portland; and the captain advertised his vessel as the first to establish regular sailings from Portland to Atlantic coast points. But reconsidering, he remained at Portland, where he soon opened a store, while Captain J. C. Flanders took over the *Madonna*, sailing her only as far as San Francisco.

During 1850 the Pacific Mail Steamship Company inaugurated a regular schedule between San Francisco and Portland, a service it was to continue through the years.

Five deep-water vessels stood in port at Milwaukie at one time in 1850. The local *Western Star* announced a "New Line of Packet Ships from Milwaukie, Oregon, to San Francisco," listing three "Fast Sailing, Coppered and Cooper Fastened Barks," the *Ocean Bird*, *Koeka*, and *Louisiana*. Lot Whitcomb, proprietor of Milwaukie townsite, was Oregon agent and was "prepared at all times to receive on board or in store at Milwaukie . . . . . Goods, Wares, Merchandise, Lumber, Agricultural Products, etc., etc.; also, to transmit remittances, make purchases, or dispose of all kinds of property . . . . . to the best advantage." To be a town proprietor in the early years of Oregon settlement meant doing business in nearly every field, a responsibility to which Whitcomb proved equal.

How prominent and necessary a part of pioneer life river shipping became along Willamette shores, is evidenced in the records of the day. Young Mary Elder, writing from her riverside home near Milwaukie in March, 1850, commented in a latter to a distant friend:

"We have passed through one winter in Oregon. We have a great deal of rain. . . . and some snow. . . .we live, . . . right on the bank of the river. We have a first rate hewed log house with three rooms below and one above and a good porch, and three of the prettiest kinds of fir trees right out in front of the house. . . . I have never been any place except to Milwaukie. We have no way of going by the river and mama is so uneasy when we go that way that we do not go very often. I have been there once to meeting, once to singing school, once to a party and once to temperance.

"A gentleman and his family stayed here night before last from California. . . . they say that all the newcomers in California are coming here next summer. There have been as many as five vessels at Milwaukie at once this winter. I went aboard two of them. . . ."

The industrial surge resulting from the gold rush to California ended the almost primeval simplicity of the Oregon farmer. His sense of isolation and deprivation was removed. As the several thousand Oregon miners returned—some not financially benefitted, others with an abundance—settlements increased in population, industry quickened and additional towns were founded. Every male citizen eighteen years of age or over could occupy 320 acres of land. If married, he and his wife might claim twice that amount—it was theirs for the taking, under the Federal donation land act of September 27, 1850. By 1851, land hunger and town building had largely replaced the lust for gold.

Because of the still meager population of the Oregon Country, skilled mechanics and the tools for fine craftsmanship were scarce. With the exception of the *Star of Oregon*, no worthy ship came from the ways until the *Columbia* was built at Astoria in the spring of 1850 by James Frost and General John Adair. That boat, ninety feet long, with French engines brought up from San Francisco, made her maiden voyage up the Columbia to Portland, arriving on July 4 at 3 p.m. She continued to Oregon City, arriving at 8 o'clock twilight, and was welcomed with brief but clamorous celebration. With a speed of four to five miles an hour, she beat all wind-driven craft, batteaux, and canoes then on the two rivers. She went into immediate twice-a-week schedule between Oregon City and Astoria, with Portland and Vancouver important ports of call—charging a straight $25 per passenger or ton of freight. By June, 1856, the *Columbia* had completed one hundred trips to Portland, making over $500,000 for her owners. But her engines so "shivered her timbers" that she soon ceased operation.

Making the year 1850 even more eventful in river history was the construction of the *Lot Whitcomb* at Milwaukie, first steam-powered craft built on the Willamette. The builder, Lot Whitcomb, believed that if Milwaukie, struggling toward river supremacy, could establish a local steamboat line giving regular service, her nearby rival, Portland, could be outdone as a competing town. Whitcomb, with Berryman Jennings, S. S. White, and several cooperating assistants, most of whom went in arrears on wages, undertook to build the boat. Their endeavors soon became "intricately cooperative": stock was sold to interested settlers, some of whom paid with produce which in turn was consumed by the laboring crew or sold for their benefit. Whitcomb pledged very nearly all of his possessions before the craft was completed.

The *Lot Whitcomb*, with machinery purchased at San Francisco for $15,000, was jubilantly launched on Christmas Day, 1850. At 3 p.m. of that sunny afternoon the props were knocked from under her hull and she slid down the ways. Oregon's territorial governor, John P. Gaines, christened her and made a speech. Mayor Kilbourne of Milwaukie presented a set of colors donated by Oregon City. Then the brass band from Fort Vancouver—but recently made a United States Military post to guard the rights of settlers in a country now fully claimed by the American government— played the "Star Spangled Banner" and "Hail, Columbia."

Witnesses of this event declared the *Lot Whitcomb*—bright with paint and vivid in the holiday sunshine—was a proud sight as she rode the winter-swollen waters. She was, her builders said, soundly constructed and everyone agreed that she was beautifully modeled. She was 160 feet long with a 24-foot beam; a man could stand upright in her hold, which was 5 feet 8 inches deep. Her draft was 6 feet 2 inches; and her great side-wheels measured 18 feet in diameter.

The one unfortunate event of the launching was the accidental death of Captain Frederick Morse of the schooner *Merchantman*, loading lumber at Whitcomb's Milwaukie sawmill. While he was firing a small and infrequently used ship's cannon loaned from his vessel, the rusty weapon exploded; a cast-iron piece struck Morse in the neck, nearly decapitating him. He died instantly. No one else was hurt. Despite the tragic occurrence festivities continued for three days.

The *Lot Whitcomb*, following a pleasure excursion to Astoria, began at once to ply the river but was handicapped by lack of government papers necessary to legalize her business. It was then American law that no papers could be issued a boat until all outstanding indebtedness against her had been paid. So for some time the *Lot Whitcomb* was obliged to operate "on the dodge," and meanwhile steer clear of the Astoria Custom-house in charge of General Adair, co-owner of the rival steamer *Columbia*. When at last, thanks to settlers' subscriptions, all debts were discharged, Adair gave the boat a clean bill. Jacob Kamm, for what money was due him for installing her boilers, was offered an interest in the vessel, but refused; whereupon J. C. Ainsworth, recently arrived from Sacramento, accepted the investment and became captain. Kamm signed on as engineer. The public felt that the *Whitcomb* was a "crack boat and ain't to be beat."

The trade route of the *Lot Whitcomb* was between Milwaukie and Astoria, two trips weekly. Where the *Columbia* charged $25 for the run from Portland, her competitor reduced this fare to $15, then to $12. From the start she enjoyed abundant patronage; she was once sunk opposite her home port, but soon raised. For a time she completely ignored Portland, hoping thereby to hinder the growth of that place both as a competing town and as a deep-sea port. As a consequence, Portland's civic-minded townsite proprietors—Coffin, Lownsdale and Chapman—bought the California steamer *Goldhunter*, 172 feet long, for $60,000. The *Goldhunter* and the *Caroline* were the first ocean steam vessels to land at frontier Portland. The *Caroline* arrived in the Willamette a few months earlier than the *Goldhunter*, with mail received at the Isthmus of Panama. The *Goldhunter*, plying between Oregon and California points, gave Portland such a boom that Lot Whitcomb hastily recognized the rival port. Soon thereafter he ceased to make his own town of Milwaukie a port of call, finding better business elsewhere. But after little more than a year the *Goldhunter* was sold to a block of minority stockholders in San Francisco, thus depriving the Portland investors of their partly paid-for property and the village of Portland of its principal boat service. Meanwhile the *Lot Whitcomb* connected her runs with the Cowlitz River Canoe and Batteau Line, but not profitably. On long runs she proved expensive to operate, and in the summer of 1854 was disposed of in California.

To the Oregon Country in the spring of 1851 came five lady school teachers, recruited in New England. Their destination was the Clackamas County Female Seminary at Oregon City. *En route,* they traversed the Isthmus of Panama, in company with other Oregon-bound travelers. A handful of these died of fever, including Oregon's territorial representative, Samuel Thurston, who was returning home from the national capital. The five teachers made the journey safely. One of them, Elizabeth Miller, who later married Joseph G. Wilson, set down on paper in 1899 an account of that trip. Of their entry into the Columbia and Willamette Rivers, she wrote:

". . . The trip was quite favorable. Our entrance over the bar was a prosperous one. We landed at Astoria. Saw Gen. Adair who first come there as a collector of customs and his family. Then shifting our belongings to the newly-built *Lot Whitcomb,* we made our way up the river. The impression on my memory is more of homesickness than of the majesty and beauty of the lordly river. There were but a very few woodsmen's huts on the banks between Astoria and Vancouver, and the less said of any thoughts or feelings the better, but the dread of the end of the journey was becoming heavier and heavier as it approached. . . A little diversion was agreeably given at Vancouver, then occupied by the Rifle Regiment under Col. Loring, afterward of the Egyptian Service called Loring Bey. Mrs. Preston had a cousin among the officers, and we were taken to the commandant's quarters, but, though we were kindly invited to stay longer, and everything looked beautiful there, the *Lot Whitcomb* was ready and we must go.

"The Hudson's Bay Company's buildings and stockades were then all complete and full of interest. We were soon at Portland and walked up from the steamer's plank through a double line of gazers composed of the entire population of Portland. No arrival had yet taken place of so many women. The one-sided community was exceedingly interested. I suppose the rest of the party were allowed to be and look just as they pleased without criticism. But the teachers, who had been sent for, and who had accepted the invitation, were the objects of many remarks. We heard of these afterward. They seemed to think we had too much experience among us, and some seemed to think the limit should have been set that none should have been accepted who were not of their teens.

"Again on the river, this time in a whale boat, expecting to reach Oregon City, the then capital and our destination at 4 p.m. I had a heavy blanket shawl. The sun was very warm and seeing my trunk, unlocked it and put the shawl away. We approached the Clackamas, but much later than had been planned, and then found ourselves fast on the bar. I do not remember much of the efforts to dislodge the boat. The boatmen were under the influence of whiskey, and when the lights of Oregon City shone out brightly, we, in full view, lay there all night supperless. I had no wrap. Some blankets were divided among the ladies. The men had reached the shore and started a monstrous fire, which dissipated the gloom a little but not the chill. The blanket did not reach me and I became very ill. Youth and a fine constitution carried me through, but my trip was nearly ended that night for all time. I never felt worse in my life.

"Now we can look back and see some of the dangers that were incurred by some of our party, who could not content themselves to lie there, or rather stalk about in the wet woods, for a cold rain set in with nightfall, while the lights of Oregon City were within full view. Several of them started. There was only a trail. They groped their way to the Clackamas . . . where they found a canoe. Wholly unused to such a boat they, not by their own skill or wisdom,

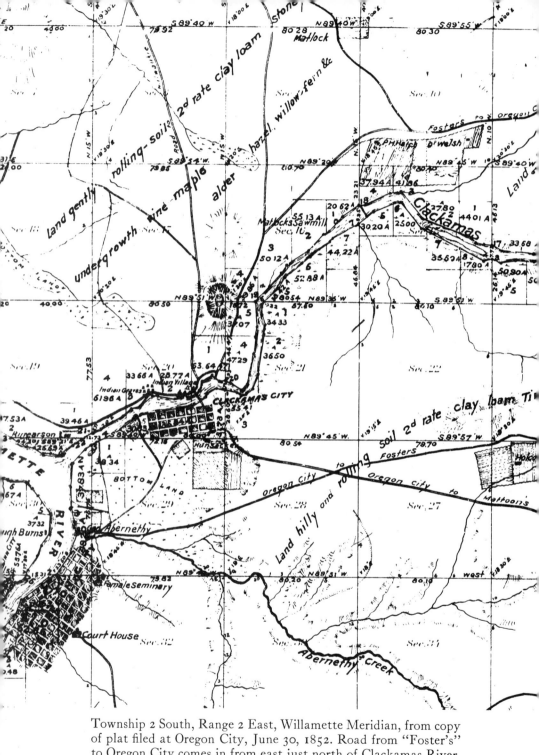

Township 2 South, Range 2 East, Willamette Meridian, from copy of plat filed at Oregon City, June 30, 1852. Road from "Foster's" to Oregon City comes in from east just north of Clackamas River, which enters Willamette just below Oregon City. Willamette Falls appears at extreme lower left. (U.S. BLM files.)

got across without capsizing. There were then only blind trails, cow paths, impassable gullies, piles of burnt logs crossing the ways in all directions, but in the rain and darkness, in five hours they finally reached the streets of Oregon City, gave the news . . . that we were stuck on the rapids and then, we may suppose, tumbled into bed. Early next morning measures were taken for our relief. A collection was taken and eatables sent down in a small boat. There seemed to be a great quantity of mince pie, and a very good breakfast, that is for supperless people. I was too ill to eat, but there was cheer in the thought that some one cared for us. We as soon as possible started on the path to the City. With my after experiences I often wondered that we all were safely canoed over the whirling torrent with inexperienced boatmen, but we found ourselves trudging along."

Between 1850 and 1853, anticipating the growth of river commerce, the Federal government spent about $30,000 clearing rock from the Clackamas Rapids. It was hoped that the Willamette could thus be made readily navigable by ocean vessels to the foot of the falls. Although this failed, the waters were deepened somewhat at this point.

Portland, stumptown of early ridicule, had meanwhile become accepted as the feasible head of navigation for ocean-going vessels. The freight of the upper country poured down by batteau and boat and was reloaded from her wharves. Also in her favor was the opening of a road across the western hills into the Tualatin Valley in 1849, a crude but vital artery that aided in giving her first place over her rival, Milwaukie. There were no widely cultivated and fertile prairies back of the latter village, such as those in the broad areas of the Tualatin. The pulse of commerce slowed for Milwaukie; but it was Portland's dawning day, and her builders envisioned the future with hopes that soared as high as the tall-masted schooners at her laden wharves.

The ships that entered the lower Willamette from the ocean in those early years were, with few exceptions, all sailing brigs, sloops or barks, lofty-masted, with clouds of sail. Appearing in sharp contrast were the squat riverboats —although often equally long—and designed to offer as little resistance to the wind as possible. Where ocean skippers, leaning hard on the tiller, watched the stars through the rigging, the river pilot glimpsed those same constellations through a wavering pillar of smoke or a shower of sparks. More often, however, the latter's vision was on the narrow course of journey; it was the flow and the rip of the current that he watched, the scarcely submerged gravelbar and the sunken or floating snag.

Thus the riverboats commenced their heyday on the Willamette, in a land of increasing agricultural enterprises, of river landings and growing towns. Of those small centers of trade, some would grow on through years of promise to permanence and recognition. But some—almost as many—would flourish for a time only, then vanish or gradually decline. Of these, a few are today nearly forgotten, others seldom recalled.

It is their stories which are the substance of these chapters.

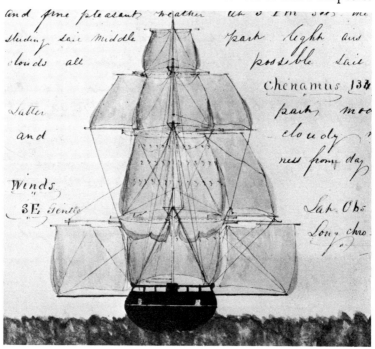

Brig *Chenamus* on the way to Oregon, sketched by Capt. John Couch in his log. (See p. 18.) OHS Cols.

Milwaukie, above, viewed in 1850s from ferry landing on west shore. Its mills and warehouses were conspicuous river landmarks in 1850s and 1860s. Records show the town then had two gristmills, two sawmills, a shipyard, two hotels and fruit tree nursery. Promoter was Lot Whitcomb, who built and was source of name of steamer below, pictured in early 1850s. (OHS Collections)

Riverboats docked for loading on east shore at Oregon City, just below the Falls, in 1867. (Watkins photo, OHS Cols.)

Unfinished steamer in the boat basin at Oregon City, 1867.
Man stands shading face with hat, at rear of ship, where
wheel will be placed; others at work on roof. Across river
another landing area. (Watkins, OHS Cols.)

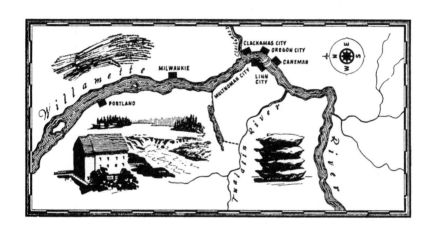

LOST TOWNS OF WILLAMETTE FALLS . . . .

In the hazy light of late summer, in his great house over-looking the Willamette at Oregon City, John McLoughlin lay dying. He was seventy-three. In the old age of his stout-hearted career he had founded the town, sprawled half on the rising levels and half on the narrow strip of hard earth and rock at the river's margin. Across the unquiet waters stood the opposing town of Linn City, founded by Robert Moore. Each town had known the guiding wisdom of a single hand. On September 2, 1857, half up the slope of the fir-clad hill behind Linn City, in the simple dwelling named by him "Robin's Nest," Robert Moore died. John McLoughlin, ex-factor of the Hudson's Bay Company in the Oregon Country, died one day after.

Four years later came the "great flood." When New Year's Day, 1862, dawned cold with a clear, pale sun, a light mantling of snow overlay Oregon City. But Linn City had vanished.

Robert Moore came to Oregon in the fall of 1840, as a member of the Peoria Party. Pleased by the prospect of owning the green flat lying along the west bank of the Willamette River at the falls, he negotiated for its purchase from Chief Wanaxha, of the Clough-we-wallah, or Wallamut Indians. In this act he differed from the majority of his fellow settlers, who took without payment the land they chose, sometimes finding their lives imperilled for doing so. Moreover, Moore had later to file entry on the property with the Federal land office. The one thousand acres he selected was two miles long and a half-mile wide, but because his wife, Margaret, had remained in Illinois, where she later died, he was compelled in 1850 to relinquish all but three hundred and twenty acres.

Major Moore was fifty-nine years old when he came to Oregon. He was a heavy set man, with rotund stomach, florid face and bald head. He was somewhat irascible, opinionated and domineering, and stubborn enough for others to find it difficult to get along with him. Notwithstanding, he was honest and on occasions kindly. William H. Gray pictured the Major as ". . . . . an old gray-headed man with a fair complexion, bald head, light eyes, full face, frequent spasmodic nodding forward of the head, and a large amount of self-importance, not very intellectual developments, with a superabundance of flesh . . . . dressed in fustian pants, large blue vest, and striped shirt, and a common brown coat . . . ."

Born in Pennsylvania of Scotch-Irish parentage, October 2, 1781, he had served as a major in the War of 1812. Settling in Missouri in 1822, he became a friend of Dr. Lewis F. Linn, afterwards senator from the state. He removed to Illinois in 1835 and platted Osceola, a "paper" town which the westward movement passed by unheeding. Disappointed but still optimistic, he joined the Peoria Party, migrating to Oregon. His family did not accompany him.

The log cabin which Moore built for himself stood on the east slope of the hill overlooking the falls. Partly because of its situation among the trees and partly after his own first name, he called his home "Robin's Nest." It peered down on the rocky flat stretching from north to south at the river level. Here for generations, Indians had maintained a fishing village. In the spring and fall their slab and bark structures were supplemented by the temporary shelters of the more restless Indian families, come to spear salmon.

Above the fishing grounds, still visited by Indian fishermen for years after Moore purchased the site, the oak, fir and spruce forest rose green and dark, climbing the steep slopes of the hills that range into the Tuality country.

At the time of purchase Moore must have seen the townsite advantages of his claim, but the platting of lots was not immediately undertaken. We learn from Wilkes, visiting the valley in 1841, that Major Moore was a man of "some shrewdness" and "exceedingly talkative." In describing the falls region Wilkes, remarking on the character of the rocks, observed that there was "Much volcanic scoria, vesicular lava, and pudding stone, intermingled with blasts of trap, and many crystals of quartz. . . My attention has been called to this by old Mr. Moore, who set up his claim to the west side of the falls, communicating to me in confidence that he intended to erect furnaces for smelting iron, etc.

Although I saw the old man some time afterwards, and told
him of his mistake, he would not believe that he had been
in error." As it turned out, Wilkes was the one in error,
although the smelting of iron ore at Oswego, six miles down
the river, did not begin until 1867, after Moore's death.

Shrewdly eyeing the development of "the Falls," Robert
Moore, pacing his rocky flat across the river, conceived of a
competing town, his own, situated on his equally accessible
claim. Water traffic, he reasoned, could as conveniently
beach for rest, for purchase of supplies, and for portage on
his side of the river, as on the opposite one. Mills, stores, a
warehouse, even an overnight house, all operated by him or
by purchasers of lots, could bring to the west side of the
Willamette a share of the prosperity that seemed dawning
for the sprawling village on the east shore.

Moore's donation land claim extended westward from the
water 1,340 feet, and from one-fourth of a mile below the
falls to one and three-fourths miles above the falls. From
the northeast corner of this property the owner carved his
townsite, in 1843. Originally there were twenty-five blocks.
Of that number, he reserved two; a block facing on the river
and one directly behind it. These were omitted in the plat
of the town, which was never recorded. All blocks were 320
by 220 feet, with twenty-foot alleys running both ways.
The streets were sixty feet wide and were named for the
presidents of the United States, and for local geographical
points. The entire townsite occupied between forty and fifty
acres, and extended part way up the tree-crowded slope
where Moore's dwelling stood.

A limited immediate sale of lots apparently took place;
concerted emigration from the East had begun, and some
homeseekers preferred the amenities of settlement commerce
to the hardships of land tilling. Early Clackamas County
records show sale to eight persons of twelve parcels in the
first twelve blocks. It is probable that little cash changed
hands in these transactions; a number of lots being sold to
individuals who received bonds for deeds, none of which was
ever recorded. That a number of buyers later defaulted, was
indicated by the advertisements in 1850 in the *Oregon Spectator*, demanding payments from delinquents.

In 1844, while Moore's town was in the first flush of construction, Willamette Falls, in its progress toward greater prominence, was incorporated as Oregon City—the first incorporated town west of the Missouri River. This did not deter the stubborn Scotch ardor of Robert Moore. Early the succeeding year his embryonic town had two commodious log houses and a large number of tents occupied by settlers who had arrived the autumn before. Some of these newcomers must have remained, for by 1846 there were about fifteen houses standing on the rocky shelf at the river's edge. These rough dwellings were occupied principally by mechanics—men employed in the flour and lumber mills built by Moore, and on the ferry he operated across the river, just below the falls. The charter for this latter enterprise, he had secured from the Provisional Legislature in June, 1844.

Thus encouraged, Major Moore, by an act of the Provisional Legislature, on December 22, 1845, changed the name of his town from Robin's Nest to Linn City in honor of his friend, Dr. Lewis F. Linn of Missouri.

The *Spectator* observed on February 19, 1846, that "On the west side of the river immediately opposite the falls . . . . at Linn City . . . . improvements are going ahead. We are informed that Mr. Moore has sold one-half of the interest he claims in the water power . . . . to a Mr. Palmer of Indiana . . . . Linn City contains one tavern, one chair manufactory, one cabinet shop, one gunsmith shop and one wagon shop."

The same issue of the *Spectator* reported that Oregon City had a "population of no less than 500 souls . . . . with about eighty houses . . . . and two churches." There were "two taverns, two blacksmith shops, two cooper shops, one tannery, three shoe shops, two silversmiths and a number of other mechanics, four stores, two flouring mills and two sawmills, and a lath machine." The single newspaper was an obvious addition to the list. Oregon City was well in the lead among pioneer towns situated at the falls of the Willamette.

General Joel Palmer tarried briefly in the vicinity and judged then that Linn City had a fair outlook. In his *Journal of Travels over the Rocky Mountains, 1845-46*, he stated that

Major Moore's refusal to sell water power was doubtless
one of the reasons why immigrants, in greater numbers, did
not settle at Linn City. Palmer had not succeeded in purchasing the water rights, although the *Spectator* had erroneously reported the sale as consummated.

Linn City continued to grow with slow but aggressive
pace. Moore had confidence in his own foresight; if the falls
region prospered at all, Linn City could and would prosper
with it.

Toward that end, Moore encouraged A. H. Frier to locate
at Linn City. Frier operated the Linn City Hotel, the
former Washington Hotel, which had been operated for a
time by Stephen H. L. Meek, who also ran an "8 ox power"
freighting line to Hillsboro. Frier made his entry known in
the *Spectator* for October 15, 1846, announcing also that he
had purchased the ferry and would fulfill the various contracts entered into by former operators. Customers of the
hotel he gladly ferried free of charge.

By 1848, many matters of local concern that previously
had engaged the provisional legislature, had passed to the
province of the county courts. The "Tualaty County Court
Records," under date of August 21, carries the following:

> Ordered by the Court that Robert Moore and John McLaughlin
> receive a license to ferry one year between Linn City and Oregon City
> in Oregon Territory at the rates of Ferriage following, to-wit:

A single Passenger	12½
One man and Horse or mule	25
Every single horse, Cow or Mule, or ass Colts and Calves included	10
Each waggon drawn by two horses or oxen and its load	50
Each waggon drawn by four horses or oxen and its load	75
Each waggon drawn by six horses or oxen, and its load	87½
Every additional pair of horses or oxen to waggon	12½
One horse or mule and waggon	37½
Every sheep, goat or hogg, lambs, kids, and piggs, included	3
Each 100 lbs. goods, wares, merchandise or produce	3

> And that the said license commence on the first day of September
> A. D. 1848 and that a tax of fifteen dollars be assessed upon said
> ferry for the aforesaid year—lincense to commence on the first day
> of September A. D. 1848 and to terminate on the first day of Septem-
> ber A. D. 1849.

At this time Moore was road supervisor of the Multnomah and Linn City District, which extended from his townsite to the Butte (Mount Sylvania) on the road to Tuality Plains, and below on the Willamette River to Sucker Creek, and south to the Tuality-Yamhill line, at Tuality River.

Captain James D. Miller, in his "Early Oregon Scenes: A Pioneer Narrative" in the *Oregon Historical Quarterly* for June, 1930, recalls that in 1848, as a youth of eighteen, he arrived at the falls with his parents. There the elder Miller purchased a house and lot in Linn City. The son relates: ". . . . we moved into it soon after we arrived, and commenced the sale of our boots and shoes, Kentucky jeans and cloth that we brought with us. For fine boots we got $5 per pair, shoes for men, women and children in proportion. If we had held them for six months they would have brought double the price."

In that year, business establishments at Linn City included a store owned by David Burnside, who had moved in from his homestead in the west hills. His stock of merchandise was less than $100 in value. The following year, the town added to its commercial ventures the store of W. P. Day & Robinson. This establishment carried a full line of dry-goods and groceries, advertised at "cheap prices." A newly-arrived physician, Dr. Henry Saffarrans, in 1849 married a widow, Mrs. Almira Ward. He remained to practice medicine, at least through 1850. Justin Chenoweth, a surveyor, was also a resident at that time.

James Marshall Moore, a son of Robert Moore, arrived in Oregon in 1847. He took the claim next above his father's and situated at the mouth of the Tualaty River. There in 1849 he built a lumber mill and a grist mill, and on November 1 advertised for twenty laborers. These were asked to apply at his store at Linn City, where he kept "constantly on hand a full assortment of Dry Goods & Groceries." Lumber cut at the Moore mill was for sale both at the mill and the Linn City ferry landing. All of the mill buildings at the upper site were connected by docks, nearly a mile long.

In 1848 the headlong exodus of able-bodied men from Linn City to the California goldfields began. Everyone would soon be so rich, the gold-seekers argued, that land would no longer be needed at least no more than enough for a homesite. And Linn City and the land would still be there when they got back.

By the winter of 1849–50, the argonauts began to return, many of them demoralized by their suddenly acquired wealth. Home again, they refused to work; they had the "dust" they went to find—and there was plenty more where they got it. Anyway, winter was the time to loaf. In the spring, if their money didn't hold out, they could go back and make another haul, or get to work. . . . With this attitude, they lived recklessly and spent wildly. Everywhere gambling was rampant.

During the gold days of inflated prosperity thousands of bushels of apples, peaches, pears and plums were gathered from the orchards of the homesteaders in the central Willamette Valley. Apples sold locally at $12 a bushel; after being shipped down the coast or hauled over the mountains to the gold fields, a thousand miles distant, they sold at fifty cents to one dollar apiece. Lumber sold for fifty dollars per thousand feet, and carpenters, if any could be found, drew wages of sixteen dollars a day. Wheat, which previously by Provisional law had been declared legal tender (one bushel, one dollar), now brought five dollars a bushel, while flour cost the retail purchaser eleven dollars a hundred weight and was difficult to obtain. Farms had been inadequately cared for by the stay-at-homes, and produce was not equal to the suddenly speeded-up demand. Gold dust, at a declared value of sixteen dollars an ounce, was rapidly becoming legal tender, and gold scales appeared in every place of business. Occasionally a fifty-dollar gold slug passed in trade.

Indians were still numerous in the falls region. In 1848, salmon of from twenty to thirty pounds, caught by the redskins, were bought by local settlers for twenty-five cents each. Sometimes the native would accept old clothes as payment. Meanwhile, the Indians grew more nondescript in appearance, drinking liquor when and wherever it could be secured. Always taciturn, they now grew sullen, a few of them unruly. In that year, Oregon City's population included a generous number of Indians and half-breeds. The

Chinook jargon, early Northwest trade language among the natives, was used frequently by the whites.

A post office was established at Linn City on January 1, 1850. Robert Moore was then 69 years old, but still an active leader. He no longer took part in the affairs of government, but gave all his attention to the development of his town. With the object of encouraging its growth, as well as that of the entire falls area, Moore, on April 18, 1850, purchased the *Spectator*, which had been temporarily suspended after discouraging five editors. Moore did not remove the paper's offices to Linn City, as might have been expected, but continued to publish it at Oregon City where it had been founded. He had, however, secured a mouthpiece through which to direct public interest and private capital toward the one town in which he was vitally concerned.

A pertinent news note appeared in the *Spectator* for June 27, 1850. Under the head of "New Road" it read:

> The citizens of Linn City just completed a very excellent road around the falls. As the track on the road is just above high water mark and ware houses will soon be erected, the portage at this place can hereafter be affected without the difficulties heretofore attending it. And by opening the road down the Tualitin River, the hill back of Linn City can be entirely avoided by the traveler from Yam Hill and Tualitin Plains.

Following this, on July 11, a second announcement appeared:

> We would say, for the information those concerned that goods intended to be carted over the portage on the Linn City road, should be landed above the upper ferry landing, as the cost of cartage from the lower ferry is necessarily much greater. Teams are always in readiness in Linn City to convey merchandise over this road.

Major Moore's first editor was the Reverend Wilson Blain, whom he had hired as early as December, 1848, to preach to him on Sunday mornings in the schoolhouse at Linn City. (Moore had withdrawn from the congregation at Oregon City when that body changed its name and affiliations from Presbyterian to Congregational.) In 1850 there were struck off each week 500 to 600 copies of the *Spectator*. It was published as a semi-monthly until September 12, 1851, when it became a weekly in order to compete with the *Oregonian*, newly launched at Portland.

Editor Blain appears to have been generally wise in his promotional statements, which usually had the tone of commendatory observations rather than of fulsome apostrophe. In an issue of December, 1850, for example, he wrote: "On the opposite side of the river is a town of considerable importance, called Linn City. Although not so large as Oregon City, it has the facilities and elements with proper developments to become a rival."

Again, on June 19, 1851, Moore advertised that he was "proprietor of one of the finest water powers in the world," and that he proposed "to have the same developed." He went on to say that "The wants of the country seem to demand a speedy completion of the said improvements in the erection of flouring mills, and almost all kinds of machinery that can be propelled by water, and the water privileges being so extensive, the undersigned would propose to capitalists that he is desirous of making arrangements for having said water brought into immediate use. . . . ."

Years later, C. W. Smith, a typesetter for the *Spectator* in 1851, recalled that "Mr. Moore himself sometimes took a hand, when anything in particular interested him. He was not a facile writer but a man of good strong common sense. He looked to be about 80 years old at that time, a good deal older than Dr. McLoughlin, who sometimes visited the office." On one occasion, Mr. Smith recalled, Dr. McLoughlin brought a letter over to the *Spectator* office, with a wish to have it printed in the paper. He was so pleased with Moore's willing acceptance that he invited the publisher over to his great house beneath the bluffs to enjoy a glass of wine.

Robert Moore's town-building interests, however, occupied most of his attention. On December 15, 1851, he made a present of the *Spectator* to his daughter, Mrs. Jean A. Painter, who had come to Oregon the previous year.

In 1851 the Rev. Ezra Fisher, Baptist preacher at Oregon City, said in a report to the American Baptist Home Missionary Society: "I have discontinued service in Linn City because of the small attendance due to so many people being away this summer." He had been preaching there twice a month. The second gold rush, this time to the Rogue River mines of southern Oregon, had taken much of the male population.

The Linn City Works, as they soon became known, were built by Major Moore in 1852 and 1853. A grist mill, a sawmill, a warehouse, wharves and a breakwater were constructed below the falls. The breakwater created a basin where river boats could tie in for loading and unloading at the mills and warehouse. Freight had then to be carried around the falls, where at their head a similar basin was constructed with a protecting breakwater, with wharves extending to the works and mills owned by Major Moore's son. The entire cost of these developments was stated to be nearly $100,000; and the combined enterprise was named the Willamette Falls Canal, Milling and Transportation Company.

The first suggestion of catastrophe which was later to destroy Linn City came with the high water of November, 1853. At that time the *Weekly Oregonian*, at Portland, observed that it "never had seen the Willamette so high so early in the season." About six weeks later, in January, the water below the falls rose out of its banks, did considerable damage to Oregon City, and broke over the breakwater at Linn City. Again the *Weekly Oregonian* observed that "following a heavy snowfall, the upper Willamette and its tributaries never have been known to be so high as they have been the last week. General Palmer's grist mill at Dayton was swept away and several of the houses of the mechanics at Linn City." Actually, seven houses were destroyed at the latter place, and the town generally inundated. It was a warning of the river's powers.

In the boat-building fever of the early 'fifties, the ill-fated *Gazelle*, a side-wheeler with disconnected engines, was built at Linn City by the Willamette Falls Canal, Milling and Transportation Company. She made her first run from Canemah on March 18, 1854, after being lifted around the falls at Linn City.

But in the mid-1850s, with his dreamed-of city still little

more than a place of mills and a transfer point for river traffic, Moore's aggressive spirit flagged. He became less active, less the self-willed individualist; he was growing old. "Old Mr. Moore," Lieutenant Wilkes had called him, as far back as 1841. He had lived on three American frontiers; and as his life approached its close, in 1857, he was weary. From his vine-covered house halfway up the hill back of Linn City, Major Moore gazed across his small town and on across the Willamette's low waters to the growing Oregon City. Seemingly, the latter had the more fortunate location. His was an industrial site, it would never be the town he had dreamed of. Never in his day, at least.

After the death of its principal citizen, Linn City seemed to lag in importance. Often, news rightly attributable to the town was carelessly or greedily claimed by Oregon City and was so reported by the press. One item, however, could not be refused its true significance. On September 13, 1858, the sheriff of Clackamas County sold for taxes forty-nine lots in Linn City, all situated in the first twelve blocks, the half-section that Moore had been permitted to keep. Sale prices ranged from a maximum of $270 to as low as $15 a lot. After charges and interest were added, purchasers paid as much as $512 a lot and as little as $75.

A final column-long notice of the sale of these lots appeared in the *Oregon Argus* of April 20, 1861, listing each lot by number. It was printed for the purpose of giving original owners an opportunity to redeem their lots, by "payment of the amount for which they had been sold, and interest and charges. By the census of the year before, the population of the Linn City district, which comprised a large orbit west of the falls, was only 225 persons.

On April 6, 1861, the *Oregon Argus* observed briefly:

> On the opposite side of the river is Linn City—one of those town sites of which much was said and written some ten years ago. There are a few pleasant residences on the site—but the expectations of its rapid growth have long since ceased.

On the night of Tuesday, April 23, 1861, fire—later said to be of incendiary origin—broke out in the lower warehouse and soon spread to the grist mill. There William

Overholtzer, the caretaker, was asleep on an upper floor. Half-choked by smoke, he fought his way to a window, from which he lowered himself to the gound by a rope tied to his bedstead. The rope burned off just as he reached firm earth. Already Linn City's residents were awake and aware of the destruction that threatened. A strong south wind was blowing and equipment at hand was poor and inadequate. The conflagration was soon out of hand and spreading from the grist mill to the sawmill.

Two river boats, that had come in only that afternoon, were docked in the upper Linn City basin: the steamer *James Clinton*, which was then supplying the Yamhill River trade, and the *Relief*, a smaller vessel. With the entire Linn City Works afire and the wharf planks burning, the vessels were endangered. Someone heroically chopped the mooring ropes of the *Relief*, and it was towed away by rowboats. The *James Clinton*, however, was larger and less manageable. Frantic efforts to cut it loose were thwarted by flame, which leaped from rail to cabin and swept along the decks. In a few hours it burned to the water's edge and sank, a loss of $6,000. Damage to the *Relief* amounted to about $500. Owners of the boats were Captains J. D. Miller and J. T. Apperson.

The grist mill was a total loss. In it were six hundred barrels of flour and fifteen hundred bushels of wheat, owned by W. C. Dement & Company and Ainsworth & Dierdorff, of Oregon City. Abernethy, Clark & Company, who, since Major Moore's death, had operated the Works under the name of the Oregon Milling and Transportation Company, suffered the greatest loss in property damage. However, there were several holders of liens on mills and warehouses, who also suffered losses. In the warehouse, which was not entirely consumed, was a large quantity of merchandise awaiting shipment; much of this was burned or badly damaged. The total loss was computed at nearly $100,000.

Earlier that day, the *James Clinton* had unloaded into the warehouse about twenty-five tons of bacon from up-river farmers. Each parcel was wrapped in burlap and it was thought for awhile that a spark from the chimney of one of the vessels, or from a laborer's pipe or cigar, had fallen in the inflammable material, had smouldered and finally broken into flame.

But Linn City's industries had been destroyed. The books and papers of the Oregon Milling & Transportation Company had been consumed. It was the loss of these, the evidence of much indebtedness on the part of individuals, that raised the suspicion of incendiarism. In reporting the disaster the *Oregon Argus,* published at Oregon City, said: "We doubt whether there is another establishment north of San Francisco the destruction of which would involve such an amount of suffering and inconvenience."

At least a few of the town's business leaders refused to be discouraged. Robert Pentland, by the right of his equity in the Works, laid claim, with James K. Kelly, to the property. If the warehouse and freight handling facilities were restored, Linn City could regain its lost trade; and Pentland announced on July 6 that he intended to reconstruct the partly burned warehouse. As before, the building was largely of timbers, with very little stone. However, more modern apparatus was installed to facilitate the transportation of freight around the falls. There was a hoist of forty feet to the basin above. The entire cost was $5,000. Handling charges for freight around the falls were one dollar a ton.

Meanwhile, there was a world of affairs beyond Linn City and beyond Oregon—a world whose events colored both the social and political life of the remote frontier. In the eastern states the first battles of the Civil War had been fought. In Oregon, differences of opinion and loyalty often reached heated controversy just short of open conflict. Community flag poles were erected; and sometimes the Stars and Stripes floating there was torn down, and the flag of the Confederacy was flown. At Linn City, on Monday, July 1, a spirited group of citizens, led by steamboat Captains Miller and Pease, assisted by Union men from Oregon City and Canemah, raised a 132-foot pole somewhere near the center of town. At its top floated an American flag made by the ladies of Linn City. It swept vividly on the breeze, over the gala celebration of July Fourth—and it seemed that Linn City enthusiasm, too, was rising to its former level.

The fall of 1861 opened with but little precipitation; late

in October the customary rains began. During November, however, rain fell almost continuously over northwestern Oregon. It was a cold rain and in the still colder mountains a vast amount of snow accumulated. In the closing days of the month the temperature softened, but a humid downpour that melted the snow continued. The Willamette rose at a rapid rate and was soon lapping over its banks for its entire 150-mile length.

At Portland, the *Weekly Oregonian* of November 30 observed, in a remark addressed facetiously "To Mariners," that "several of our principal streets in the Third Ward are now in a navigable condition." On Monday, December 2, boat schedules on the lower river were begun as usual. The steamer *Rival* left Oregon City for Portland, and the *Onward* started up river from Canemah. Both immediately met with difficulties, for the river was already cluttered with debris and floating wreckage of small landings and unsecured property. The *Onward* continued a journey which soon became one of succor for persons stranded on the lowlands. The *Rival* lay over a few miles from its point of departure.

As darkness settled on Monday, water was rising over the lower Linn City streets. "The ceaseless roar of the stream made a fearful sort of elemental music, widely different from the ordinary monotone of the Falls," a spectator reported through the *Oregonian* a few days later, "while the darkness was made more visible by the glare of torches and hurrying lights." The eerie atmosphere was intensified by the shouts of people from windows of houses surrounded by water rising at the rate of almost a foot an hour.

In the early half-light of Tuesday morning, the wooden bridge from Abernethy Island on the Oregon City side, where the Island Mills were situated, was carried away. Strained faces peered through the drenched daybreak at the still-rising river, now more thickly strewn with debris. Log rafts, splintered landings, an ungainly scow filled with apples, swept past. On a sheaf of oats that turned precariously in the roily waters, a rooster stood and crowed.

The mills, the warehouse, and all of the stores and houses on the rocky flat of Linn City were deep in the mounting flood. All day stranded people were removed through win-

Above photo of Oregon City, taken by Lt. Lorenzo Lorain about 1857-58, before great flood of 1861, shows falls and Linn City buildings on west side. Later view below, across Oregon City boat basin, reveals bare rock at Linn City site. Sternwheeler *Alice* in foreground (see p. 66). (OHS Collections)

dows of their houses by boats courageously manned but precariously controlled in the driving current. Floating timbers and drift of every sort endangered rescue efforts, while household goods and prized possessions were snatched away from frantic fingers.

During that afternoon a large part of the breakwater protecting the Works gave way before the immense pressure of water. At intervals, great masses of timbers forming the cribwork broke up and were swept away. Gradually the flood's force became too great to resist; walls of houses and stores were crushed or were picked up bodily and borne away. With the breakwater gone, the grist mill and the sawmill collapsed and their wreckage was sucked into the current.

For a time on Tuesday afternoon the William Day building, a two-story structure used as a dwelling, stood above flood. As other buildings and houses became imperilled and were carried away, their occupants fled to the supposed security of the Day house, where Captain J. D. Miller and his family lived. The rain had stopped and many believed the flood crest had been reached. By the time those crowded into the Day house had finished supper it became obvious to all that the building must be vacated; water was streaming under the house, almost at floor level. Furniture and stored possessions were hustled out, the last of them with the movers knee-deep in water. Later, encamped on the side of the hill, the refugees were twice forced to move to higher ground. Sometime in the night the Day Building went down.

Miller later recalled that on the last eventful afternoon, "There were two houses besides the one I occupied yet left in Linn City, so all residents that had lost their homes were divided up between the three of us, some going up on top of the hill or mountain to find homes up there for the night."

Finally, with the gray break of Wednesday morning, the extent of the destruction was fully apparent. At Linn City only two dwellings and the warehouse at the Works remained standing. The breakwater, above and below the falls, had been carried away at a loss of $50,000. In the mill, quantities of wheat and flour had been gulped down by the waters. All of the houses of the mechanics were gone. Only the lower and upper mills remained standing.

Oregon City had suffered far less, about a third of the lower town being under water. A half dozen buildings, at the most, were demolished. At the flood's height, water coursed down Main Street for half a mile and many buildings were temporarily abandoned. The Clackamas bottoms north of the town, as well as the west shore levels below Linn City, were inundated, with houses deeply submerged or carried away. The Willamette's streaming level stood fifty-five feet higher than its lowest twelve-foot stage reached in summer; it was twelve feet higher than the flood of 1853–54. The falls were so deeply covered as to seem no more than a turbulent rapids. Only the Indians, when questioned, recalled a greater deluge, many, many moons before.

On December 7, the waters ceased to rise; but almost a week more passed before the river was again within its banks.

The *Argus* announced on December 14 that the destruction of the Linn City Works meant an impairment of freight transportation, since with the loss of its freight-handling paraphernalia "freight must be hauled in wagons from Canemah to Oregon City, a distance of a mile, at a large expense and necessarily considerable damage. . . . ." In the future, it was stated, the construction of a breakwater would be "on more philosophical principles."

During the Christmas week there was a light fall of snow over the mid-Willamette country. The white flakes fell, almost without obstruction, upon the denuded flat where Linn City had so recently stood. Even the thin surface of earth which before had covered the harsh rocks had been licked away.

Thereafter, until 1868, little was heard of the former townsite. In that year the Willamette Transportation & Locks Company began excavation for a locks, long contemplated; when finished in 1873, it cut through the rocks at the river's western margin and provided a passageway for boats around the falls. In the late 1880s the industrial development, now lying close to the water's edge on the west bank, was begun. The Crown-Willamette Pulp &

Paper Company mills and an electric plant today stand partly on the site of the lost town.

The present highway to Portland crosses by bridge from Oregon City to the west shore, at a point approximately where Robert Moore operated his early ferry, near the northeast corner of his townsite. Well above the highway and the waters of the river, the modern town of West Linn stands on the same green hill that watched above the havoc of 1861.

HUGH BURNS'S MULTNOMAH CITY

DEEP in pioneer lore lies the history of Multnomah City, long since disappeared and not to be confused with the comparatively modern town of Multnomah, situated ten miles to the northwest on the outskirts of Portland.

Just below Linn City and the falls, Hugh Burns platted a town on his 640-acre land claim. The date was October 9, 1842. He named it after the lower river—called by the Indians, Multnomah.

Today, knowledge of the town is fragmentary and meager. The second issue of the *Spectator*, then edited by W. G. T'Vault, observed on February 19, 1846, that Multnomah City was located on a "beautiful site" and "must in a short time, be a city in appearance as well as in name." Fronting the eastern sky and the river, it faced not so much the daily sunrise, as the hardier ascendancy of its rival, Oregon City; no easy opposition, as time proved.

Hugh Burns recorded his claim first on December 11, 1843, at "Willamette Falls"; again on March 24, 1847; and a third time on April 17, 1850, with the clerk and recorder of Tuality County. The three entries were made in compliance with the several land laws passed by the Provisional and Territorial legislatures. As described, boundary lines began "at a small White Oak on the Waters edge," the adopted corner between Robert Moore's property and that of the claimant. It ran to a stake, thence west to a stake and two witness trees, thence due north to another stake standing forty-one links from a fir tree; from that point it ran to the

Willamette River, up which it meandered to the place of beginning.

A boat landing was Multnomah City's first development, following erection of the log dwelling of the proprietor. The lot lines through the dense evergreens and the thick undergrowth of Oregon grape, salal and salmonberry, must have been but vaguely defined. Improvements on the part of purchasers were not a condition of sale. As proprietor, Burns would defend the rights of his town inhabitants, but industrial growth devolved solely upon lot owners. Joe Meek, the frontiersman and collector of revenue for territorial Oregon, in 1844 paid taxes on "a property in the city of Multnomah."

We learn from Palmer's *Journal* that Hugh Burns was a "native of Ireland, but lately an emigrant from Missouri." He was born in Westmeath, Ireland, in 1807. From the time he came to Oregon he was active in community affairs. Prior to June, 1843, he served as magistrate and justice of the peace for the Yamhill district, which then included the west central Willamette Valley, commonly called the "cow country." On that date, according to Bancroft's *History of Oregon*, Burns resigned; and his town-building competitor on the west bank, Robert Moore, was named in his stead.

In 1845, soon after the organization of the house of representatives of the Provisional Government, Burns and Moore each proposed to locate the seat of government on his respective townsite. Robert Newell at Champoeg, twenty miles up the river, also petitioned that his town be made the capital. Burns offered to donate thirty-two lots and erect a building fifteen by thirty-five feet, and one and one-half stories high. The vote to consider a choice among the three was in favor of the Multnomah City site. But no decision was made; by petition, sixty men from Champoeg and the middle valley caused a deferment of choice. This session of the Provisional Legislature was held at Oregon City, and consequently there the seat of government remained. At the 1846 session, Burns acted as a conciliatory agent, defending the claims of his site and the other townsites at the falls. Also in that year, he signed a petition to incorporate the Multnomah Circulating Library, at Oregon City. He served as judge of elections, first for Tuality County in 1844–46, and in 1849 for the Multnomah precinct, Washington County. On one occasion—January 17, 1846—an election for district justice of the peace and constable was held at Burns's home. The Provisional Government, on December 23, 1847, appointed him one of three Commissioners to handle the financing of the Cayuse War.

From these civil and public activities, Hugh Burns the man, does not emerge clearly individualized from the ten or a dozen major property holders and community builders of his day. J. W. Nesmith spoke of him as a "shrewd Hibernian and the principal blacksmith west of the Rocky Mts." He appears to have been pacific by nature and, at least in his early Oregon years, confident.

In the *Spectator* for February 5, 1846, Burns advertised that the postmaster general, W. G. T'Vault, had contracted with him to "carry mail from Oregon City to Weston, Missouri, for one trip only." Postage was fifty cents on single sheets, and letters, he assured prospective senders, would reach Weston "early in the season;" from there they would be forwarded to any part of the United States. He urged this opportunity upon all wishing to correspond with their friends in the East. Clearly, the affairs of his town were not consuming his time. But neither did mail-carrying, for it was unprofitable and after a few trips he gave it up.

Sometimes early in 1846, or possibly sooner, Wesley Mulkey kept a tavern and tannery at Multnomah City. On April 30, C. D. Smith advertised in the *Spectator* that he was now "occupying the stand formerly kept by Mulky, on the west side of the river and hopes to give general satisfaction to all who may call on him." His terms were "Ready pay, 25 cents per meal. Price for horse over night 75 cents." He accepted all kinds of produce as payment, announcing that he was in the market for one thousand hides, which he would tan on shares or pay for in cash or in "store pay." This meant that he carried at least a partial supply of food stuffs, such as black sugar from the Sandwich Islands, put up in seaweed bags, rice, salt, and necessary staple articles of diet not to be raised on home acreage. Rope, boots, harness and denim cloth may also have been part of his stock in trade.

On June 10 of the following year Mulkey's name again appears. In the *Spectator* for that date he announced that he had purchased the "lower Ferry across the Willamette River at Oregon City, for the term of 15 months," and offered to "ferry everything at reduced prices for ready pay." His charges were "wheat two cents per bushel, wagons fifty cents per trip, man and horse twenty cents per trip, lumber and everything else in proportion." He was willing to deliver the wheat at "either of the mills" for the same price. The mills were at Linn City and Oregon City; there was none at Multnomah City. In that day of meager cash, wheat and all kinds of produce were acceptable payment for services rendered. He invited prospective trade to "take the left hand road about one and a half miles from Oregon City," where a "first rate road down to Multnomah City" was to be found. Such instructions guided the homesteader and the traveler to the ferry's east-shore connection, on property owned by John McLoughlin and so across river to the timbered streets of Hugh Burns's small hamlet. The court records of 1847 show that Mulkey was also sheriff of Tuality County.

It was in that year that Joel Palmer, later Superintendent of Indian Affairs for Oregon Territory, while passing down river prior to returning East, saw at Multnomah City "but few buildings, and some mechanics settled in it." These latter were the operatives of the adjacent mills, docks and tanneries, most of them located at Linn City, adjoining on the south. The term mechanic, in that day, applied to anyone engaged in a manual trade, as distinguished from professions and farming.

That Burns negotiated the sale of at least a handful of his town lots is indicated by his "Stop Thief" advertisement, dated June 12, 1847, and published in the *Spectator*—wherein he reported, that among various articles of clothing and bedding stolen out of his house, was his pocket book, which contained a small sheaf of notes payable to him "or bearer." These, as itemized, bore dates as early as 1845 and were for amounts as high as $431.75. He listed ten documents. It is not known whether the thief was ever apprehended or the bills finally collected.

Late in 1847 or early in 1848, Burns came into possession of the "lower ferry," previously operated by Mulkey. For the right to operate, the County Court of Tuality, on May 9, 1848, ordered that he be "taxed the sum of fifteen dollars . . . . . for each year he had received his charter from the Legislature." But the date of the charter is not given among the multitudinous notations of court transactions, orders and applications. The same court, on the day previous, had ruled that James M. Moore, son of the owner of the rival townsite of Linn City, was "appointed supervisor of Mult-nomah and Linn City District, which said district extends to the Bute (Mount Sylvania) on the road to Tualaty Plains and below in the Willamette River to Sucker Creek, and south to the County Line." Multnomah City, it would appear, had been prospering mildly.

The following year, James Moore, fortified by the prominence of his position applied for a license to keep the lower ferry; his application was opposed by Burns and was refused. Consequently, when Burns sought to renew his license, on August 6, 1850, he was contested by Moore, with the result that the matter was laid over until September 2. With the matter left to the pleasure of the court, Burns was, for no stated reason, denied a renewal of his license.

Soon after that, Robert Moore, proprietor of Linn City, was granted a renewal of ferry rights for the "upper ferry," which he had operated for several years, and in which McLoughlin also had an interest. The west shore ferry point, as designated by this grant, was from the lower end of Linn City and the upper end of Multnomah City. This act probably consolidated the two services. Moore's license was for one year, and he was assessed $100 and held in bond of $1000 to operate with "proper boats." One may surmise that the lack of water-worthy equipment caused the cancellation of the lower ferry service, or that McLoughlin, interested in both ferries, wished to avoid unnecessary duplication.

From a document dated August 23, but with the year omitted—presumably 1849—we learn that Hugh Burns petitioned the legislative body "now in session" for charter rights to construct a bridge across the Willamette at the falls. The signature of Walter Pomeroy appeared as a second name, with that of John McLoughlin scratched out. The paper asked that the enterprise be chartered under the name of the *Multnomah Bridge Company*. Construction was to be of wood, or of chains, or both, at the discretion of the builders. The document read in part: "That the growing importance of the falls of the Willamette, increase of travel in and through the towns adjacent, dangers of delays of ferriage across said river below and near the falls, require for the public good and convenience the speedy construction of a bridge . . . . . which shall . . . . . connect the cities of Multnomah and Oregon. . ." However, the *Oregon Archives* do not show the entry of this petition. If it was acted upon it was soon dispensed with. The bridge was never built.

The lots of Burns's town, after a fairly promising start, gradually diminished in sale. On August 7, 1851, he gave to John March Smith, an "esteemed friend" living in distant Baltimore, Maryland, a quit claim deed for Lot 1, Block 4, in Multnomah City. Burns had just returned from San Francisco, where he had purchased coffee and sugar to sell to the Oregon trade. But the country, he said in the letter accompanying the deed East, was "almost knee deep with coffee and sugar," and he was not making a profit. The former was fourteen cents a pound, the latter six cents. Later, while in the East, visiting at Baltimore, on May 5, 1853, he further secured this parcel of property for his friend, by a second quit claim deed, personally filed. The lot was an outright gift and lay near the ferry landing on the south side of the town where a store building faced east.

Thereafter the name of Multnomah City dims upon the records. West-shore river traffic tied up at Linn City's more accommodating wharves, and Multnomah City became merely the northern environs of that growing port. A road that in 1850 was cut through from Portland—a difficult thirteen-mile course over wooded grades and through swampy hollows—carved its irregular margins through the upper level of Hugh Burns's townsite. However, industrial prosperity was nearer the falls; and the traveler hastened onward to Linn City. "The falls of the Willamette affords ample water privileges for the erection of machinery of every description, to any extent desired," *Spectator* editor T'Vault had observed in 1846. But Multnomah City was a half-mile from its driving waters.

The high water of November, 1853, which inundated the low levels about the falls on both sides of the Willamette, swept away the crude plank landings and some of the clustered buildings. There was small incentive to rebuild. Scattered log houses maintained a tenacious foothold amidst the still dense woodlands. Here and there some settler's garden plot lay fenced about by sharpened stakes to keep out the wild deer. "Stranger, where's Multnomah City?"

▨ CLACKAMAS CITY ABOVE THE RAPIDS

EASTWARD of the Willamette, on the south shore of the Clackamas River and a long half-mile upstream from where that lesser body comes to a brawling confluence with the greater stream, stood pioneer Clackamas City. Here on property claimed by the Methodist Mission and likewise by Dr. John McLoughlin, a young and sometimes brash Virginian by name of Charles E. Pickett staked off a claim of one square mile. On a portion he platted a townsite, offering the lots for sale in an advertisement in the first issue of the *Spectator*, February 5, 1846. No lot price was given but the advantages of the site were stressed to the effect that: "The situation of the ground is dry, level, and at least ten feet above the highest water mark; and from it to the crossing of the Clackamas, where a bridge will be built the coming season, an almost level road can be spread."

From this town-building enterprise, the Methodist Church, feeling theirs a prior claim, attempted to discourage young Pickett. Instead, Pickett by his acts and pertinacity, broke the local monopoly. Land-hungry settlers poured in to build homes around the falls. Incidentally, Pickett's advertisement of "Town Lots for Sale" was the first real estate advertisement to appear on the Pacific Coast.

But a few months after this the restless young man—he was twenty-five and of the Virginia family known as the "Fighting Picketts"—left overland for California.

To whom the founder left his embryo town is not known, although A. Husted advertised in the *Spectator*, January 7, 1847, that he would sell "his interest in the undisposed Town Lots of Clackamas City."

Captain James D. Miller, early riverboat pilot, recalled in a series of articles in the *Oregon Historical Quarterly*, in 1930, that soon after the arrival of his parents, "Father traded our mules and horses for one acre of land in Clackamas, a city on paper adjoining Oregon City town plat." That was in 1848.

The town early showed not only promise, but growth. In an advertisement dated July 9, 1847, but not published until August 5, in the *Spectator* under the head of "Clackamas City School," Carlos W. Shane, principal, announced: "The second session of the Clackamas City School will commence on Monday next, July 12th, and will continue twelve weeks. All the branches usually taught in common school will be attended to. Particular attention will be paid to the Intellectual, Moral and Physical habits of the pupils."

In making his bid for the "attention of Parents" he points out that his location was a "very eligible one, both for health and convenience." Also, he stated that "The playgrounds of the school will soon be arranged on the most approved plans, and everything done for the good of those taught." By his accommodations, he was limited to twenty-five scholars. Principal Shane's school was one of the first half-dozen schools opened to the public in the entire Oregon Country. Parents of pupils attending made their terms with the schoolmaster; but what, in this instance, the terms were, has not been preserved. In pioneer days the usual practice was to pay teachers of the common branches of knowledge from four to eight dollars a pupil for one season's instruction. Since actual money was scarce, rate bills, bearing a stipulated trade value, were frequently given as payment. These were then negotiable at the various places of trade within the community.

The issue of the *Spectator* that carried the advertisement of the Clackamas City School, printed also in the advertising columns the trade announcement of Norriss & Cutting. With the salute, "Oh Yes! Everybody," they informed their friends and the public of their location and that they were prepared to "carry on the Blacksmithing Business in all its various branches as follows: All kinds of wrought mill work, and farming utensils. Ironing new and repairing old Wagons, Carts, Dearborns, &c. Edge tools of every kind made and repaired, also cast steel Boaring Augurs, Bells, Gun Work, Spurs of every description. . ." They offered services "on as reasonable terms or a little cheaper than any other shop in Oregon."

Following these announcements, Clackamas City enjoyed a period of moderate prosperity. A sawmill stood on the bank of the Clackamas River and its constant cut of timber was large. There were at least a few dwellings. Of stores, there is no record. A large Clackamas Indian village and "flint factory" stood about a half-mile farther upstream.

Thereafter, for two years, references to the town that faced the Clackamas Rapids did not appear in the *Spectator*. Finally, in a three-column article extolling local town-development that Editor Blain spread over the second page of the issue of December 13, 1849, mention of Clackamas City reappeared. It was a brief paragraph in an unusually long article, as though the editor had suddenly thought it advisable to sing the praises of the communities from which his paper drew its livelihood. The paragraph read: "Between the Falls of the Willamette and the mouth of the Clackamas are situated the following places. Oregon City, Green Point, Clackamas City, Linn City and Multnomah City. These will in all probability at some future day constitute the different wards of one great city. At present the entire population is about 1,200."

Since the paper was published at Oregon City, it was of that town that the far-visioning editor was thinking, when he so tactfully referred to the "one great city."

On Sunday, April 1, 1850, the Rev. George H. Atkinson, Congregational missionary residing at Oregon City, noted in his *Diary:* "In the afternoon I commenced preaching again at Klackamas City. Had a full room." But on May 16, again a Sabbath day, he reported less sanguinely: "P. M. at Clackamas had a smaller number than usual. Found a Sabbath school of 18, 3 teachers."

And as the years passed the Reverend Atkinson was unable to report any growth in attendance at Clackamas City services, jotting in his *Diary* for February 17, 1851: "I have been employed as usual from Sabbath to Sabbath, having a cong'n of about 50 in the morning [Oregon City] & 50 to 80 in the eve. At Linn City about 20 or 25 attend, at Clackamas City, from 12 to 20 including children."

Thereafter Clackamas City as a place-name disappears from the records. There is reason to believe that the mills, damaged in the freshet of 1849, were later at least partly rebuilt. As confirmation of this belief—after the river steamer *Lot Whitcomb* went into service, she occasionally stopped to load lumber near the mouth of the Clackamas.

Today the lowlands, where the former town struggled for life, are overspread by vegetable gardens, hopyards, and pastures.

CANEMAH, "THE CANOE PLACE"

SITUATED strategically at the head of the falls and the terminus of upper-river traffic, Canemah was an important point in early river commerce. To the land-seekers the falls marked the gateway to interior Oregon; all pioneer travel halted at the foot of those cascading waters. There on the gravelly flat of the east shore, beneath the upthrusts of granite, camped Oregon's incoming homemakers, bound for locations farther up the valley. There among the cottonwoods and evergreens stood the first homes and store buildings and on the shoreward rocks, John McLoughlin's flouring mill. There, during the earliest years of white settlement, Indians—Clough-we-wallah and Clackamas tribesmen—still lingered in their fishing huts. To pass upstream on the east, the pioneers' ox-drawn wagons mounted by a difficult winding way over the shoulder of the bluffs. By that route travellers reached the flat above the falls at the water's east edge, from whence they continued by river or by trail. The area there was from ancient times an Indian encampment, claimed principally by the Calapooyas, and was known as Canemah, "the Canoe-place."

Because of the gateway position of this natural harbor,

Canemah early in the third decade of white settlement became a shipping town that flourished for a time and then, with the waning of river commerce, declined and finally ceased to exist as a separate town. Today, as a living place-name, Canemah is seldom heard.

Canemah's original claimants were a powerful clan exacting tribute of all other Indians seeking the privilege of fishing above the falls. According to local legend, other tribes resented the excessive tribute asked, and, while the Canemah's slept, made a concerted sortie upon them, killing them all—men, women, and children, some three thousand persons. When the first American settlers arrived in the 1840s not a single Canemah remained among the Indian villagers.

The earliest American to stake a land claim on the old Canemah campsite was Absalom F. Hedges. Born in Ohio, October 13, 1817, he learned the carpenter's trade and in 1844 crossed the plains to Oregon. Home-seekers were then pouring into the Willamette Valley, some of them commercially ambitious. The seeds of townhood sprouted wherever a cluster of houses, a mill, a store, or a warehouse tossed plumes of smoke skyward.

Hedges came to the embryo Oregon City late in 1844. The entire falls area appealed to him as a desirable place to get a start, but the best of Oregon City was already in other hands and much of its property was involved in unsavory dispute over ownership. Climbing above the falls, by the steep grade to the left, be confidently staked his donation claim on the flat land almost at the brink of the cascading waters.

Here he built a cabin and there all day the slow-moving oxen and heavy wagons of portagers and land-seekers labored past his door. Downstream came the canoes and flatboats, the latter manned by Indian paddlers who beached their wieldy craft at the foot of his property. Loaded on portage wagons, the produce of the first settlers was transported down the difficult Canemah trail to Oregon City. Back up Canemah hill came the reloaded wagons, bearing a miscellaneous freight for upper valley residents, or with the worldly possessions of the new arrivals.

Hedges, energetic, ambitious and adventurous, was not

the type to take to farming; it is doubtful if he ever intended
to till his land. It was timbered, a part of it rocky, some of
it steep. He had, instead, an inclination for commercial
endeavor, and the shrewd yet affable nature needed to carry
such efforts forward. As early as 1846 he ventured into
business, operating a tannery under the firm name of Pomeroy, Hedges & Kirby.

In 1846 he married Elizabeth Jane Barlow, the 16-year old
daughter of the recently arrived Mount Hood road-breaker,
Samual K. Barlow.

Hedges realized that he owned a natural townsite at his
canoe-place location. Consequently, sometime in the latter
part of 1849 he laid out into lots a sizeable portion of his
property, and invited the establishment of stores, warehouses, and other trade ventures. With William Barlow, a
brother-in-law, Hedges opened a store and sawmill. He chose
for a town name, Falls City.

In the December 13, 1849 issue of the *Spectator*, a special
number lauding the Falls area, the write-up of Falls City
commanded more space than that given Linn City or Multnomah City. It read:

"This is a new town just laid out by A. F. Hedges, Esq.
It is situated on the east side of the Willamette, immediately
above the Falls, and adjoining Oregon City. It enjoys great
commercial advantages as the terminus of the navigation of
the Willamette from above. It undoubtedly will in a few
years become a place of very considerable business. Though
Falls City was surveyed only a few weeks since, such is the
spirit of improvement, that we see several new houses
erected, now we are assured that others will be erected soon.
We are authorized to say that a lot will be cheerfully donated
to any Christian denomination that may wish to erect a
house of worship at Falls City. To those who wish to make
investments this town holds out flattering inducements. We
wish Mr. Hedges success in his enterprise."

The record of the commercial growth of Falls City is
somewhat obscure. It is known that in its early epoch the
town contained several stores, hotels, feed yards for oxen, a
blacksmith shop, a plough factory, and two or three warehouses. A board walk was laid along the waterside, con-

necting the place with Oregon City. Sometime around 1850 the native name reasserted itself; Falls City was gradually discontinued in favor of Canemah.

Meanwhile, the farm produce of the upper valley was coming down river in greater and greater quantity. Enough settlers were now tilling the fertile bottomlands and prairies to make agriculture important. The chief market for Oregon-grown goods was the California gold fields, and Willamette Valley producers were shipping all they did not themselves consume or sell or trade locally. Much of that produce came to lower river ports by way of the long artery of the Willamette River, much of it being trans-shipped at Canemah.

When Willamette Valley shipments increased to a point where the small Indian-manned boats and farmers' craft could not handle the volume, and produce accumulated at landings and in riverside warehouses, alert minds realized that steamboats were necessary if freight was to be moved with the needed dispatch.

Hedges was one of the first fall's residents to see the promising river-traffic opportunities. A depression in the rocks at Canemah offered a natural harbor for boats; there the water was deep and still just before its plunge. Hedges had accumulated some money from his ventures into business and town-building, and had friends with additional funds. Riverboats could be built right at the Canemah dockside at comparatively low cost. The machinery for powering such craft must be procured in the distant East, however, and required a cash outlay. Purchase, Hedges believed, should be made personally by the buyer. Obtaining several thousand dollars of the newly-coined Beaver money, in five and ten dollar gold pieces, he put them in a satchel and embarked by vessel late in 1849, via the Isthmus of Panama, for New York City. When he arrived there, he found that the Oregon territorial money, privately minted, although literally worth more than its face value, was not legal tender in the East. He therefore had to go to the United States mint at New Orleans, where he changed his gold coins into proper money.

In the meantime word reached the *Spectator* late in July,

1850, that Hedges had purchased two 30-horsepower engines in the Louisiana city, and that these were soon to be shipped *via* Cape Horn to Canemah. Returning overland late that year, Hedges and his partners—Captain Charles Bennett, Alanson Beers, Hamilton Campbell, and John McClosky—constructed their first steamer, the *Canemah*.

That boat, however, was not the first steam-powered vessel on the upper river. In May, 1851, the small steamer *Hoosier*—that long-boat of a sailing vessel with a pile-driver engine—was the first to go into service from the Canemah docks and the first above Willamette Falls. There followed the *Washington*, brought north from San Francisco on the deck of a windjammer. Third was the *Multnomah*, built of Jersey oak shipped West, with a barrel hull that required no calking. Put together at Canemah, she began service late in 1851.

The *Canemah* was launched about the end of September, 1851. She was built of Oregon native woods and was of good workmanship; a sidewheeler, 135 feet long, 19 feet beam, with 4 feet of hold. Her bows were blunt, her stern square. Fitted to carry passengers and freight, she went into immediate and profitable service, piloted by Captains Bennett and McClosky. Illustrative of her profits is the twenty-cent-per-bushel rate she received for transporting grain from Avery & Company, Corvallis, handlers of a large part of the grain then raised in Benton County. She became the first traveling post office in Oregon when her owners were awarded the contract for carrying the upper-river mails. Nathaniel Coe, appointed postal agent for Oregon Territory in 1852, took up his quarters on board, where he sorted the letters and papers and packages for Willamette Valley points as the boat steamed from landing to landing.

A contributing factor in the town's growth was the blasting of a new portage road out of the solid rock, almost at the water's edge from Oregon City to Canemah. It eliminated the sharp grade of the old road, over which trade had grown so heavy it utilized sometimes three score wagons a day. Construction of the new road was authorized jointly by the people of Canemah and Oregon City, who raised $20,000 by popular subscription; Peter H. Hatch was com-

missioned to do the job. Throughout 1853 and 1854 the
new road, which was shorter and provided a nearly level
route, was used day and night by a never-ending line of
transfer wagons. Although traffic was considerably speeded,
teamsters had a difficult time passing one another on the
narrow rock shelf. At night great flares burned continually
beside the portage way. About this time, at the Oregon City
end, to further assist the handling of freight, D. P. Thompson, Asa L. Lovejoy, and the Dement brothers, William and
John, built a wooden-strap railway along what was then
Main and Water streets, to a warehouse dock at the foot of
Eighth Street. Mules furnished power for the small open
cars.

Trans-shipping trade, immigration, and the general business of a town so strategically situated, made Canemah an
important and colorful place throughout the 1850s. The
building of additional stores, warehouses and shops catering
to a variety of trade, and private residences, expanded the
town until its rear doors virtually opened against the hills
rising to the east.

Nine or ten boats were built at Canemah during the
1850s. The *Shoalwater*, better known as the *Fenix* and then
the *Franklin*, and later as the *Minnie Holmes* (for a popular
lady of Oregon City), followed Hedges' first venture. Built
by Captain Leonard White in 1852, she was owned by
McCarver & Son, Oregon City merchants. The *Shoalwater*
suffered the first boiler explosion in Oregon, a blown flue
injuring a number of persons and damaging the boat. In
hope that she would escape the jinx which had beset her, the
boat was renamed the *Fenix*, for that fabled bird hatched
from the ashes of disaster, the phonetic spelling admitting
of larger letters on the pilot house. However, the new name
failed to remove ill-luck and she was twice renamed. She
was a light draft side-wheeler about ninety feet long, propelled by two small geared engines that supplied more noise
than power.

Meanwhile the *Canemah*, cruising to and fro on the upper
Willamette, in the summer of 1853 blew a boiler flue below
Champoeg, the explosion killing one passenger, Marion
Holcroft, and scalding two or three others. The following

year the *Canemah* was bought by Captains Fred Cole, J. C. Ainsworth, Chris Sweitzer and George A. Pease, and put under the command of Captain Theodore Wygant.

After the disposal of the *Canemah*, Hedges and his associates built the *Wallamet*. That large side-wheeler was constructed at a time—1853–54—when labor costs were high—from $5 to $6 a day, because of the heavy exodus of men to the southern Oregon gold fields. Once in the river she was quite unwieldy and difficult to manoeuver, especially among the snags and gravel bars which obstructed the Willamette at that time. Built for larger traffic demands than the Willamette could furnish, she soon proved too expensive to run. Within a year she had lost so much money for her owners that she was taken below the falls for use on the Portland-Astoria run, but soon went to San Francisco and later to the Sacramento River. At the time of her removal she was successfully lined over the Willamette Falls, Captain George Jerome aboard.

While the ship-building fever was at its height and competition was keen, the most tragic disaster in Willamette steamboat history occurred at the Canemah dockside. The *Gazelle*, a side-wheeler built by Page, Bacon & Company for the Willamette Falls Canal, Milling and Transportation Company of Linn City, made her trial run on March 18, 1854. She went into immediate regular service, in charge of Captain Robert Hereford. At 6:30 on April 8, 1854, the *Gazelle* had come over from the long wharf above Linn City, on the west shore and was tied up for a 15-minute stop at the Canemah docks, prior to her up-river run. In preparation for rapid departure, the engineer crowded on a heavy head of steam without opening the safety valves. Some sixty persons were aboard when at 6:40 both her boilers went up with a deafening explosion, killing twenty persons outright, and injuring everyone else aboard; four others died later. Among the casualties were John Clemens, the pilot, David Page, part-owner, Judge Samuel L. Burch of Polk County, and the Rev. J. P. Miller of Takenah, later Albany. Many of the victims were hurled into the water. J. M. Pudge, pilot of the *Wallamet* lying alongside, was killed by flying debris. The *Gazelle* sank where she was tied. Some blamed the steamship company for poor equipment, but the tragedy was generally chargeable to the engineer, who had tied-down the safety valve so that no steam could escape.

A coroner's jury found the explosion "resulted from the gross and culpable negligence of First Engineer, Moses Tonie, in knowingly carrying more steam than was safe and neglecting to keep sufficient water in the boilers."

The wreck of the *Gazelle* was sold, lined over the Falls in August, and restored as the *Senorita*.

Canemah was at the peak of its prosperity when the flood of 1861 struck. The town, almost at river level, suffered more than any other community excepting Linn City and Champoeg. Practically every building was washed away. For some unknown reason the few papers of the day gave Canemah small mention in that catastrophe, and a detailed analysis of destruction is lacking from the records.

One event, however, did capture journalistic attention and has not been forgotten. When the flood was at its greatest, the daring Captain George W. Taylor rode the small steamer *St. Claire* from Canemah over the falls and into the lower river. The women and children of Canemah, since the men were busily engaged in salvaging, lit beacon fires at their retreat atop the bluffs, in celebration of the boat's plunge through the boiling waters. It was agreed that Captain Taylor should pull the whistle as he entered the lower stream if he were still alive and his boat dry. As the triumphant toot-toot-toot came echoing over the river and against the rocks, a shout went up from the massed onlookers.

After the flood Canemah emerged from the receding waters and a number of buildings were restored and the wharves rebuilt. River transportation was resumed. While the flood had removed some of the smaller riverside towns, the larger ones, more fortunately situated, now grew rapidly. At Canemah, essentially a portage point, commercial activity revived quickly despite an unacknowledged feeling that something of community promise had "gone over the Falls."

With upper valley residents demanding an outlet for their produce, the People's Transportation Company, with sixty-five stockholders variously located between Oregon City and Eugene, was organized. That combine constructed an improved basin above the falls and a canal of sorts below, thereby somewhat shortening the portage distance. At Canemah a new boat-building program was begun. A more prosperous future was anticipated.

In 1865 a portage railway was built around the Falls on the east bank. Over the iron track moved a hoisting car for the handling of freight.

Meanwhile, in 1863, the *Enterprise*, constructed in Canemah's tranquil waters was launched by a group which included Captain George A. Pease, C. E. Pope, and Nathaniel Lane, Sr. Three years later the boat passed to the People's Company. The *Reliance*, launched in 1864, was built by the latter organization. The *Active* also entered the waters here, constructed by the competing Willamette Steam Navigation Company in 1865. Three years later the *Success*, built by Captain E. W. Baughman, D. P. Thompson, and J. Winston, was launched to compete with the boats of the People's line. But when she came to grief a short time after, she was taken over by that monopoly. In 1868 the People's Company fashioned the *Albany* on the Canemah ways, while the Willamette line launched the *Echo*. Within ten years the People's Company spent more than one million dollars in steamboat and dock construction, and other improvements, maintaining a virtual monopoly on the upper river.

But the uncertain portage facilities between Oregon City and Canemah were doomed when in 1870 the State Legislature granted an allotment of $200,000 to the Willamette Transportation and Locks Company, operating on the opposite side of the river, for the building of boat-locks there. In 1871, while construction work was in progress, the dispirited People's interests sold out to Ben Holladay, then building the Oregon Central Railway.

Two years later the west-side locks were opened for travel.

Boat building declined on the upper river in the 'seventies, only three boats being built at Canemah in that decade: the *Shoo-Fly*, the *Alice*, 150 feet long and among the largest boats to navigate the upper river, and the *McMinnville*, 132 feet in length built in 1877. All three operated under the People's banner. Those were the last boats constructed above the falls.

Absalom Hedges was no longer an important figure in the town he had founded. The flood had swept away much of his investment. Soon after he lost heavily when loans he had made in gold were repaid in greenbacks at a time when they had depreciated in value, and debts as a consequence could be discharged at fifty cents on the dollar. In the 'seventies his health failed and he moved to eastern Oregon, where he acquired a minor position in the Indian Service, in Malheur County. He died of consumption at North Yakima, Washington, in 1890, at the age of 73.

With the diminishing of river transportation, Canemah, as a separate community, gradually faded. In the 1880s the warehouses, corrals, and a few commercial establishments stood like aging monuments to past greatness, a few dwellings scattered among them. On the green hill that rose sharply behind the flat were the comfortable, sometimes pretentious dwellings of retired merchants and river captains. Canemah, referred to less often by name, gradually became known as a part of Oregon City, a merger so subtle as to cause no protest.

In the *Oregon City Enterprise* for December 11, 1891, this item appeared:

"There worked up through the mud of Main Street the other day a section of the old rails of the tramway that did duty three or four years in the early 60s in transferring freight around the falls between the upper and lower river. D. P. Thompson, A. L. Lovejoy and the Dements built and operated that road and it made more money than any other mile of railway in the Northwest. The motive power was mules. The rails were wood. The road extended from Canemah down the river, traversing Main street to Fourth, and, turning then to the river bank, following down to the present wharf of the Oregon City Transportation company. In 1865 the 'basin' was completed so that boats could come to the present Imperial mill. Arrangements were made for transferring freight there, passing it through the warehouse and down to steamers below the falls. Then the old tramway went into disuse and the street was graded over it. That mode of transfer continued till the locks were completed in 1872. There was no steam railway in the valley in those days and the river transportation business was immense in volume and in the profit it yielded."

The same newspaper, in its New Years Day edition for 1892 remarked that, "Oregon City, the seat of justice of Clackamas county has a population of about 5,000 souls. There is a cluster of communities that have names of their own but which are practically part of this city. Canemah, Elyville, Park Place, Gladstone and Paper Mill on the east side and the village on the west side of the river connected with Oregon City by a suspension bridge are among these, ..."

View of west side locks, Oregon City, with suspension bridge in background. *N. R. Lang* is sternwheeler at right in front of paper mills. (SP Col., OHS)

Of these early steamboats on the Willamette, the *Multnomah*, shown below in lower Portland harbor, was assembled in 1851 at Canemah. Short and square, she was not easy to handle in the sometimes swift current of the lower Willamette. The *Wallamet* was constructed 1853-54 for Willamette use, but soon moved below the falls. (Both prints from original OHS daguerreotypes.)

1860s view of *Enterprise* near Corvallis,
with full load, probably wheat.
(Fred W. Wilson Collection, OHS.)

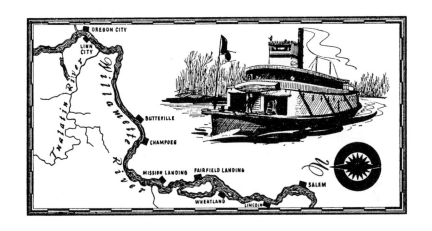

WHEAT PORTS OF THE MIDDLE RIVER...

Butteville of Yesterday

Old Champoeg

Fairfield Landing

Wheatland at Matheny's Ferry

Lincoln, Metropolis of Wheat

"EIGHT miles from Pudding River is a village called Butes. It was laid out by Messrs. Abernethy and Beers. There were but a few cabins in it when I left. The proprietor had erected a warehouse to store wheat they might purchase of the settlers, who should find it convenient to sell their crops at this point. At this place are some conical hills called Butes, which rise to considerable heights; the sides and tops of them are clothed with tall fir trees, which can be seen from the valley for sixty miles."

So wrote Joel Palmer in his *Journal* of 1845, published in 1847. That was the first printed mention of the river hamlet that soon became known as La Butte and, by 1850, as Butteville. The most prominent of the hills mentioned, standing about a mile to the southwest, is today still called LaButte, but cannot be seen from any such distance as Palmer declared, since its height does not exceed 427 feet. One "t" in Butte was, until about 1860, frequently omitted or overlooked, even by the newspapers of the day and region.

As staked out by George Abernethy and Alanson Beers, of the Methodist Missionary forces, Butteville expected to grow rapidly into a metropolis. It lay at the extreme northern edge of French Prairie, sixteen miles above Oregon City, and much of its trade was drawn from the prairie ranchers, retired French-Canadian trappers of the Hudson's Bay Company. Wheat and other produce of the settlers was handled at the Butteville warehouse and shipped north for export to the Sandwich Islands and China. The founders planned a town that would compete with Champoeg, three miles up the river.

Much of the story of Butteville's early commercial and social life is lost. In early years the name frequently referred to the entire Butteville district, an area of about fifteen square miles. At its best, Butteville was, through the 'forties, little more than a river landing, with a warehouse and a few dwellings.

It attained its majority when Francois Xavier Matthieu opened a general mercantile business there in 1850 or 1851. Matthieu had been a "mountain man," trapping in the

Yellowstone Country from 1839 to 1841, for the American
Fur Company. Coming to the French Prairie in 1842, he
had lived for two years on the ranch of Etienne Lucier, in
the Champoeg district. There he farmed, made wagons and
did carpentry work for his neighbors; more than one rancher
had a home built by Matthieu. Also, during that time he
played an important role in establishing the Provisional
Government of Oregon, casting a favorable vote in the historic Champoeg meeting of May 2, 1843. At that time
Matthieu was chosen a constable for the district. It was
said that he frequently settled unneighborly differences by
inviting the parties to his board for dinner.

In 1844 Matthieu married Rose Osant, the daughter of a
nearby trapper-settler. Two years later he took a donation
claim, about a mile southwest of the river landing, then most
commonly called La Butte. He had many friends among his
own people, the Canadian-French, and when he opened his
store, in a building half of logs and half of crude boards, he
numbered many of them among his customers. Some came
from a considerable distance to trade with him. A day-by-
day journal of the store's business, which he kept from its
opening date through 1853, reveals that he carried the
accounts of many of the valley's leading citizens. Among
these were George Gay, early English settler, Michael La-
Framboise, long-trusted emissary of the Hudson's Bay Company, and Robert Newell. In partnership with Matthieu
for two years was George LaRoque, owner of the claim lying
at the west edge of town.

So significant was the advent of this store that it has
sometimes been erroneously stated that Francois Matthieu
was Butteville's founder. There is, however, some evidence
that the storekeeper may have been responsible for the first
actual platting of the town, in 1851. At any rate, the plat
showed sixteen blocks of eight lots each, lots being sixty by
one hundred feet. Alleys ran lengthwise of the blocks. Lots
in the three riverfront blocks were 190 feet deep, and were
without alleys. Streets sixty feet wide separated the blocks;
few of them were then built on, some were partly tree-clad.
Street names were Lane, Butte and Marion; and Main,
Second and Third, the latter three running at right angles

to the river. Matthieu's store stood on lot 1, on the corner of Butte Avenue and Front Street. His property ran to the river's abrupt edge.

At least a portion of Matthieu's store sales were paid for in trade. This meant that trappers, settlers and Indians exchanged such products as beaver skins, buckskin, salt salmon, wheat, shingles and saw logs, for staple commodities; or, as frequently occurred, that they gave these as payment for indebtedness contracted with one another. Not until the mid-1850s did gold pass from hand to hand as the standard medium of exchange.

In more than one way, Matthieu was the early life-spirit of the river hamlet. Sometimes his business ability and acumen called him into usefulness elsewhere. Sydney Smith, of Chehalem, in the 'fifties, some years after he had pre-empted the land claim left at Ewing Young's death, called upon the French-Canadian to help him make out a bill of sale for a lot of white-fir logs destined for the Oregon City mills. When Smith attempted to float them, the first out, heavy with sap, sank deeply into the waters of Chehalem Creek. With some effort he dragged a log out, bored a hole in one end and inserted a cedar plug. The log then floated, one end at water level. He treated each one similarly. Smith, whatever the problem, could get his logs to market, but he needed a "mind for figures" to help him make out the bill of sale.

Although canoes, keelboats and flatboats had brought and taken produce for several years previously, the first steamboats touched at Butteville wharves in 1851. Increased settlement of the region brought added produce to all the river landings, for shipment. Likewise, the convenience and economy of river transit invited passenger travel to an extent unknown before. Unfortunately many of the earliest boats were of flimsy construction and accidents were not uncommon. Calamity befell the *Shoalwater*, when a flue collapsed at a point near Butteville, on her upward trip, on Saturday, April 30, 1853. The *Statesman* reported a week later that "Twelve or fifteen persons were blown into the water, but no one materially injured."

In 1853 the mail routes for the Willamette Valley and

adjacent Oregon, were published in the territorial newspapers; the route from Portland to Salem progressed "to a
point opposite Butteville, thence across the Willamette River
to Champoeg, to Fairfield, to Salem."

Some idea of the importance of the town is to be gained
from the Fourth of July celebration held there in 1853. As
reported in the *Statesman* for July 12: "The 4th was celebrated at Butteville, in this county, in good style. Dr. White
was president of the day. David Crawford, Marshall, Rev.
Mr. Fackler, Chaplain, J. D. Moores read the Declaration,
and Hon. G. L. Curry delivered an address, after which the
assemblage partook of a sumptuous repast. There were
about 300 persons in attendance. The "shooting" on the
occasion is said to have been loud, and the toasts excellent.
(No rain)."

The same issue of the *Statesman* carried in its third page
advertising columns a lengthy "Notice to Travelers," which
opened:

"Charles Banget (more generally known as Cheff) the
well-known French teamster, at Oregon City, having located
himself at Butteville, Marion County, Oregon, would
respectfully inform the traveling public that he is now prepared to convey passengers from Butteville to Salem, by
stage, in the shortest time possible; his horses being of a
good selection, and his carriage large and comfortable."

Also, Banget had in readiness a "goodly number of bag-
gage wagons" and "horses for the saddle, both for ladies and
gentlemen." He remarked that "the road from Butteville
to Salem is level the entire distance, and the two places are
more easy of access to each other than any point below the
head of low water navigation."

The 1857 Fourth of July celebration was recorded in the
regional press. Dr. William Keil, his fellow townsmen, and
the German Brass Band came from the recently established
community of Aurora, about four miles to the east, through
the timber and wild meadows of the lower Pudding River
country. The visitors, while at some distance from the scene
of the festivities, were met and escorted into town. Around
the liberty pole raised in the square a large crowd already
stood gathered. With the opening of the "Star Spangled

Butteville's convenient river location at head of French Prairie made it important in the valley's pioneer life. Present (1972) peaceful aspect, above, contrasts with activity of town's 1894 Fourth of July celebration below. Both views look toward riverfront location of former docks.

Banner," which every one sang heartily, the flag was run up; heads stood bared until the song was concluded. Thereupon a throaty cheer was hurled abroad to the morning. Finally, the town cannon, a small ship's howitzer, was fired, to the great delight of the small boys and the assurance of all present. Thereafter, the day progressed with speeches by the Reverend S. M. Fackler, of the Episcopal Church, and Amory Holbrook of Oregon City. The Declaration of Independence was declaimed by J. H. Stevens. Grand marshal for the day was W. H. Rees, a local resident. The picnic dinner followed in the grove, where four tables each seated 150 persons, happy with this opportunity for social intercourse. Speechmaker for the afternoon was the Reverend Hoyt, of Salem. Butteville was doing itself proud.

In November, 1859, Butteville was resurveyed by R. V. Short, and an addition called St. Alexcie was laid out, adjoining on the southwest. As a matter of fact, the plat which Short filed with the County Recorder showed the former town included under the St. Alexcie banner. But that, as it soon developed, was an extravagant ambition, for the new name never came into use. It was undoubtedly derived from the first name of Alexis Aubichon, out of whose claim and that of Joseph La Forte, the two towns were carved. Lane Street was rechristened Union, and new streets were French and American. At least twenty blocks were added, seven of them facing the river. It is plausible to believe that a good many more residents then claimed Butteville as their home.

In the same year Butteville Academy was incorporated by an act of the State Legislature. Matthieu was listed as a trustee, with eight others: George L. Curry, G. A. Cone, George Hibler, Ely Cooley, J. W. Grimm, F. W. Geer and J. C. Geer. There is no record that the academy ever opened its doors; probably it was a large name for a small public school.

Under the religious stimulation that from the first was common on the frontier, an Episcopal church was organized and built at Butteville in 1860. The Rev. St. Michael Fackler, prominent for the many addresses he made throughout the mid-Willamette Valley on National holidays was for awhile its pastor. Prior to the building of the church structure, its membership gathered for worship in private homes. When the great flood of 1861 destroyed the sister church at Champoeg, the bell that until then had hung there was found in debris in a nearby creek. It was rescued and hung in the tower of the Butteville church. An auspicious religious attitude, however, did not prevail for long, for in the November 30, 1865 issue of the *Spirit of Missions*, the Episcopal publication of the day, the Rev. J. W. Sellwood mournfully observed in a field report: "This town, like most of the small towns of Oregon, is composed of such a confused mass of beliefs and unbeliefs . . . . . It is indeed a moral wilderness, all denominations here deserted. It is a place smitten with the curse of God. The field is left wholly to us. . . . ."

In the early 'sixties, L. and A. W. Rynearson—probably father and son—made ploughs and advertised the fact to the agricultural community in the *Argus*, claiming that they were "some of the best cast steel plows ever made on the coast," for sale at "prices to suite the Times." They boasted a substantial trade and announced that they intended to "keep up with the rapidly increasing demand. If you want a good plow," they concluded, "of easy draft, and sure to scour, get one of Rynearson's Butteville plows."

When the great flood of 1861 surged down the Willamette, it brought devastation to Butteville, inundating much of the town. There is no record of the amount of damage done but it was considerable. A few buildings, at least, withstood the water's force; sufficient to provide a nucleus for rebuilding. This the town did, slowly but with pertinacity. Following the destruction of the Oregon City headquarters of Multnomah Lodge No. 1, AF&AM, that body made its home at Butteville.

In 1862, G. A. Cone moved into town and opened a general store. He served also as postmaster, adding to his duties the office of justice of the peace. Meanwhile, Matthieu continued in business until the middle 60s, when he sold his store and retired to his farm. He had been a merchant for fifteen years and the town's central figure.

Butteville, which, for a quarter of a century, was a large shipper of wheat and other produce, met discouragement when, in 1871, the Oregon & California Railroad passed it by, several miles to the east. After that, the community's agricultural output that had previously gone by the river route, went largely by rail. As a consequence, population drifted toward the railroad points, and Butteville began to decline. Nevertheless, a *Historical Atlas Map of Marion &* *Linn Counties*, published in 1878, pictured the town with the following structures, closely grouped and largely within the limits of the first platting: an Episcopal church, public school, Masonic hall and Odd Fellows hall, post office, Grange hall, vinegar factory, and a warehouse still carrying the name La Roque. This publication listed Butteville as a regional "grape and wine center."

Butteville is still a sleepy village by the river, but as early as 1873 it looked to the past instead of toward the future. On October 18 of that year the first meeting of the Oregon Pioneer Association met there, with former Governor George Law Curry addressing a large assemblage. The years of pioneer settlement were over. Now remained a recounting and a recording, that future generations might not forget.

OLD CHAMPOEG

EIGHTEEN miles above Willamette Falls and a short distance below the mouth of Chehalem Creek, where it smears a streak of yellow on the meandering Willamette, there was, a century ago, the only riverside opening in the forests of fir and oak, spruce and black ash, that lined the shores of the wilderness stream. This forest-fringed area was the northern-most extremity of a series of prairies that extended southward along the east bank of the Willamette, almost to the Indian village of Chemeketa, twenty-five miles distant. Although rimmed by forests, there were few trees and little brush on these prairies, kept open by the wandering Cala-pooya Indians, who, each fall, fired the high dry grass. Such fires served manifold purposes: they destroyed cover that might secrete lurking enemies, provided a renewal of green pasturage for the ponies, cooked the tarweed pods ready for the squaws to gather as a part of the winter food supply, and, if counter-blazes were properly set, rounded up the fat game animals for easy killing. As a consequence, this was coveted country.

On the ridge by the river, among the scattered trees of the northernmost prairie, stood the Indian village of Cham-poeg, or Cham-poo-ick, where each spring the tribes gathered preparatory to going to the falls to spear salmon. Later, came the summer game hunts and the fall berry trek to the high mountains. The Calapooyas were usually a peaceful people, but they fought doggedly to hold the region of abundance against encroaching tribes. At last, however, it was not their neighboring tribes who took it from them, but the palefaces.

This prairie district was known to the white man at least seventeen years before Etienne Lucier, newly retired from the Hudson's Bay Company employ, settled among its pleasant groves in 1829, at a point near the river and a short distance from present-day St. Paul. Prior to that date, in April 1812, Donald McKenzie and William W. Matthews, of Astor's ill-fated Pacific Fur Company, had passed up the river. Joined later by a second party headed by William Wallace and J. C. Halsey, they had established a hunting camp and trading post, immediately above the locality later chosen by Lucier.

Others to pass through the valley—or portions of it—in early decades were the redoubtable Peter Skene Ogden, ex-ploring for the Hudson's Bay Company, David Douglas, the English naturalist of the pensive mood; both in 1826. Two years later Governor George Simpson of the Hudson's Bay Company in North America, and Jedediah Strong Smith, the Bible-reading explorer, traversed the Willamette region; but neither tarried. Finally, Dr. John McLoughlin, with his assistant, Donald Manson, shrewd Scotsmen both, gave impetus to settlement. With a view to determining its adaptability to agricultural purposes, the two men in 1829 made an extended tour of the Willamette Valley, laying claim to property at the Falls, and pronouncing the rich-soiled prairies to the south the Northwest's most desirable region for settlement.

Under its British charter, the Hudson's Bay Company was required to return all employees, when their term of service expired, to the place of their enlistment. Such a course, however, was not always desirable, for many trappers had taken Indian girls as wives, and consequently did not wish to return to Canada or England. To meet this social problem, chief factor McLoughlin continued many of his former trappers on the Company's books, allowing them to settle on the land with their Indian half-breed families. Most of these men chose the fertile prairie region of the middle Willamette, fifty-odd miles south of Fort Vancouver. To those first land claimers Dr. McLoughlin gave the necessary seeds and implements, on credit, with the understanding that all surplus produce raised was to come as payment to the Company.

About seventy-five former trappers accepted the opportunity for settlement in the valley. Following Lucier's entry, Joseph Gervais built a log house at Chemeway in 1830. Near him, two years later, his friend Louis LaBonte planted a home in the bush. Joseph Delor and Jean Perrault soon followed. Below, near the Indian village of Encampment du Sable, Jean Baptist Desportes McKay, squawman and trapper, in 1832 took up his abode. Three or four Canadians were visited by the Boston trader, Nathaniel Wyeth, in 1832, and mentioned as living "22 miles from the falls." Actually there were two separate communities, known for some time as the "settlement at McKay's" and the "settlement at Gervais."

The first settlers, who for a time knew less of farming than of hunting, fared so well as tillers of the soil that it soon became necessary to provide a warehouse at the Encampment du Sable, in which to store surplus food stuffs. The place took the name of the Indian village, Champoeg. For these surpluses, Dr. McLoughlin found a ready market among the Russian settlements on the upper Northwest Coast. "In those days," says an unsigned article in the *Oregon Pioneer Association Transactions* for 1888, "the Canadian pioneer delivered his wheat at Champoeg and received sixty cents for every imperial bushel, 'paying in the goods of the Company at Vancouver.' The principal crop, as later and elsewhere in the middle valley was 'old white winter wheat.' "

As with many other matters concerning Champoeg, the origin of the name is subject to dispute. Argument has been advanced that the word is a corruption or mispronunciation of the words "campment du sable." Another explanation is that it is a combination of the Indian words "Champoo" (root), and "coich" (a weed). A third claims that Champoeg is a single Indian word. The bulk of the evidence points to one of the two latter explanations.

When William A. Slacum visited the Willamette Valley in December 1836, he estimated that a cargo of at least 5,500 bushels of wheat could be obtained from the sixty or more settlers, and that all of it could be readily sold to the Russian settlements, in the Sandwich Islands, or in Peru. The year before the Rev. Samuel Parker entered the country and commented on the region of French settlement. "It is well diversified with woods and prairies, the soil is rich and sufficiently dry for cultivation and at the same time well watered with small streams and springs." Of the residents there, he noted: "These hunters recently turned to farmers, cultivate the most commonly useful productions—wheat of the first quality to as great an extent as their wants require." He mentioned seeing "on the way (to Gervais) a large number of horses, lately brought from California, fattening upon the fresh luxuriant grass of the prairies."

Parker found twenty families living in the district that had come to be known as French Prairie. That number grew to twenty-six families in 1838, to fifty in 1840, and sixty-one by 1841; none of them were too arduously employed. Most of the families—on the paternal side at least—were of French origin. A few, however, were fathered by Americans and Englishmen. Prominent among the latter was William Johnson, a veteran of the war of 1812. Johnson took an Indian wife, who bore him several children. There was also William Cannon, a former member of the Wilson Price Hunt party, sent west in 1811 by Astor, the fur trader. Another was George (Squire) Ebbert, blacksmith and gunsmith, who in 1839 was the first American settler on land he sold to Andre Longtain in 1841 and that soon thereafter became a part of the Champoeg townsite. Caleb Wilkins, a former Mountain Man and warm friend of Ebbert, was an American neighbor.

Other French Prairie residents of American blood were the members of the Jason Lee Indian Mission, seventeen miles to the south. Dr. William J. Bailey, another resident, was a Scotsman and physician, who in 1835 had fought his way up from California through Indian affrays that nearly took his life. Two years later he married Margaret Smith, a teacher at the Mission, and they went to live in a cabin a few miles east of the Hudson's Bay Company warehouse at Champoeg. There were few others of American stock. In 1841, between four and five hundred Indians still wandered about the prairies of the Willamette.

At either side of Dr. McLoughlin's Champoeg warehouse, which stood on the first ledge of the bank with one timbered end extending over the water, there grew up in the 1830s and 1840s a cluster of buildings. The structures were strung out along the route, named Napoleon Boulevard by the Factor—the route that today leads from the highway into Champoeg Memorial Park. Gradually the settlement grew to some ten or a dozen cabins, mostly of logs, "of French style;" one-story structures with low-pitched roofs. There were, in addition to the warehouse, a general store and a blacksmith shop. With increasing business, the Company added a fur depot that carried the customary trade commodities. Soon a private store was established.

At that stage in the town's growth, the population numbered about twenty-five white men, chiefly with Indian families. The village was surrounded with much the same coverage as the site shows today: scattered fir and spruce trees, oaks hung with mistletoe, alders and balms and a few black ash trees. Beneath the larger trees grew the willow, hazelbrush and salmonberry that still blanket the margins of nearly all Willamette Valley streams. Deer and elk came down to drink and were preyed upon by panthers and wolves, who soon learned to relish equally well the tamer blood of the ranchers' domesticated stock.

The production of grain around Champoeg, all of which was stored in its warehouse, rose to a harvest in 1841 of 10,000 hectoliters (33,000 bushels) of wheat and 3,000 hectoliters (10,000 bushels) of other grains, according to a report made by the De Mofras exploration party, visiting the region in that year.

Because of the scattered nature of settlement in these

early years, the term Champoeg soon came to mean not only the trading point of that name, but a wide surrounding area. The first grist mill in the valley was "at Champoeg," though it stood at the confluence of Champoeg and Mission Creeks, three-quarters of a mile to the southeast. Built in 1834 by Webley Hauxhurst, on funds furnished by McLoughlin, it was a great improvement over the primitive method of pounding wheat and barley in a mortar. Likewise, the first public school in Oregon, established by the Methodist missionaries in the home of Joseph Gervais, eighteen miles distant, was later vaguely reckoned as at "Wheatland (Champoeg)," although Wheatland was across the river on the west shore, and a mile from the Mission "at Champoeg." So also were Fairfield Landing, a good fifteen miles crowflight from Champoeg, and St. Paul, center of Catholic enterprise in the community, six miles to the south.

Champoeg was a popular meeting place. The Rev. Jason Lee and the Rev. Samuel Parker, of the American Mission Board, and the Rev. Bishop Francis N. Blanchet, of the Catholic Church at St. Paul, all preached, and nearly all of the settlers of the district, of whatever faith, came to hear each of them. When the explorer Eugene de Mofras visited Champoeg in 1841, the settlers of French birth assembled there to meet him, showing an almost pathetic yearning for news from the motherland—of friends they could not forget, of events that were new and strange. For lack of indoor quarters, such meetings usually took place in the open.

By far the most memorable of these outdoor gatherings, assembled by appointment, was that of May 2, 1843, at which first steps were taken toward formation of civil government west of the Missouri River. Indeed, it was this eventful meeting—leading to the July 5 meeting of actual organization, at Oregon City—that has perpetuated the memory of Champoeg.

Since early in 1841, meetings of one kind or another among the settlers of the Prairie and adjacent regions, principally to the west, had been common. The death in that year, of Ewing Young, most prosperous of the ranchers, had precipitated a need for adjudication of property rights. A meeting was called and an executor appointed. Meanwhile his farm stock ran wild in the Chehalem Valley, bringing the wolves and panthers deeper into the central Willamette and the settlements. Cows and their calves were killed, and many colts. The first "wolf meeting" was called and met at the Oregon Institute, on February 2, 1843. An assessment of five dollars was levied on each member present, to pay bounties on all wolves, lynx, bear and panther killed. A second "wolf meeting" convened at the home of Joseph Gervais, on March 6, when the real intent of many was revealed; a resolution was unanimously adopted for the appointment of a committee of twelve to "take into consideration the propriety of taking measures for civil and military protection of this colony." The committee then appointed met at Willamette Falls a few days later. It should be noted that the American population of the Oregon country at this time was a little less than two hundred and fifty persons, most of whom lived south of the Columbia River.

The meeting that followed on May 2 was dramatic from the start. An attempt to hold it in the too-small quarters of the Hudson's Bay Company office in the corner of the storehouse, caused such confusion at first that many voted contrary to their convictions and a motion to adopt the report of the committee calling for steps to be taken toward organizing themselves into a civil community were lost. Those not American by birth were nearly all opposed to any official government. Amid much wrangling over matters of personal freedom and former loyalties, the meeting was adjourned to the field outside the office. Then the lusty voice of trapper Joe Meek rose above the clamor of the assembled group, urging consideration of a divided count. It was officially moved by G. W. Le Breton that division of the group of dissenters be effected. The motion was seconded by William Gray, Methodist Mission assistant.

Tradition, possibly tinctured with fancy through many repetitions, records that the division resulted in a tie. Of the 102 persons present, fifty settlers chose to follow Joe Meek to his side of the field. Of the remaining fifty-two, the story goes, all but two decided to stand firm against Meek's appeal. The uncertain two were Etienne Lucier and F. X. Matthieu, both French-Canadians. Lucier was hesitant

about joining Meek's party because he had heard that if the
United States assumed control of the territory even the
windows of his house would be taxed. Matthieu, apparently
not so gullible as Lucier, refused to believe the report and
convinced Lucier that his fears were groundless. The two
then joined Meek's followers, thus breaking the tie in favor
of those for local government. The defeated dissenters, most
of whom were French-Canadians and former Company
trappers, withdrew from the field or further voice in the
matter. A legislative committee of nine Americans were
named to prepare a program of principles of self-government.
Two months later Champoeg settlement was declared the
judicial center of a legislative district that extended east to
the Rocky Mountains.

In his *History of Oregon, 1792-1849*, William H. Gray,
wrote, ". . . A primitive State House was built with posts set
upright, one end in the ground, grooved on two sides and
filled with poles and split timber, such as would be suitable
for fence rails; with plates and poles across the top. Rafters
and horizontal poles held the cedar bark which was used
instead of shingles for covering. It was 20 x 40 feet. At one
end some puncheons were put up for a platform for the
president; some poles and slabs were placed for seats; three
planks, one foot wide, and about 12 feet long, placed upon a
sort of stake platform for a table, for the use of the Legislative Committee and clerks . . ."

With civil government partly if not yet adequately realized
and with the tide of American immigration rising to new
levels each year, Robert Newell, a Mountain Man, who in
1842 had taken the 360-acre claim of Walter Pomeroy
adjoining Champoeg on the south, secured and fitted up two
old batteaux, which he ran between Champoeg and the head
of the Falls. These, the *Mogul* and the *Ben Franklin*, were
propelled by Indian paddlers and his service was referred to
as the "Passengers' Own Line." Under that head, Newell,
in an advertisement carried in the *Spectator*, October, 1845,
said:

"We beg leave to tender our thanks to the public for the
liberal support received during the last season, particularly
for the provisions furnished by the passengers. The *Mogul*

and *Ben Franklin* have just been slipped into the water, after a thorough gumming, and intend to ply regularly between Oregon City and Champoeg this season. The boats will leave Champoeg on Mondays and Thursdays—from Oregon City on Wednesdays and Saturdays during the season, passengers or no passengers. As the proprietors intend, as they have always done, to keep the best boats on the waters above the falls, they hope to receive a share of public patronage. XYZ can have two passages free gratis for nothing. The first lieutenant will attend to all business in the absence of the Captain. NB. A reasonable price will be paid for a quantity of good gum."

Two years later the prospect of continued community growth was such that "Doc" Newell optimistically laid out the townsite of Oxford on the sidehill about a quarter of a mile from Champoeg boat landing. Soon thereafter the provisional legislature authorized construction of a stage road from Salem (formerly Chemeketa) to Oxford. Surveyed in 1850, it became the Salem-St. Paul-Champoeg stage road, and exists today.

But Oxford was not fortunately situated to become a competitor of Champoeg, and Newell, strategically including the then developed area of the settlement with an extensive portion of his own adjoining property, platted an enlarged townsite in November, 1852. The surveyor was S. D. Snowden, and the plat was filed and recorded on January 19, 1853, with E. J. Harding, clerk of Marion County (Champooick had been changed to Marion in 1849). The town had eight full blocks and five fractional ones. Lots were fifty by one hundred feet, with sixty-foot streets and ten-foot alleys. A strip, sixty to eighty feet deep, was reserved along the waterfront for wharves. The town's center was near the present memorial monument.

The early streets all bore names of celebrated men. East and West streets were Napoleon, Jefferson, Madison and Monroe (misspelled Munroe); those running North and South were Montcalm, Washington and John, the last probably for John McLoughlin. The fact that four of the seven names were for Americans illustrates how rapidly French and British preferences were waning from the district. An unofficial population count in 1845 had placed the Canadian French, including a large Indian admixture by marriage and birth, at between six hundred and seven hundred individuals. Five years later a similar count revealed that the number of inhabitants of French extraction had increased to 1,200. The Americans, who previously had taken holdings principally west of the Willamette, had begun buying such Prairie farms as were for sale. More than ten thousand American settlers had arrived, and French Prairie had lost its former character.

In 1851, steamboat service reached Champoeg from Canemah Landing, and was gradually extended to upriver points. A fever of development seized every hamlet and landing and Robert Newell readily sold a number of his best lots. A few he gave away; one, at the corner of Montcalm Street and Napoleon Boulevard, soon bore the town's most impressive building, the Masonic Hall. Edward Dupuis' stage station, erected at the east end of town, carried overhead in big black letters: "Through By Daylight, Champoeg to Salem." Newell himself began merchandising there in 1853, and in 1855 operated the Hauxhurst grist mill nearby.

From about 1847 through the early 1850s, Champoeg reached its peak of economic importance. In addition to the concerns already mentioned, it had a store owned by Crosby & Smith, a public house, saloons and several livery stables. Three stage lines reached the town from the south, one continuing to the rival town of Butteville, a few miles down river. A news item in the *Statesman* in 1853 remarked that "the two stage lines to Champoeg and one to Butteville are carrying passengers free with a free meal thrown in at Champoeg. Certainly that is cheap traveling."

In the spring of 1850, soon after Oregon became a Territory of the United States, a post office was established at Champoeg, but the aspiring town of Butteville soon claimed it. The office, however, was re-established the following year.

The town's trade, at that date, must have been considerable, for Francois Matthieu, who for a time prior to 1850 was a purchasing agent for the Hudson's Bay Company store there, recalled years later that there were between one hundred and one hundred and fifty houses, including stores "at Champoeg." But this undoubtedly included a considerable territory and not merely the town, since in 1852 the Rev. Ezra Fisher said in a letter to New York that Champoeg was then a small settlement of eight or ten houses, principally log built. This latter appraisal, however, must have been as far under the facts as Matthieu's was in excess.

Champoeg, through the thirty years of its existence, occupied a prominent place in the commerce and trade of the section. The Hudson's Bay Company valued their Champoeg investment at £1,700, as Peter Skene Ogden and James Douglas reported in 1847. Property became increasingly valuable. In the five years between 1847 and 1852 the Company's holdings at Champoeg, according to an appraisal by Sir George Simpson when the Company relinquished its American enterprises, had grown to be worth £3,400.

Newspapers of the day carry reports of two disastrous fires in the Champoeg vicinity in the early 'fifties. In September, 1851, a fire entailed a loss of $7,000 in merchandise in a store owned by Ed Dupuis though operated by two Germans. In 1853 fire destroyed the home of Dr. Bailey. The loss was considerable as it was a new dwelling. Compounding the Doctor's misfortune, a runaway horse crossed the yard where the Doctor's medicines and implements, all that was rescued from the flames, were strewn. These the horse's flying hoofs largely destroyed, completing the ruin.

Patriotism was not a hidden virtue in those days. On the Fourth of July, 1854, a gala celebration was held at Champoeg. The citizens formed a parade at the center of town and marched through the streets to the Ed Dupuis home. Here Dr. Edward Shiel read the *Declaration of Independence* to the assembled patriots. The *Statesman*, reporting the day's activities, said: ". . . the celebrants enjoyed the sumptuous dinner . . . given beneath the roof where the first celebration took place in Oregon, and where the first laws . . . were enacted. After dinner the guests proceeded on a pleasure excursion, three miles up the river, on board the steamer *Fenix*."

When the *Fenix* returned to Champoeg, the celebration reached enthusiastic heights. Impromptu orations were roundly cheered and the explosions of firearms echoed and re-echoed from the surrounding forest. Upon conclusion of the day's festivities, the good steamer *Fenix* loosed her lines to the accompaniment of a half-dozen vociferous cheers, and chugged off for Canemah. Those remaining made merry at the ball which followed.

George T. Allan and Archibald McKinlay, general merchants, owned for a time after 1855 the Champoeg Flour Mill, purchased from Robert Newell. "Attached to the mill," their advertisement read in the Oregon City *Argus*, "is a granary for receiving and storing wheat, a dwelling house and garden for the use of the person in charge. The whole property embraces about five acres." They were particularly proud of their mill machinery, which was of "very superior quality, having been imported from Rochester, N. Y." There were "two runs of the best French Burrs, and an extra patent run of smaller Burrs for chopped feed."

During November 1861, as noted in previous chapters, the whole Willamette Valley watershed experienced an unprecedented rainfall, and on December 2, the river broke over its banks. The next day and the day following the inundated lowlands from Albany north bore a raging torrent, sucking and sweeping everything into its path. The village of Champoeg was under seven feet of swirling water.

Here, as elsewhere, so swiftly did the waters rise that many residents were marooned in their homes and places of business. When they became endangered, Isaac Ogden, Peter Hae, Alex Michel and Joseph Gary, by the use of two small rowboats, succeeded in saving all of the stranded people. Gradually the heavy hewn timbers of the town's buildings loosened and were swept away. Only two saloons on the high south side withstood the waters.

Some days later, in appraising the Valley's losses, the *Argus* observed of Champoeg: "The flood swept this town entirely clean of houses, and the site is now as bare as a sand beach. Mr. McKinley would do well, we think to lay out a town on his side of the river."

So the town vanished. Two hundred houses, some say three hundred and fifty, were washed away. The *Argus* noted that "Waccom Umphroville rescued 30 persons between Champoeg and Fairfield, taking fifteen of them from one house, to which they had fled for refuge."

"Doc" Newell, disheartened by his ill luck in Oregon, moved to Idaho territory, where he remained until his death.

But despite tragedy and the mutations of time and circumstance, Champoeg was not forgotten. No longer a town, it lived on remembered by a few as a "place," called Newellsville, once known as "Champoeg." The single store that was rebuilt and conveniently remained through the years, was prudently located on the bluff, a quarter of a mile back from the river. Over the front of the building the name of the dead town still lingered.

Champoeg, by name, was optimistically replatted, November 4, 1886, by the estate of Donald Manson, then seven years dead, who had purchased Newell's property in 1857 and 1862. All the former townsite and eighty acres more were included in a composite of fifty-one full blocks and eight fractional blocks. North and south streets were Lafayette, Orleans, LaSalle, Montcalm and De Grasse; those running east and west were Wilson, Alder, Maple, Langtain, Napoleon, and two left unnamed. This time most of the names were of French origin and distinction; already the region was remembering the past. But very few lots sold in the reclaimed town and none was developed. Champoeg belonged to the pioneer yesterdays.

Acclaimed by Oregonians as the State's most celebrated historic spot, Champoeg is visited year after year by many people. Early each May on the grounds of the Champoeg Memorial Park and in the large pavilion, the anniversary of the organization of the first American civil government west of the Rocky Mountains is celebrated. Carved in the granite of the shaft that stands near to the gravelled roadway of old Napoleon Boulevard, are the names of the fifty-two men— perhaps not infallibly chosen—who took part in that event more than one hundred years ago.

FAIRFIELD LANDING

A GRAY frame church, the district schoolhouse, and a decaying tangle of huge squared timbers mark the site of Fairfield. These stand beside the Salem-St. Paul road, on a high bluff overlooking the Willamette where its channel is split by large Grand Island. Here as early as 1851, half on the high land and half on a bench near the water's edge to the west and sixteen miles below Salem, stood one of the most important of the pioneer landings. For years it was a teeming shipping point, but passing its zenith, it declined gradually until now only vague tracings of foundations remain.

In the 1840s the increasing harvest of wheat from French Prairie required more convenient shipping points than Champoeg, some distance to the north. True, there were scattered landings along the meandering Willamette; crude plank affairs under fir trees or anchored among willows; but there were no warehouses at these points and grain and produce stacked on the riverbank had to be sheltered from the weather and guarded from thieving Indians and despoiling game. Besides, once the grower's shipment was assembled at the waterside, he must wait with it for one of the few flatboats not too heavily loaded to take his produce aboard—sometimes a wait of several days not easily spared from other duties. At best, transportation was arduous and uncertain. Often too, these loading platforms were carried away by freshet, which necessitated a rebuilding. A landing used one season might not be there the next year.

For nearly a decade the scattered ranchers had been hauling their wheat to Fairfield Landing—for the fields of the Prairie were fair and broad behind it. It lay in a quiet arm of the river, within reasonable hauling distance for many. Firs and spruce of enormous size sheltered the spot below the bluff, which rose to a height of more than one hundred feet. Emerging from the Prairie, a road crept around from the south, crossing John C. Peebles donation land claim to water-level and the loading platforms.

By 1852 Fairfield Landing had become a considerable wheat-shipping port, with a trade activity sufficient to encourage Ben Simpson and a company of farmers to build—in the small slough just to the south of the landing—the little steamer *Oregon*. Simpson then set about building a warehouse. A resident on French Prairie since 1847, he had been operating a general store at Parkersville, twelve miles to the east, on Pudding River. There he constantly took a great quantity of wheat in trade. He then had to ship the surplus out of the valley in order to realize the cash he needed to pay for staple commodities brought up from San Francisco. Those who hauled wheat to him at Parkersville could just as well haul it to Fairfield, he reasoned. Shipment down river would then be the only labor.

When he opened his Fairfield warehouse in the spring of 1853, Ben Simpson announced, in the advertisement in the *Statesman* that he "kept on hand a supply of drygoods and groceries for sale cheap," for the convenience of his trade hauling to this point. The new warehouse, he declared, was "commodious." With some pride he reminded the public that "The main body of French Prairie (the Granary of Oregon) laying contiguous to this point renders it a desirable place to purchase and forward produce from."

Simpson, however, soon had competition in the warehousing business. In the same Salem newspaper, for July 17, 1853, J. C. Waldo & Company announced that there was then "being completed a good substantial and commodious two-story warehouse, placed above high water mark. . . ." That concern would "always be found ready to attend to business pertaining to forwarding and commission. Also to the purchase of grain at the most reasonable rates." Like its competitor, it kept on hand "goods, groceries, etc. to accommodate customers."

Although there must have been a few log and frame houses at the Landing in those early years, Fairfield was primarily a place of warehouses and commerce. Much of the roustabouting was done by the ranchers themselves, and although they were sometimes obliged to remain overnight, no tavern or lodging house is mentioned in the fragmentary records of the day.

The peak of river transportation came in the fall months when boat traffic, forced to "lay by" for months during the rainless summer season of low water, was again resumed. From ranches near and far, the loaded wagons came creaking onto the planks of the wharf, which sagged under the increasing weight of the stacked goods: grain, potatoes, bacon in burlap wrappings, an occasional side of beef. All that could not at once be loaded onto boats or stacked in sheltered piles for early shipping was carried into the warehouses. Gradually the rains came on, heavier, steadier. Loaded wagons continued to arrive, their teams of horses and oxen weary from the journey over the miry roads. But there was protection for the rancher's produce, once it arrived at Fairfield Landing, and to Fairfield Landing much of the Prairie's abundance came—wheat and perishable goods to the warehouses, swine and steers to the waterside pens. There was a calling of orders interspersed with oaths, a dickering among parties for a fair and remunerative deal, a constant stir of trade activity. The yearly harvest was going to market!

Through the mists and increasing rains of winter, the valley's produce moved down-river by steamboat. Gradually the surplus stock was emptied from the warehouses, until by spring little was left. But there was incoming upriver freight, too, and new settlers. Fairfield Landing became economically, if not socially important, to a wide area. As early as 1852 it was on the twice-weekly mail route from Oregon City to Salem, served by Nathaniel Coe aboard the *Canemah*.

But either Ben Simpson was restless or the prospect of remaining in business at the Landing did not promise all he had at first anticipated, for in a few years he moved from the Willamette Valley to Grand Ronde Indian Reservation in the western part of Polk County. There he built a sawmill and operated the suttler's store at Fort Yamhill, then in charge of Lieut. Phil H. Sheridan.

Commerce on the river grew and Fairfield Landing handled a substantial share of the trade. But the rapidly increasing prosperity of such river towns as Oregon City and Salem, more favorably located and with community and industrial advantages lacking to Fairfield, gradually and consistently drew the rancher trade away. Roads were being corduroyed, travel was less laborious, distances seemed shorter. Moreover, the social appeal was stronger in the thriving towns; there were educational opportunities there for the children of ranchers who could afford it. Fairfield Landing began to lag.

Fairfield maintained a reasonably prosperous status for three or four decades. It suffered little in the great winter flood of 1861–62. Seventeen years after that event, the place was mentioned in a descriptive atlas as being among Marion County's dozen or so most important trade centers. "Fairfield is located on the high land on the bank of the Willamette River, eight miles west of Woodburn, and is distant sixteen miles from Salem. There are extensive warehouses for the storage and shipment of grain, and a store which does an extensive business with the surrounding country. Steamboats have little difficulty in reaching this point at ordinary stages of water." Apparently it was still very much the trade settlement it had been in the 1850's.

In the *Pacific Coast Directory* for 1880, the general merchandising firm of E. A. Breyman & Company, was, however, the sole commercial listing for Fairfield. A population of fifty persons was reported, but some of them may have been ranch families living nearby.

As late as 1910, the census reports gave Fairfield—the term Landing had been dropped years before—a population of twenty-six persons, a figure that undoubtedly included at least a few residents of the surrounding district. By this late date much less wheat was produced than formerly; there was less grain to be shipped away. Instead, orchards flourished on soil that had been "grained to death." Bands of sheep likewise grazed over the once stubbly fields, where clover sought now to restore the soil.

Meanwhile, river traffic had declined more sharply than wheat production. Long ago the railroad had come up the valley, its speedy rails spanning the long length of French Prairie on the east, through a region that had sprouted a number of small but prosperous towns.

As a small boy Samuel L. Simpson, Oregon's first well-recognized poet, played around the wharves of Fairfield Landing. Then at ten years of age he moved with his parents to the Grand Ronde Indian Reservation. When at sixteen he returned to the central valley, to attend Willamette University at Salem, the river of his boyhood reentered his life.

After graduation, going to Albany to practice law with J. Quinn Thornton, a leading barrister of the day and prominent in Oregon governmental affairs, something reclaimed from the past and the river beset Simpson's spirit. He turned to poetry. And the Willamette that he loved came to life in his singing lines. In four memorable if not great stanzas he wrote the poem "Beautiful Willamette." He was only twenty-two. Sam Simpson died in Portland in 1899.

Ben Simpson died in 1910. In a varied career he had been steamboat and warehouse builder and operator; surveyor, storekeeper and sawmill owner; Indian agent, newspaper publisher, postal inspector, and for a time in Alabama before coming to Oregon, operator of a cotton plantation, as well as being a volunteer Baptist preacher. He had lived at Clacka-mas City, Parkersville, Fairfield Landing, Grand Ronde, Siletz, Yaquina Bay and Santiam City—nearly all of which became ghost towns. His second wife was a grand-daughter of Colonel Cooper, an associate of Daniel Boone in the settling of Kentucky. For a while he had been Surveyor General of Oregon and was spoken of as the Honorable Ben-jamin Simpson. With the passage of time Fairfield's few and later residents knew little or nothing of the days when the two Simpsons, father and son, had lived there. It was an even score, however, for elsewhere Fairfield was seldom mentioned.

WHEATLAND AT MATHENY'S FERRY

SALE OF TOWN LOTS

A public sale of Lots in the town of Atchison, in Yamhill County, on the west bank of the Willamette river, at Matheny's Ferry, will take place on the 15th of May next (1847) on the premises. Wheat will be taken in payment. Further particulars as to terms &c. will be made known the day of sale.

DANIEL MATHENY

THIS notice first appeared in the advertising columns of the *Spectator*, April 29, 1847, but Atchison is not to be found on any map of Oregon, past or present. Lying at a point about twelve miles below Salem, Atchison made a quick growth to regional importance. Its local residents, however, thought Atchison City an unlikely name for a wheat-shipping center and took to calling the place Wheatland. Wheatland, al-though still a name on the Oregon map, is gone—its site covered by a peach orchard that spreads along the bench-land. Only the ferry landing and the road to it remain.

Like many another early Oregon town, Wheatland was the ambitious undertaking of a single individual. Its founder, Daniel Matheny, was born in Virginia, December 11, 1793. Following adventurous years in the War of 1812, in the Black Hawk War of Illinois, and in a minor fracas of 1839 referred to as the Mormon War, in which he moved from a lieutenancy to a captaincy, Matheny learned of the free land to the west in the Oregon Country. It was in the spring of 1843 that he and his brother Henry allied themselves with the overland wagon train that became known as the "Great Migration." In the journey westward Matheny's sound judgment was often depended upon.

Evidently Matheny brought some money with him to Oregon; for in the spring of 1844 he purchased the squatter rights to the donation land claim of James O'Neal, situated on the west bank of the Willamette River at a point about seventeen miles above Champoeg. That was just across the river and slightly north of the first Methodist Mission, then recently abandoned in favor of Salem. Of greater advantage was the fact that the O'Neal claim also lay just southwest of French Prairie, a district of growing settlement.

During the previous year, a party of immigrants, including the three families of Jesse, Lindsay, and Charles Applegate, had stopped at the old mission, occupying one of the buildings for the winter. While there, Lindsay Applegate "built a ferry boat for A. Beers and James O'Neil [O'Neal]." Jesse A. Applegate, son of Lindsay, related later: "He first caulked the openings between the planks in the bottom of the boat, and then poured in hot pitch. As it was a large boat he used a bushel or two of literature he found in the old house. Tracts and other pamphlets that had been left there by the missionaries were forced into the cracks with a chisel and hammer." This boat Matheny secured when he purchased O'Neal's claim.

Captain Matheny came accompanied by his wife and seven children: four sons—Adam, Daniel, Isaiah, and Jasper; three daughters—Elizabeth (married to Henry Hewitt), Mary and Charlotte.

Though the Captain's primary intention was the cultivation of the land, the location of his claim offered commercial opportunities. On the far shore, a warehouse stood—then probably the only one above Champoeg. Ranchers coming from the west, the so-called "cow country," with produce for warehouse storage or shipment, faced the difficulty of getting it across the river. Few of them had boats—which necessitated renting or borrowing one, often from Matheny. Incoming settlers, too, wished to be transported to the west side, to continute into the rich Chehalem Hills and the Yamhill country.

Already George Gay—a native of England, married to an Indian woman following his arrival in 1835—had built the first brick dwelling in Oregon, amid the maples and oaks on the west shore of the river. Parents had held a meeting at Garrison's Landing, a mile and a half above O'Neal's on February 1, 1842, to consider means for establishing a school for white children, since the Methodists in the vicinity had been concerned only with educating the Indian youth. Easier communication was imperative; a ferry was needed, and Matheny installed one at the foot of his claim. Begun in 1844, it was the first ferryboat on the Willamette equipped to carry a wagon and ox team.

With the assistance of his growing sons, Matheny cleared timber and worked his widening land, meanwhile keeping his ferry in more or less regular service, which at first meant "on call." More and more the ranchers from the interior districts came lumbering down to the willow-clad shore with wagon-loads of wheat, for the Mission Bottom warehouse and for shipment downriver to Oregon City and Vancouver. Between 1844 and 1847, a great many wagons crossed Matheny's claim to the ferry landing. At times, at the height of the wheat-hauling season, there was a considerable overnight camp of the wagoners, waiting their turns to be ferried over. In those intervals barter and exchange were common. Occasionally a flat-boat put in at the ferry platform and loaded the wheat directly aboard. With his property thus becoming a focal point in river transportation, Matheny staked out the town of Atchison.

Although there are no existing records of the early sale of lots, there presumably was an almost immediate disposal of the more favorably situated ones. A warehouse was erected and the town that was to call itself Wheatland was begun.

As the years passed—there are regrettable omissions in the early record—Wheatland gathered together an imposing group of shops, stores, mills, warehouses and hotels. With the coming of the steamboats in the early 'fifties, commerce took a noticeable upswing at all the river ports, and Wheatland shared in this mounting prosperity. Almost daily, boats stopped at its wharves, bringing freight and new settlers upriver, and taking aboard cargoes of grain and farm produce for Portland and export trade.

One of Wheatland's early residents, Al Zieber, born in Maryland in 1830, opened a store there sometime in the 'fifties. One of the community's younger merchants, he served also as a member of the 1857 Territorial Legislature, and of the first State Legislature. The following year he married Charlotte Manoir. He remained in business at Wheatland, presumably until the flooding waters of December, 1861 carried out the lower portion of the town, devastating his establishment and destroying the local warehouse containing 7,000 bushels of wheat. In 1862, Zieber moved to Portland, became sheriff of Multnomah County, operated a hotel and transfer business, and was a United States Marshal under President Johnson.

Whether the first grist mill was built by M. B. Hendricks or came later into his possession is unknown. At any rate, he had been shipping flour to Portland and was the mill's owner when it burned in 1872. Not discouraged by his loss, he rebuilt the mill and added a general merchandising business. A warehouse, erected by him, was operated until it was wrecked by high water in 1890. After that he built a second warehouse, this time below the town. In later years Hendricks planted the first peach orchard in the community.

Proper wheat winnowing was a serious problem with the Oregon pioneers, and the mechanically-minded among them frequently experimented with cleaning devices. At Wheatland, a Mr. Drury was among the more successful manufacturers of grain cleaners, which he offered for general sale. But just when he lived there and for how long has been forgotten; certainly it was in the early years of settlement.

There were several families of Smiths and Fowlers in the town. A. J. Smith was blacksmith; and a harness and saddle shop was operated by John Smith and John Fowler, who also made boots and shoes. Charles Fowler had a wagon shop, W. J. Fowler had a shingle factory, while Mark and Jim Fowler ran a saloon, serving the local and transient thirsty. Prominent also were the Williamsons: C. S. (Charley) Williamson was the town druggist who also carried a line of "fancy goods;" L. C. Williamson was postmaster, until the office was moved to Hopewell, to the west, in the early 'eighties. The Oregon Central Railroad was slanting down the west-side valley then, and most of the small river ports were conceded to be on the decline.

In its heyday, Wheatland boasted two hotels—much better overnight accommodations than could be found at any other river hamlet between Salem and Oregon City. The *Occidental* was owned and operated by James T. Isham; F. M. Adair was proprietor of the *Wheatland House*. The houses did a large business in the fall and spring shipping seasons; and rancher and tradesman alike, as well as the occasional visiting evangelist, must have appreciated their comfort and hospitality and the opportunity for sociability that a brief stay provided.

In listing Wheatland, Polk's *Pacific Coast Directory* for 1881 observed that it was "entirely dependent on the river for transportation." It had then a population of 319 persons, at least fifteen business concerns, an Evangelical church and a good district school with about thirty pupils. This same issue stated that the miller "M. B. Hendricks has steam power to his cleaner and elevator, and last year shipped between 30,000 and 40,000 barrels of flour, besides doing a large amount of custom work." New enterprises in the town were a saloon with T. T. Cooper as proprietor; a general merchandising store kept by S. C. Forest; and a one-man shingle-making plant owned by J. McCaughy. A Dr. Kirkland was then the town's physician, and William Gardner and M. E. Hendricks were wood merchants. The name of B. M. Fowler, appearing as ferry operator, would imply that Daniel Matheny was then no longer Wheatland's central figure.

With the gradual abandoning of the Willamette River as a trade artery, the town's years were numbered; it had no place in the changing, more progressive economic order. Since agriculture had given Wheatland its birth and growth, it was in the nature of things that the land, when river commerce declined, should absorb much of the town's identity. One by one its business houses were closed, their owners either tilling the adjacent acreage or moving away to more prosperous commercial centers. *Wheatland House* and the *Occidental* locked their doors and boarded up their windows; squirrels and pack-rats lived in the dusty rooms. The roofs, grown heavy with moss, caved in, and under the warring elements the walls fell awry.

Wheat was no longer the prevailing harvest of the country between the meandering Willamette and the lovely Eola Hills to the west; hopyards and berry fields ran their long trellises over the cleared landscape, and orchards spread out burdened with crimson and gold. Sheep grazed over the tired soil. Eventually, the commercial raising of chickens and turkeys would further diversify the products of the former wheat regions. The golden age of river commerce had passed away.

Today a power ferry crosses the Willamette at Wheatland to the district that is still sometimes called Mission Bottom; and this flat, workaday craft, shuttling patiently between the banks, is named *Daniel Matheny*. Thus Oregon's oldest ferry service—the crude boat which Matheny, with great labor, shunted across the uncertain waters in 1844—is remembered casually, but appropriately.

The place is still called Wheatland, but the town that stood there for a half a century razed its final timbers long ago.

LINCOLN, METROPOLIS OF WHEAT

LINCOLN—originally known as Doak's Ferry—was once the largest wheat shipping port on the Willamette River above Portland. Located in Polk County, about six miles downriver from Salem, this landing place was named for Abraham

Lincoln, shortly after his election as President of the United States and some years before the town itself was planned. Farmers from a wide area hauled their grain to Lincoln; and at the height of its prosperity, when river shipping was at its best, the town had five large warehouses, a grist mill, sawmill, beehive factory, blacksmith shop, tin shop, shoe and harness shop, store, lodge hall, church, school and several dwellings, as well as the ferry that had operated since the early forties. Essentially a place of commerce, Lincoln one year shipped 350,000 bushels of wheat from its warehouses—a record never equalled by any shipping point in the Willamette Valley except Portland.

Andrew Jackson Doak may be credited with establishment of the town. Doak took up a donation land claim on the west bank of the Willamette at this point, built a ferry boat, and soon engaged in transporting travelers across the river. When mail service was established between Salem and Lafayette, in 1850, the route was via Doak's Ferry. He sold his land and ferry privilege in 1860 to Jesse Walling who laid out the Lincoln townsite.

Walling had removed from Salem, believing the ferry point offered better business opportunities. As laid out, Lincoln was mostly in an apple orchard previously set out by Ben Windsor. The trees left in the streets by the town plat were claimed by lot purchasers, each man selecting his own trees.

The first warehouse to be constructed on the river bank was that of Hamilton & Son, who also erected a store; but the date of their initial venture is forgotten. The property was sold in 1867 to Cooper Brothers, of the nearby village of Zena, who operated the property for one year. Selling it to Jesse Walling, they then acquired new property at the south edge of the town.

Lewis Abrams soon became Walling's partner. From the day of his arrival—1869—Abrams took an active part in the life of the community. Abrams and Walling opened a store; their partnership continued until Abrams, in 1877, took over the business. At that time he also acquired complete control of the warehouse and ferry property, obtaining the latter by deed from the Walling heirs.

For many years the ferry business provided the community with its keenest business rivalry. It began when the Spong family settled on the east side of the river opposite Lincoln on property that included the ferry landing. With this foothold, they built their own ferry and launched a competing enterprise. Both the Spongs and the Abrams then withheld landing privilege from the opposing party. Tradition has it that trade competition finally became so bitter that a shooting affray between crews took place, in which, however, there were no casualties.

As a result, Abrams, in the interests of peace, withdrew from the ferry business. The single boat remaining in operation became known as Spong's Ferry. The names Spong's Ferry and Spong's Landing, are still used to designate a spot on the east bank of the river.

Lewis Abrams prospered, despite his retirement from the ferry business. With his store and warehouse he built up a large business as wheat shipper and merchant, an accomplishment all the more remarkable in that his business was built almost entirely on the confidence of an entire community in one man. Growers brought their wheat to his warehouse, accepted a receipt for it signed by Abrams, and thought no more of the matter until they wanted to sell. When a man sold his stored wheat, Abrams gave a check for it and reported a certain number of bushels delivered to his Portland representative. Funds were forwarded from Portland to cover the transaction, although the wheat itself might not be shipped until some months later. Much of the wheat cargo moved down-river during high water seasons, in the winter and spring, when laden boats could operate with maximum speed and safety.

In time, increasing business brought about the construction of additional warehouses. Even with those in use, however, it was sometimes necessary, in bumper crop years, to stack the bulging sacks in piles on the river bank, covering them with tarpaulin until boats could carry them away. The more recently developed westside wheat region was outrivaling the long-famed French Prairie district.

Wheat hauling to Lincoln was a two-months' job in the fall. Some of the grain came from as far away as Willamina, twenty-five miles to the northwest. Farmers living in the Rickreal country, to the south and west, frequently drove their laden carts and wagons past the Salem Ferry and continued down the river road to Lincoln.

In the season of wheat hauling, the wagoners started for Lincoln before daybreak and often darkness had fallen again before the return trip brought them to their home acreage. Wagons would then be loaded anew, for another early morning start. Once wheat hauling was begun, it was arduous, ceaseless labor. Often more than one hundred awaited their turn at the warehouses, forming a line of restless teams and high-heaped wagons that extended from the shore to the wooded bluff, a half-mile to the west.

A considerable amount of wheat was also brought across from the east side of the valley; Abrams for a time paid the ferry charges, to place these growers on the same selling level as those living on his side of the river—a concession both generous and shrewd.

Lincoln grew consistently during the 'sixties, 'seventies, and 'eighties, and for a time had a half-mile waterfront of warehouses and wharves. A lengthy succession of boats served the town; and as late as the 'nineties, long after river transportation had been reduced almost to the vanishing point by the railroads, there were three boats each way, stopping daily at Lincoln to discharge and load freight. Boats leaving Portland in the morning, passing through the locks at the falls, usually stopped at Lincoln at about 3 o'clock in the afternoon. But occasionally one made better time.

The fastest schedule ever made on the river was probably achieved by the steamer *Ruth*, launched in 1895 and commanded by Captain Miles Bell. Captain John Spong, operator of the ferry, told of hearing a boat coming up the river while he was at lunch. Believing that his watch had failed him, he rushed out onto the bank, where the *Ruth* was just drawing in, and asked the crew aboard for the time of day. Captain Bell answered: "12:25, Johnny, and don't forget that!" The standing record had been surpassed by more than two hours.

The grist mill at Lincoln was established in a small way

by a man named Walker—probably W. M. Walker—in 1861. Its grinding stones—as was true of many early mills—were imported from Scotland and it is believed to have been operated by horse power. Joshua Whitten acquired the mill property in 1870 and added a sawmill with a daily capacity of 5,000 board feet. Aided by John Roark, Whitten undertook to develop water power to operate the two mills. The men spent a small fortune digging a ditch from a broad lake lying in Spring Valley, to the west, carrying the flow to the top of the bluff above Lincoln. From there a flume was built to the mills at the river's edge. But the minor engineering feat was a failure, because the lake did not refill fast enough to provide the water necessary for continuous operation and was soon drained.

The failure of the project, coupled with exposure received in the work, resulted in Whitten's death. Lewis Abrams, his son-in-law, succeeded to part ownership and operated the mills from 1877 to 1883. The heirs then sold the property to Fred Hurst, who, under the firm name of Hurst and Dane, operated it for many years with steam power. The Whitten's, during these years, kept a boarding house and hotel.

When later Hurst and Dane sold the mill properties, Dr. E. Y. Chase, of Salem, was the purchaser; under the name of E. Y. Chase and Company he spent a large sum of money building a beehive factory which he operated in connection with the sawmill. The combined business was conducted in a rather satisfactory manner for five or six years until the sawmill and beehive factory were destroyed by fire. That tragedy ruined Dr. Chase financially, and in 1890, he sold his property rights to Charles Muths and Charles Dodge. For several years the two operated the grist mill, undamaged by the fire, but when the mill later lost business and became unprofitable, they abandoned it.

During the height of the Grange movement in Oregon, that order established warehouse facilities at Lincoln. For that purpose a building with 162 feet of river frontage was purchased from Abrams. Under the name of the Lincoln Warehouse and Shipping Company, the Grange conducted a grain shipping business from 1874 to 1882. That cooperative enterprise did not prosper as expected and the Grange resold the property to Abrams and withdrew from the shipping trade at Lincoln.

Meanwhile, Abrams had built an additional warehouse, providing space that was completely utilized when the Abrams general store burned in 1886. Lincoln warehouses provided for both bulk and sack storage. In the beginning, power to operate the cleaners and elevate the grain into bins was furnished by horse and sweep. Later steam power was used.

With the construction of the westside railroad in the late 'seventies and early 'eighties, the wheat shipping at Lincoln fell off sharply and the mercantile business declined in proportion. Undaunted, Abrams had the townsite officially surveyed by T. L. Butler, on November 12, 1887; the plat was filed at the Polk County courthouse, at Dallas, on May 4, 1888.

In 1886, Lincoln had a population of fifty persons, and stages ran daily to Salem, on the south, and to McCoy, nearest railroad station and banking point, eight miles to the west. The 1889 school census showed twenty-eight pupils living in the Lincoln district. The school itself was established in 1880, on a rear corner of the mill block, on the south side of the town. When, later, Lincoln shrank until it was no longer a bustling trade center, a new school house was erected on the bluff near the Lincoln-Zena Highway.

The Methodist Episcopal denomination organized a church at Lincoln in the early 'eighties, and in 1882 bought a house and two lots in Block Four, near the center of town. A parsonage was on the first floor and quarters for services on the second. Religious services were conducted for several years but the activities were gradually discontinued. Later, Captain John Spong, moving over from the opposite side of the river, bought the building and lived in it for a number of years.

The first blacksmith shop was built and operated by Charles Weeks. The exact dates of his enterprise are unknown, but he was succeeded in 1884 by Clemens Gerth, who tended his smithy until 1915. Gerth, who had been a tool-maker in Germany prior to coming to America, was both expert and successful. From all parts of the valley, broken plow mould-boards of chilled steel were brought to him to be repaired. He seemed the only blacksmith able to make a drill bit of sufficient hardness to drill through the mould boards.

Lincoln once had a flourishing lodge of the Order of Maccabees, organized in 1900. The lodge constructed a hall on land donated by John Walling, west of the blacksmith shop, on Main Street. However, in 1912, with improved methods of travel drawing the local residents to other points of greater social appeal, the Order felt that the interest of the local members could best be served by a transfer of activities to Salem. Abandoned, the hall was later sold and razed for its lumber.

When Lewis Abrams died in 1905, his estate showed a book value of over $50,000. Much of that was in accounts with people scattered over the wide territory once served by the Abrams' warehouses and store. The bulk of these accounts proved uncollectable. In 1910, the estate sold the store and warehouses to M. A. Albin, who operated them for two or three years and then went bankrupt. The Abrams estate reclaimed the property, reselling it to a man named Larson. But final tragedy beset the buildings when a short time afterward they were destroyed by fire.

In the halcyon days of Lincoln, when the entire waterfront was lined with wharves and warehouses, and vivid with the movements of loaded wagons, wheat storing and boat loading, the Abrams' house, which stood on a lot just south of the store and like the store and all other buildings on First Street, faced the warehouses and the river, was quite pretentious, probably the finest in town. There were then between fifteen and twenty houses at Lincoln and nearly as many other buildings. Probably many of the warehouse laborers roomed, in season, in the warehouses, as was the custom elsewhere. Lincoln was a center of commerce, not a place of homes. Indeed, its commercial promise, at one time, surpassed Salem's, or any other river town above Oregon City.

Today, the house pointed out as Abrams' is not the original home of the family, but a dwelling occupied by them after fire destroyed the old house in 1903. Only one of the dwellings identified with the pioneer families of the town remains, that of John Walling's; but this is not one of the earliest houses. Both stand on the second level, above the flat where the warehouses skirted the river.

But all of the places of business, the mills and the wharves, are gone. Along the abandoned streets still stand a few of the ancient apple trees, planted more than a half century ago. Now on the upper levels and rolling back against the western skyline, are the countless trees of younger, more expansive orchards. Lincoln, wheat city in an orchard, like the era of of wheat that it served, has passed away.

PLAT OF LINCOLN

George Gay's home, built early in 1840s near Wheatland, was first brick house in Oregon. (Author's 1972 search failed to turn up a surviving brick.) Another pioneer also previously involved in fur trade was Robert Newell, who built on his Champoeg townsite. His house, as reconstructed by D.A.R., adds charm for visitors to Oregon's first "bread basket" area.

Marion-Linn County Atlas, 1878, includes Butteville plat, left, with location on river to right, and Champoeg (upstream). Mission Landing and Ray's Ferry were also locations for warehouses.

Gov. T. T. Geer (left), George H. Himes and F. X. Matthieu at Champoeg, May 3, 1900, locating area of 1843 meeting to form government. Matthieu (right) was a participant. Meeting, background and development of park at site are described in John Hussey's history of *Champoeg: Place of Transition* (published by Ore. Hist. Soc. in cooperation with Ore. State Hwy. Comm. and Nat'l Park Serv.).

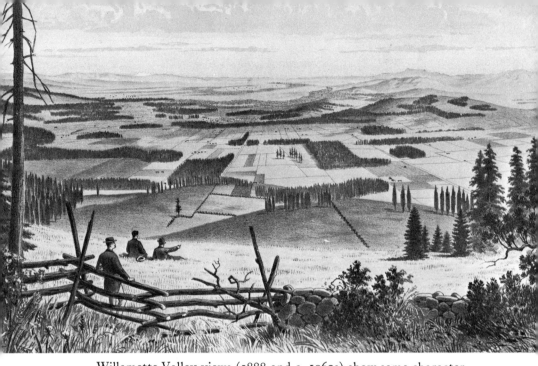

Willamette Valley views (1888 and c. 1960s) show same character. Earlier *West Shore* drawing looks south across Newberg toward Salem in distance, with Cascade peaks on left. Photo from Bunker Hill southwest of Salem, looks southwest over river and valley, with part of Coast Range visible on right. (Ore. St. Hwy. Travel Div.)

TOWNS OF THE MIDDLE AND
UPPER WILLAMETTE

THE percentage of survival among middle and upper Willamette towns from Salem south, has been greater than on the lower river. At least four towns that began as pioneer riverside villages grew into importance and some magnitude and are today among the state's most thriving cities. A few others flourish.

Salem, Oregon's capital and second largest city, had its beginnings when the Rev. Jason Lee and his evangelizing compatriots removed the Methodist Mission holdings from Mission Bottom, opposite Wheatland, on June 1, 1840, to Chemeketa, "Place of Peace" of the Indians, situated about ten miles farther up the river. On property bordering a shady creek they erected a house and nearby a combined sawmill and grist mill. Two years later the first building of the Oregon Institute was completed and, in 1844, in need of funds with which to carry on their educational plans, the missionaries laid out the town and christened it Salem, offering lots for sale. In 1845, discouraged from teaching Indian youths, the Methodists turned solely to the education of white children.

Thomas Cox, immigrant of 1847, brought in a small stock of dry goods, giving the new town a commercial air. Selecting a site near the ferry boat landing, Cox, in 1848, built a two-story house where he conducted a fairly profitable business. Thomas Black soon set up in business as a blacksmith. The two buildings were later joined to form the Union Hotel. A second merchant, J. B. McClane, brought goods north from the California mines in 1849 and within a few months had realized $6,000 from a $2,500 investment, and had still a portion of his stock remaining. Other merchants followed, although town residents were still comparatively few. Gradually more and more returning gold-seekers invested their small fortunes in business enterprises, and more settlers came to dot small dwellings over the sprawling townsite.

Impetus toward town growth came in 1851, when the legislature, meeting at Oregon City, chose Salem as capital

of the new Oregon Territory—a move that was ardently
supported by the missionaries, the Democrats, and the young
editor of the *Oregon Statesman*, Asahel Bush. The removal to
the new site, in the face of some protest by legislative members, was made in 1852, with the lawmakers and their official
documents journeying up-river aboard the new steamer
Canemah. Salem still had comparatively few houses and the
first session was held in the residence of James W. Nesmith,
later Senator from Oregon. Bush, appointed territorial
printer, moved his newspaper from Oregon City to Salem in
1853.

The state capital had not yet taken root, however, and
two years later again moved up river, this time to the still
newer town of Corvallis. But after less than one year at the
new site, the seat of government was returned to Salem,
where a small structure was erected and paid for from
United States treasury funds. When Oregon was admitted
to the Union in 1859, Salem continued as state capital.

Many territorial and state officials and legislators journeyed to and from the halls of state aboard the puffing
riverboats. In rough leather boots they tramped the plank
landings and the muddy or rutted avenues of the riverfront
town. Aboard steamers, too, came the more distant-living
students, to attend Oregon Institute, granted a charter in
1853 and renamed Willamette University. A few visiting
dramatic troupes passed through the town, *via* the waterway.

While participating in the growing river commerce, Salem
also had connections with other valley points by stagecoach,
the condition of roads permitting, and in the mid-'sixties
by telegraph. But her dawning prosperity was darkened in
1861 when the disastrous Willamette River flood poured
through the lower areas of town, carrying away much of the
business section. Although Salem was "about the least
exposed town on the river," the losses were "serious." The
Statesman spoke of the flood as "not Noah's commonly
called, but the next deepest one to that."

After a further decade of struggle, during which Salem
was largely served by the river steamers, the early 1870's
brought the railroad and a period of more rapid growth. In
1876, the town that overlay Chemeketa Prairie in the mid-

valley beheld the rising of a stone structure that became the new State Capitol.

Meanwhile, other centers were developing farther up river. The most influential of those in pioneer days was Corvallis, amid the oak openings of the central valley. On either side, some distance removed, were Eugene to the south, and Albany to the north. Of lesser importance were Harrisburg and Independence, towns whose wharves rocked in the constant nudge of the Willamette's waters.

About eight miles above Salem, Edwin A. Thorpe in the late 1840's blazed the markings of his donation land claim. On the site of this, just north of Ash Creek and on the west bank of the Willamette, he platted a small town, naming it Independence. By 1853 Independence boasted a post office on the west Willamette mail route. Among the first buildings were a store and Israel Hedges' blacksmith shop. Bill Tetherow's saloon was also used as the first church and first schoolhouse, until more suitable buildings were constructed.

Then came the 1861 flood. That havoc caused the citizens of Independence to ask Henry Hill to plat a new townsite on his higher claim, to the south of Ash Creek. Hill debated the matter until 1867, then consented. Thereafter, for a time, the two settlements stood side by side, one known as Old Town, the other as New Town.

Railroad construction, which in the early 'seventies brought renewed life to many river towns, passed up the valley far to the eastward and on the opposite side of the river from Independence. In 1870 a two-horse stage provided the town with daily mail and passenger service, connecting with the Oregon-California Stage Line and later with the Oregon and California Railroad. New Town became an incorporated city in 1878, and in 1882 Old Town was annexed. For the next few years Independence grew rapidly, acquiring a sawmill, another blacksmith shop, a brickyard and an opera house.

Diversified farming, hop growing, and dairying in the surrounding country made Independence an agricultural center, rather than a commercial one. As such the town thrived. Then in 1890, as the first week of February closed, the rampaging Willamette brought a second flood to the town, a really memorable one. Of that, the *Independence Enterprise* noted:

"The water now stands in the main street of Independence and all over North Independence. The shipping house of the farmers warehouse floated away at noon. The office of the sawmill later. $5,000 worth of hardwood lumber at 3 o'clock. At 4 o'clock the Prescott & Veness sawmill floated away taking the ferry with it . . . The water came up to within a few inches of the stores and got the A. J. Whiteaker's furniture store and the Mazeppa Saloon. Small boats pass up and down the street. The ladies have all enjoyed the privilege of a boat ride on the main street.

"Nearly all of North Independence was compelled to move out but none of the residences in this part of town had any water in them. Nearly a quarter of a million bushels of grain is safe here. The sack house of the old flouring mill is gone— the rest intact."

The flood brought Independence to the notice of the public in a manner unequalled by her agricultural activities: for three days all of the telegraph news of the district originated there.

Albany, twenty-two miles above Salem, began as a village divided against herself, and was first named Takenah—a pleasant sounding word employed by the Indians to describe the large pool or depression created by the Calapooya River as it enters the Willamette from the East. But the habit of certain individuals of translating this into "hole in the ground" so oppressed the town that on petition of the citizens to the legislature of 1855, the name was changed to Albany; the choice was promoted by Thomas Montieth, who previously had lived in "York State."

The city was established in 1848 on property owned by Walter and Thomas Montieth, although Abner Hackleman and his son Abram, had an early part in its location. Town growth, however, commenced only after the gold craze began to wane. A grist mill first turned its stone burrs there in 1851, and in 1852 the steamer *Multnomah* nosed in at the muddy landing. A courthouse for Linn County was built in

1853, the first church two years later. The first local news-paper, the *Oregon Democrat*, began publication in November of 1859. Not until after the flood of 1861, which damaged Albany less than many lower-lying towns, was the city incorporated.

During the 1850s and the 1860s, Albany was a hotbed of political intrigue. On August 20, 1856, a group called the Free State men held a meeting in the town and adopted a platform that carried the declaration: "Resolved, that we fling our banner to the breeze, inscribed free speech, free labor, a free press, and Fremont." As an outgrowth of this the Oregon Republican party was born, in the spring of 1857. The slavery issue came to a head that year, when eight counties sent delegates to Albany to prepare an address that placed the issue squarely before the people. During Civil War years pro-slavery advocates were locally numerous and vocal. On one occasion a cannon mounted on the riverbank and used for celebrations was stolen by "Joe Lane Demo-crats" who sank it in the river, thus preventing its use by the "Cayuse Republicans," who had just carried the 1861 state election. The small howitzer lay in the river's bottom for three-quarters of a century before it was dredged up, quite by chance. During that time a good many steamboats passed over it to dock at Albany wharves and discharge passengers for Steamboat Inn. Gazing across the river, a young Albany attorney, Sam Simpson, in 1867 penned the ode known to all Oregonians as "Beautiful Willamette."

Settlers entered the wide Corvallis area in 1845. The first commercially-minded was Joseph Avery, staking a donation land claim on the west bank of the Willamette, twenty-odd miles above Indian Takenah. Erecting a small cabin, he went to Oregon City for his family. He returned in 1846 and found William P. Dixon settled on adjoining property. During the next few years, Avery operated a ferry, harvested crops, built a log granary, then hustled away to the Cali-fornia gold mines. Later, purchasing a stock of goods at San Francisco, he shipped it by boat to Portland. Ox teams brought the merchandise from Portland to his homesite, and the granary became a store. He had already platted a town on a portion of his property and sold lots.

Encouraged by his neighbor's success, Dixon platted part of his own claim as a townsite. Two stores, two blacksmith shops, a school and a saloon stood on the joint properties in 1851. For a town name Avery selected Marysville, for nearby Marys River and Marys Peak.

In 1851 the territorial legislature designated Marysville as the seat of Benton County. Avery and Dixon each deeded forty acres "for the benefit of the county." A courthouse was erected and the two plats became one town. In 1852 the Baptist denomination built a church. The town cherished metropolitan dreams when the first steamboats churned noisily up to its docks, establishing the new port as the head of navigation.

From earliest years, Marysville was on the road through the west Willamette Valley, by way of Yamhill Falls and across the Rickreall, Luckiamute, and Long Tom Rivers, to the upper Willamette and the Umpqua country. From there the road proceeded through the southern Oregon settlements and over the Siskiyou Mountains into California. Along that route in the gold-crazed years moved freight wagons and pack-trains, carrying the commerce that made Marysville an important way-point. Transportation of commodities employed hundreds of animals and drivers. Because the route also passed through Marysville, California, Avery decided to avoid confusion by renaming his town Corvallis, from the Latin words *cor* and *vallis*, meaning "heart of the valley."

The city prospered. The first telegraph line was strung from Portland to Corvallis in 1856, and the next year the city was incorporated. The educational nucleus that later became Oregon State Agricultural College began in 1856 as Corvallis College. A jail was built in 1859. Corvallis was gradually transformed from a roistering frontier community of ribald freighters, saloon-keepers, and gamblers, to one of law-respecting, home-building citizens. The original land claims for miles around were purchased by capitalists, who then devoted large areas to grain-growing. Regarding those transactions, David B. Fagan, in his *History of Benton County*, comments:

"Improvements in Corvallis came to a stand-still. . . .

farms, barns and temporary dwellings fell into decay, or were mortgaged for a cayuse pony or a little ready cash to assist them in following up some mining humbug. When not chasing a golden will-o-the-wisp, they employed themselves principally in whittling, and depended upon the accidental raising of Spanish calves and colts for the support of large families. The consequence was, a few capitalists owned section upon section of land, large numbers were forced to seek other locations, which depleted the population, stopped the plough, the erection of schoolhouses and of churches. Some of the best farms and orchards in the county were marked with dilapidation and ruin."

In 1872 Corvallis had a population of one thousand. A town plat, drawn in 1874, shows almost all of the business located along Second Street: three hotels, two livery barns and a stage barn, a brewery and forty-six other places of business. Pittman's Planing Mill stood at the end of First Street. Along the river stood three warehouses, two of them equipped with horse-powered machinery for cleaning grain, Gaylord's sash and door factory, and a tannery, as well as other manufacturing plants.

Wallis Nash and a party of 26 British land-seekers disembarked at the Corvallis wharf, May 17, 1880. Of their arrival Nash wrote in 1882, in *Two Years in Oregon:*

". . . The white houses of the little city of Corvallis were nestled cosily in the bright spring green of alders and willows and oaks that fringed the river, and the morning sun flashed on the metal cupola of the court-house, and lighted up the deep-blue clear-cut mountains that rose on the right of us but a few miles off.

"When we got into the main street the low broken line of booth-like wooden one-storied stores and houses, all looking as if one man could push them down, and one strong team carry them off, grated a little I could see, on the feelings of some of the party. The redeeming feature was the trees, lining the street at long intervals, darkening the houses a little, but giving it an air of age and respectability that was lacking in many of the bare rows of shanties dignified with the title of town, that we had passed in coming here across the continent.

"The New England Hotel invited us in. . . The street in front was a wide sea of slushy mud when we arrived, with an occasional planked crossing, needing a sober head and a good conscience to navigate after dark; for, when evening closed in the only street-lighting came from the open doors, and through the filled and dressed windows of the stores."

In the 1890s Corvallis developed a permanent character as a commercial and educational center. In the winter months college attendance doubled the local population. Introduction of dairying and fruit-raising necessitated canneries and creameries, and the industrial payroll grew. The town that began amid the oak openings of the river-bottom had a census count of 4,445 in 1910. But by that date the river meant little in its life.

Until construction of the railroad in the 'seventies, the town of Harrisburg, like other up-river villages, depended almost entirely on river transportation—first by flatboat and canoe, later by steamboat. The first steam carrier, the *James Clinton*, reached Harrisburg in 1856, and then went on to Eugene, twenty more miles upriver. After her came other boats—a few at favorable times maintaining regular schedules.

Harrisburg townsite was surveyed in 1852, and was originally called Prairie City. It was renamed Thurston the following year, but that name also failed to achieve permanence. The first house was built in 1853 by the brothers David and Asa McCully, who used it as a store. During the winter of 1853–54 the Scott and d'Armond saloon cooled the tongues of the thirsty. About that date, L. Fletcher and James R. Ripperton started a second store.

The town was incorporated in 1866 under the new name of Harrisburg, after the Pennsylvania capital. By 1880 it had a population of five hundred, a figure that later doubled several times. But it lacked metropolitan hardihood and grew into the present century as a local trade center.

At the foot of a small rounded peak in the upper valley there settled in 1846 a pioneer named Eugene Skinner. The butte soon bore his name and the small settlement that grew up at its base was called Skinner's. Nearby, J. M. Risdon, later a judge, erected the first dwelling within the area which, in the early 1850s, became the corporate town of Eugene.

Skinner operated a ferry across the Willamette. His land lay so low that the new town soon bore the derogatory epithet of "Skinner's Mudhole." To avoid the continued use of so unfavorable a term, the town was renamed Eugene City in 1853 and made the county seat of Lane County.

Eugene's early industry centered around milling and agriculture. The shipping of these products to tidewater markets was greatly speeded by the coming of the steamboats. But Eugene could claim to stand at the head of navigation only when rains were sufficient to maintain adequate water-depth, which in the best years was never for more than five or six months. Some years there were less than four months of negotiable water, and at broken intervals. The Eugene *Oregon State Journal* noted on January 16, 1869: "A boat was up to this place on Wednesday, and returned on Thursday loaded with hogs." But on the 30th it stated that "the river has been so low that we have had no boat at this place for several weeks."

The same medium on April 3, 1869, reported: "The steamer *Echo* arrived at this place on Sunday evening with considerable freight, and went immediately to Springfield, where it remained overnight and returned on Monday, leaving this place with 101 tons of freight, the heaviest load ever taken by a boat from this market. Another boat came up on Wednesday and also went to Springfield, returning the same day. The two boats were not able to take near all the freight from this place and Springfield, and as the river is falling very fast, it is not likely that they will be able to reach here again until there is another rain. Rain enough for farmers in Oregon does not answer the purpose of steamboat men."

A convenient spring of cool mountain water led Elias M. Briggs, in 1849, to locate his claim on the site now occupied by Springfield, three miles above Eugene, on the east bank of the river. For many years the fenced-in portion of his claim was appropriately known as "the spring-field," and when later a settlement grew up here it was given that name.

The Briggses, father and son, ran a ferry across the Willamette. Until 1853, their home and J. N. Donald's small trading post were the only buildings on the site. However, in the previous year work was begun on a canal intended to bring water from the Middle Fork, close by, to operate a saw and grist mill already under construction. Thereafter a few additional settlers trickled into the area that is surrounded on three sides by low mountain ranges, wooded with oaks and maples and other deciduous growth. So Springfield grew slowly into a village with a future.

Springfield's pioneering epoch reached its zenith with the coming of the steamer *Relief*, riding the December flood waters of 1851. Thereafter, the depth of the river permitting —which meant when exceptional rain or melting snows increased the stream's normal flow—a few boats reached as far as Springfield.

Water transportation on the upper Willamette was practically abandoned following construction of the railroad in 1871. The milling of lumber grew in importance, while more and more grain raised by the farmers of the countryside was fed to meat stock. Manufacturing drew an increased settlement. For a time the gold and copper mines discovered in the mountains to the south added to the region's prosperity.

Concurrently, Eugene's position of prominence was assured and something of its temper was permanently fixed when in 1872 the University of Oregon was established there. The city provided the campus and the first building for the college; an amount of $50,000 was raised, part cash and part wheat and fat hogs donated by Lane County farmers. The institution weathered the panic of 1873, and in 1876 received a state grant of seventy-two sections of land.

As the years grew, varied industrial plants substantially aided the agricultural economy of the region. Southward and westward from the cottonwoods that flanked the river, grew the modern streets of the new residential Eugene. Its citizens, entering the life of the twentieth century, turned away from the waters that had motivated town growth, and toward the farms and forests that promised a better and more dependable future than the river itself could ever bring.

The old sketch of the riverside cluster of Corvallis in 1858 includes steamboat and ferry traffic. A warehouse with a chute appears on the west bank, and Marys Peak looms in the background.

The steamer *Albany* was a frequent upriver visitor after the turn of the century, here docked before the Corvallis Flouring Mills in bright winter sun, with the Willamette running full. (S.P. Collection, OHS)

Quiet, parklike banks, left, show that Albany, like Corvallis, has today (1970s) turned away from the river. (State Parks photo)

View of steamer *Occident*, below, about 1870 and before railroad bridge crossed at Red Crown Mills (white building). Uniformed band (?) on steamer and top-hatted crowd at Simpson's warehouse mark special occasion. (G. B. Abdill Collection).

Top view of Albany waterfront, about 1910, still shows river use, Red Crown mills, etc.

UNTIL 1851 no steamboats were built or in use on the upper Willamette. Yet valley farming had greatly increased and the agricultural output was constantly growing in volume. Settlements were springing up where before only bankside pontoon landings rocked in the nudging waters. Increasing numbers of wagons and carts—ox, mule or horse-drawn—hauled heaped loads of grain and other farm produce over the crude roads for shipment from those rough wharves. Flatboat service was inadequate and at many places freight piled up, awaiting transportation to down-river markets. Seeing this, shrewd men with an eye for future profits envisioned the coming of steamboats for quick and efficient service.

The first boat to go into regular service on the upper waterway—except a noisy contraption called the *Hoosier*—was the *Canemah*, built by Hedges & Company. Her story has already been told in the chapter on the town after which she was named.

Three other boats entered upper waters at about the same time. One of them, the sidewheeler *Multnomah*, was built in the East, of Jersey oak, and shipped in sections around Cape Horn and portaged around the falls to Canemah in June, 1851. Her hull was barrel-shaped and hooped with heavy bands which made calking unnecessary. She made her initial trip on the Willamette as far south as Corvallis that autumn. Thereafter she went into regular service between Canemah and Salem, taking a short side trip to Dayton on the Yamhill River. Frequently on her down-river trips she carried from 1,000 to 1,500 bushels of valley wheat. Her draft proved too deep for the shallow upper river waters, however, and in May 1852 she was again portaged around the falls to the lower river and placed on the Oregon City-Portland route. Later, she plied between Portland and the Cascades of the Columbia River, and between Portland and Astoria. She was the fastest boat of the early 'fifties, and once made the run from Portland to Vancouver, a distance of eighteen miles, in one hour and twenty minutes—a speedy trip for the period.

Steam-driven craft on the lower Willamette in 1851 or soon thereafter were the *James P. Flint*, the *Eagle*, the *Allen*, the *Washington*, the *Wallamet*, and the *Multnomah*. The *Eagle*, running between Oregon City and Portland, charged passengers $5 a trip and collected $15 per ton of freight. Trade rivalry became so keen that in 1853 the first river steamboat merger was formed by Captains George W. Hoyt and Alexander S. Murray. Their steamers were the *Multnomah* and the newly-built *Portland*.

Until 1854 all riverboats plying inland Oregon waters were side-wheelers. In that year J. C. Ainsworth and Jacob Kamm, operating the *Multnomah* and a new boat, the *Belle*, built the first sternwheeler, the *Jennie Clark*. Kamm owned a half interest, and Ainsworth and the Oregon City merchants, George Abernethy and Ransom Clark, had each a one-fourth interest. She was 115 feet long, 18 feet beam, with a depth of hold of 4 feet. Compared with sternwheelers which followed, the *Jennie Clark* was crude, yet so well planned that few of the prominent features embodied in her design could be improved on. Built in Milwaukie, where the *Lot Whitcomb* had been constructed four years earlier, she carried a pair of 12 by 15 inch engines bought in Baltimore. Captain Ainsworth was in command when she went into service between Portland and Oregon City in February, 1855.

With the building of the *Jennie Clark*, sternwheelers rapidly became the fashion on the Willamette. As the earliest-built vessels went to pieces, the county commissioners of Clackamas County announced that at Oregon City the disused boilers were being constructed into jail cells, set in thick brick walls.

In 1853 the Willamette Falls Canal and Transportation Company, with headquarters at upper Linn City, was organized to monopolize, if possible, all traffic on the upper river. However the result was only to drive all other transportation interests to form combines. In 1854 the Defiance Line was organized by Absalom Hedges and John Miller, with the *Wallamet* brought up from the lower river as chief carrier. The Citizens Accommodation Line, Captain George E. Cole and E. M. White at its head, commanded the

Canemah, recently purchased from the Hedges' interests, and the *Franklin,* formerly the *Shoalwater.* Both of those lines operated out of Canemah, on the east bank. Then in 1855, Captains J. S. Gibson, Cassidy and Cochran, forming a combine at Linn City, built the *James Clinton.*

The *James Clinton* was by no means a remarkable boat, but she made lasting fame for herself as the first steamer to navigate the Willamette as far as Eugene. When she did that in the spring of 1856, the upper river was an uncharted stream. There were unknown mud-flats and shallow sloughs to be avoided and marked for future trips. Everywhere were rocks and "sawyers," or sunken logs, and trees that thrust forth impeding arms. Considering the extreme narrowness of the channel in its upper reaches and the snaky meandering of its course it was something of a feat for the *James Clinton* to make the trip successfully and come back with a cargo aboard. It is little wonder that it took her all of three days to steam between Corvallis and Eugene, a distance of fifty-three miles.

The *Clinton* reached her destination on March 12, 1856, without serious mishaps, and the jubilant Eugenians staged a celebration. The first steamboat had been a long time in coming. Earlier, the Harrisburg merchant, David McCully, had asked Captain Archibald Jamieson of the *Enterprise* to ascend at least as far as Harrisburg. But the wary captain had refused to venture any farther than Orleans, opposite Corvallis. The refusal meant that McCully and his fellow merchants were obliged to haul their produce over the few rough and miry roads to navigable water, often as much as sixty or seventy miles.

But when the *James Clinton* slid into the river, McCully hastened to ask Captain Cochran to make the run, not only to Harrisburg but to Eugene. To this the captain agreed— if the two towns could subscribe to a steamboat line he planned to organize. The shrewd McCully agreed to induce his associates to buy stock and he himself promised to join the venture. As it turned out, Eugene alone took $5,000 worth of shares, while Harrisburg, some thirty miles below, subscribed liberally. Those stock subscriptions became the financial foundation of the People's Transportation Company. With a part of the money Captain Cochran and his partners built the *Surprise* at Canemah in 1857—a 120-ton boat, 130 feet long. Others connected with the line were Absalom Hedges, W. C. Dement, Charles C. Felton, J. Harding, Robert Patton and Theodore Wygant. At Portland, the moving spirit was Stephen Coffin.

The days were days of growth. But all was not smooth paddling for the little river craft and some of them came to grief. A few suffered boiler and stack explosions; others ran aground on gravel bars or struck snags which tore holes in their hulls; several of them encountered major tragedy.

On July 2, 1853, an unlucky boat, the *Portland*, was launched on the lower Willamette by Captain A. S. Murray, who had arrived in Oregon in 1851, attracted by the developing steamboat possibilities. The vessel, a small sidewheel steamer, was put on the Oregon City-Portland route, making connections with the *Multnomah*. In October 1856 she was brought around the falls and placed on the upper river, where she ran until March 17, 1857. On that day she left Canemah in command of Archibald Jamieson, who intended to take her into the basin above Oregon City to discharge freight.

The river was unusually high and the current strong. In swinging into the basin the current caught the *Portland* and took her too far out. Before the men aboard could do anything to prevent it, almost before they were aware of their danger, the boat began drifting toward the falls. When the crew saw this they tried with all effort to regain control of the steamer, but could make no headway against the surging waters, mainly because the steam was low in the boat's boiler. George Pease was standing on shore nearby and realized the peril of the boat and crew. He grabbed a rope close at hand, threw the end into the water as far as he could and shouted to the men to jump overboard and seize it. Peter Anderson, the fireman, took his advice, and Captain Pease hauled him ashore. Captain Jamieson and Bell, the deckhand, hesitated too long before jumping, and were swept to their death.

The *Portland* went over the falls and her upper works were carried away. These floated down the river and came ashore at Portland; the pilot house was picked up by a steamer near the mouth of the Willamette.

The steamer *Gazelle*, built by Page, Bacon & Company, newly organized as the Willamette Falls Company, with docks above and below the falls at Linn City, made her trial trip in March 1854. On April 8 she came to the tragic end already noted—the river's most fatal disaster.

Despite those, and other less fateful accidents, the fever of boat construction grew. Among notable sternwheelers built on the lower river in 1858 were the *Relief* and the *Carrie Ladd*. The latter was designed by John T. Thomas, a boatwright with United States Navy training. She was fitted to accommodate over two hundred passengers, and her speed amazed local steamboatmen. The *Relief*, launched at Oregon City and placed in command of Captain Cassidy, ran opposition to the *Carrie Ladd*, Captain Ainsworth at her helm. Shrewdly, Ainsworth soon acquired all of the outstanding stock of the *Relief* and so made himself chief owner. Thereupon he cut competition by ordering Cassidy to run his boat every other week.

The apparent trend toward steamboat monopolies filled skippers and the independent boat owners with apprehension. The Dements, William and John, Oregon City merchants, determined to enter the competition. Building the steamer *Rival* in 1860, they announced with fanfare that this boat had come to stay and would not be bought up as other small company boats had been. Captain George Pease was placed in charge on a route running between Oregon City and Portland. The owners were willing, they said, to make long term contracts, and announced their rates at $2 per ton of freight, and fifty cents a head for passengers. Such moderate rates were unheard of, and for awhile patronage was enormous. The *Rival*, only 110 feet long, carried the unbelievable load of seven hundred persons on her first trip, July 4, from Oregon City to Vancouver. Captain Pease afterward said he was mighty glad to see that crowd of merrymakers unloaded safely. Two years later, however, the Dement Brothers failed in their attempt to buck the opposing steamboat pools, and the *Rival* passed into the hands of the People's Transportation Company.

In 1860 there were two influential combines on the river. The People's line, organized in 1857 and reorganized in 1860, was incorporated in 1862. Its purpose from the start was to reduce freight rates. In this, its most persistent opposition came from the Oregon Steam Navigation Company, incorporated in 1860, the year in which corporation laws first became effective in Oregon. The People's line had three boats, the *Senator*, the *Rival*, and the *Fannie Patton*, on the lower river in 1865, and operated a small fleet above the falls. In 1865 a third line, the Willamette Steam Navigation Company, ran the steamers *Active*, *Alert*, and *Echo* between Portland and Eugene. In March, 1866, however, these were sold to the People's line.

With assets valued at $175,000, the O. S. N. Company had among its shareholders such locally prominent men as Captain J. C. Ainsworth, Simeon G. Reed, William S. Ladd, R. R. Thompson, George W. Hoyt, Laurence Coe and Jacob Kamm. It was their intent to make Portland the shipping center of the Columbia and its tributary valleys. The O. S. N. Company was to be the welding instrument of a great empire. The combine, at the start, was not totalitarian in its control, for such independent owners as did not join found it profitable to continue operating their own boats. The *Success*, the *Elk*, the *Onward*, the *Relief*, had Theodore Wygant for Portland agent. The P. T. Company, purchasing some of the boats of the W. T. Company, bucked the stronger Oregon Steam line for more than a decade.

Perhaps the strangest river craft that ever appeared on the Willamette River was the cattle-powered boat *"Hay Burner."* Steam vessels had been plying the Willamette and Columbia rivers for fully a decade, when in 1860, a "genius" at Corvallis decided that they were too expensive to operate. So he rigged a scow with treadmill machinery, using cattle and hay for motive power. Coming downstream on her first trip, the vessel ran aground—or, rather, walked ashore—at McGooglin's Slough, where she remained until the cattle had devoured nearly all the fuel. She was finally pulled off by a steamer appropriately named *Onward* and then continued down the river to Canemah. But once there she lacked sufficient power to return to Corvallis against the current. The skipper sold his oxen and abandoned his enterprise.

In 1862–63 the People's Transportation Company constructed a breakwater above the Willamette Falls on the Canemah side. Within this thousand-foot barrier four steamers could lie at one time, safe from the hazard of being carried over the falls. Over an incline freight was hauled from one level to the other, greatly expediting commerce.

The autumn of 1863 was almost rainless and December found the upper Willamette without water enough to float steamers. Transportation was at a standstill, with boats tied to their wharves. Mills closed for want of grain to grind and the stocks of country merchants ran low. However, steamboat building went merrily on and continued during the years following. Canemah saw the most craft slide into the water, but Oregon City, Milwaukie and Portland were also boatbuilding ports. The steamers, whether built by private parties or small combines for the most part found their way into the hands of either the P. T. Company or the O. S. N. Company.

During the 'sixties and 'seventies, when steamboat traffic on the upper river was at its height, there was considerable racing between rival steamers. The People's line had four boats on the Portland-Corvallis run. The Willamette line put up stiff competition in rate slashing and fast running. The fare from Portland to Salem dropped to fifty cents, with meals and berths free; to Albany, $1; to Corvallis, $1.50. Speed contests became almost daily occurrences, sometimes drawing considerable criticism from the newspapers. The *Oregonian* of January 19, 1866, said:

"Thus far the waters of Oregon have not been the scene of steamboat racing to any extent, and the lives of many have no doubt been spared on that account. The scenes of the Sacramento last year should be sufficient check to the dangerous policy of testing the speed of rival steamers at the risk of life. Opposition is to be despised if it brings matters to this, and the company, or the officers of a company, who so far neglect the safety of those under their charge for the purposes of racing one another should be held strictly accountable for their acts. On last Saturday the steamer

Reliance of the People's Transportation company, and the *Active* of the Willamette Steam Navigation company had an exciting race from Canemah to Salem, which is thus noticed by the *Salem Statesman:* 'The time was about seven hours and five minutes, and the race so close that both boats claim the victory. We enter our protest against steamboat men endangering the lives of the insignificant little dug-outs they run on the Willamette river. The people don't care a fig which can run from Canemah to Salem in five minutes least time, but they do care when their lives and freight are endangered by racing. If it continues, another special session of the legislature, to make it as criminal in law as it is in fact, would be justifiable.' "

The riverboats multiplied in numbers. In 1867, the P. T. Company, with its monopoly on quick portage of freight and passengers through its basin at the falls, swallowed the W. S. N. Company and bought its boats. In the following year, another steamboat line, with the vessels *Success* and *Ann*, offered brief competition to the People's line, but was absorbed in 1869. For a time the Long Tom Transportation Company operated the steamer *Ann* up the Long Tom River; the first boat to navigate this stream, she reached Monroe City—an ambitious name for former Starr's Settlement—on February 17, 1869. Of that occasion the *Oregon State Journal* of Eugene City, jested sarcastically on April 3: "The Long Tom people were so infatuated with the presence of a steamboat on the placid waters of their quiet stream that they did not let the *Ann* leave, but have tied it up somewhere in the Long Tom now. They probably think that if a boat is a good thing they will keep this one while they have it. Good idea. It might not have been able to get back if it had been allowed to leave." The Long Tom soon proved itself unnavigable and the career of the *Ann* ended two months later when she sank near Harrisburg with a thousand bushels of wheat aboard.

In 1868, eight steamboats, privately owned, and a similar number belonging to the O. S. N. Company, transacted freight and passenger business centering at Portland. Even then, some of the boats were forced to engage in towing barges and ocean vessels to make expenses. Two years later more than a dozen boats churned through the placid lower waters; fewer plied the upper stream. Although there were not so many towns to serve, following the devastation of the "great flood", most of those that survived were growing vigorously.

In the fall of 1868 the P. T. Company beheld the approaching cloud that was to obscure their prosperity. This was the Willamette Falls Canal & Locks Company—an organization formed on September 14, with a capital of $30,000, plus $40,000 in aid from the Oregon Legislature. Work was begun immediately on a canal and locks around the falls on the west shore. It was no secret that the undertaking had as its main purpose the breaking of the monopoly of the P. T. Company at the falls.

However, the People's line went ahead with its program of building and buying steamers. This was the more remarkable since two railroads—the Oregon Central and the Oregon & California—were building south from Portland and were sure to make their bids for part of the tonnage carried by the Company's steamers. To top it all, the Willamette Navigation Company was formed in 1870 by indignant valley farmers who hated the P. T. Company. The new organization built the 100-foot steamer *Calliope* at Corvallis and placed her on the upper-river route. She made one unsuccessful venture up the Santiam River in 1870.

Before the Willamette Locks were completed, Ben Holladay, representing the railroad interests, blasted a right of way under the bluffs at Oregon City, close to the water. Along this grade the first train steamed on New Year's Day, 1870. It was ironic that with the improvement of the river, expediting water travel, a competing land agency was born that was eventually to put the riverboats out of business. Meanwhile, the fleet of ten or more boats owned by the P. T. Company was suddenly sold to the Holladay interests, which then held many of the ships, boats and railroads of Oregon in their control.

The locks at Oregon City, situated on the opposite shore, were opened to traffic on New Year's Day, 1873. The promoters did their best to hire a steamboat sufficiently well appointed and commodious to hold all the distinguished people invited to view the locks on this occasion. But all suitable boats were busy elsewhere, only the *Marie Wilkins* being available. She was little more than a tugboat, built at Portland in 1872. With Captain Charles Kellogg at the wheel, George Marshall as engineer, and with Lewis, one of her owners, at the throttle, she made the momentous trip. Invited guests included Governor Lafayette Grover, Portland's Mayor P. Wasserman, Henry Failing, former governor John Whiteaker, Harvey Scott, then editor of the *Portland Bulletin*, Jacob Kamm, S. B. Parrish, and others of prominence.

It was a raw, windy and rainy morning when the viewing party assembled at the Oregon Steam Navigation Company's wharf at Portland; it was nearly nine-thirty before all had arrived. Space aboard the craft was soon at a premium, since the boat was only seventy-five feet long; so chairs were set around the boiler on the engine-room deck. To make people forget their discomfort, cigars and whisky were passed around, and soon the group thawed and talk became general.

The first part of the trip went smoothly enough, but at the Clackamas Rapids the small *Marie Wilkins* encountered difficulties. Again and again she was driven back by the current as she tried the ascent. Finally, as the Captain was about to give up the effort, the boat managed to climb the rapids. She arrived at the foot of the locks near noon.

Along either shore of the river enthusiastic people from shelters and from under umbrellas cheered the *Marie Wilkins* and the guests aboard her. Governor Grover made a speech and proposed three cheers for the locks, their builders, backers, and planners, after which the crowd, despite the falling rain, cheered everything and everybody.

And thus the Willamette became a stream of continuous passage. Meanwhile, another steamship company—the Willamette Transportation Company—had been incorporated, with Bernard Goldsmith, president of the locks' company, as head. It began business on the upper Willamette on March 18, 1873, with the *Governor Grover*, 140 feet long, launched at Portland on January 28, 1873, the first large steamer to run as far as Harrisburg.

In rapid succession the W. T. Company bought the steamers *Vancouver* and *Shoshone*, built the *Beaver* and launched her at Portland on August 21, 1873. Then in 1874, the *Willamette Chief*, 163 feet in length, entered the water at the same place. She was intended to run from the mouth of the Columbia to the head of navigation on the Willamette, and her owners thought to revolutionize transportation with her. On her first run, under Captain Charles Holman and Engineer John Marshall, she left Corvallis with 200 tons of wheat and thirty passengers, picking up one hundred and thirty more at Albany and Salem, chiefly farmers who were accompanying their grain to Astoria. Colonel Joe Teal of the locks company, and also of the Farmers Wharf Company, a concern related to the W. T. Company, was aboard the *Willamette Chief* and announced that in the future the entire wheat crop of the Willamette Valley would be transported from Corvallis to Astoria for $4 per ton, and that all grain ships for ocean points would land at the Astoria wharves. But that did not come to pass, as the company ceased to do business the next year.

During the year or so of its existence, the W. T. Company went after the business of the Ben Holladay line, the Oregon Steamship Company, and also after the Oregon Steam Navigation Company. It placed the *Beaver* on the Astoria run, the *Governor Grover* on the Corvallis route, the *Willamette Chief* on the Albany course, and the *Shoshone* on the Yamhill River. As a consequence, reckless competition was again in full swing among the several companies. More boat racing ensued and rates between Astoria and Portland went down to one dollar per person and ton of freight. The speed of traffic brought many collisions.

In the year immediately following, new ownerships and corporations were a frequent recurrence. The most important of the new corporations was the Willamette Transportation & Locks Company, which came into existence on December 29, 1875, with a capital stock of one million dollars. It soon acquired most of the combines and rival interests on the river. With this company and the O. S. N. Company almost monopolizing river traffic, independent competition died out and steamship building declined. In

1879, monopoly of transportation facilities was further strengthened when the O. S. N. Company passed out of existence and the still greater Oregon Railway & Navigation Company emerged, with a capital of six million dollars.

Many are the stories told of the boats that plied Willamette waters. The *Success* built at Canemah in 1868, the first boat to navigate the narrow Duran Chute between Salem and Eola, had all her windows broken by the obtruding tree-growth. The boiler of the *Resolute* exploded at Portland in 1872; everything went through the bottom of the boat, sinking her instantly. More tragically, the *Senator* blew up while pulling into Alder Street dock at Portland; seven passengers were killed and as many injured. The *Occident* and *Orient*, built at Portland by the Oregon Steam line, were called the "Willamette Twins." Launched in 1875, the *Occident* later nosed up the narrow Santiam River as far as Jefferson, a trip also made that year by the *City of Salem*. This was something of an accomplishment, since the Santiam, rapid and dashing, was practically unnavigable except during extreme high water and then for only a few days at a time. Men there were who boasted of the accomplishments of the *Alice*, which in 1875 hung up a record of thirty-three landings between Oregon City and Albany on a single trip. The *Alice* became known in her day as the "queen of the river," and in February 1876 outdistanced both the *City of Salem* and the *Willamette Chief* in a race from Albany to Corvallis.

Then there was the *Ohio*, built in 1873 by U. B. Scott, a veteran of the Ohio and Mississippi Rivers, and a seasoned and sometimes profane pilot and captain. The panic of 1873 was at its height but Scott managed to induce enough capital to join him in construction of a "light draft" vessel, which at first was a joke then a reassuring success. That flat-bottomed scow was one of the few boats that could go as far as Eugene, and during her first three months, for all the facts of her ridiculous difficulties—she several times lost her paddle wheel—coined her owners $10,000 in clear profit. As a consequence, Scott, who had almost to beg for money with which to build the *Ohio*, now found money pushed his way to build more boats of the same type.

For a time, construction of Willamette Valley railroads

boomed lower river traffic. So much so that by 1878 nearly
a score of craft were in service on the lower waters alone.
Besides these, an average of sixty cars a day came into
Portland from up-river points, with grain and passengers
and livestock. Besides the railroads, numerous sailing vessels
and a few steamships, their numbers increasing with the
years, carried Oregon produce to coastal and foreign ports.
At least two ocean-going barks each month cleared from the
port of Portland with lumber.

In a period of approximately thirty years fifty-two sidewheel and sternwheel steamers were built along the Willamette—twenty-seven at Canemah, thirteen at Oregon City,
five at Milwaukie, and one each at Oswego, Linn City,
Newberg, New Era, and Tualatin; and two at Sucker or
Oswego Lake. Besides these, a handful were built at Portland.

A number of boats were built over succeeding years for
operation on the lower Willamette, plying also into the
Columbia. Most noteworthy was the *T. J. Potter*, launched
in 1888 and for more than a quarter of a century the fastest
sidewheeler in the Pacific Northwest. She was 230 feet in
length and 35 feet in beam, and was lighted by electricity.
Other boats of speed and admiration were the *R. R. Thompson*, the *Wide West*, the *Bailey Gatzert*, the *Telephone*, the
Harvest Queen, the *Lurline* and the *Undine*. Nearly all
carried pleasure-seeking Oregonians to the breezy summer
beaches, or on moonlight excursions up the Columbia or
Willamette.

Humor and sentiment were often compounded in the
river's many-mooded story. Intermingled with matter-of-
fact events and daily occurrences, were incidents that sometimes partook of the tragic, sometimes of the heroic. Recalling the early days, T. S. Wilkes wrote years later in the
Hillsboro Argus:

"I have seen the deckhands out in the fields helping to
round up cattle that were to be shipped, and the heartiest
laugh I ever enjoyed was when they tried to get a bull ashore
at Scappoose Landing. He resisted all efforts of the deckhands until Charles Kellogg, who had as usual another
'cargo' on board which does not tend to increase one's

patience, said, 'Make that rope fast to that stump. Damn him, I'll land him!' Two strokes on the big gong in the engine room, followed by a tinkle of the slow bell followed the casting off of the spring-line, and soon the bull found the boat slowly creeping out from under him. He set his feet and slid along the deck until he was drawn up to the bitts, where he saw the inevitable and did the high jump. The splash when he struck the water went higher than the hurricane deck and when he came up he was willing to climb the bank without urging."

More sentimental is the story of a group of young people who were descending the river by boat from Oregon City to Portland in the late 'seventies. At that date the forests still darkened the shores, with scattered grassy openings. Gleeful, the young people pointed out sites that pleased them. One would exclaim, "I'm going to have that spot for my house." Another would shout, "There's my future home over there." And so it progressed until the boat approached an island a short distance above Portland, when a girl jumped to the rail, exclaiming, "That island's mine. I always did want an island." Immediately a young man called out, "Well, if you want that island you'll have to take me along with it, for I own that island." The reply came, "I'll take you." Shortly after the trip the two were married. The young man was Sherry Ross, and the island is still called Ross Island.

The *City of Salem*, built in 1875 by the U. B. Scott Steamship Co., could carry immense loads over shallow water, and even went up the Santiam to Jefferson in 1876. A different type was the palatial *T. J. Potter*, with the diningroom shown below. The *Potter* ran on the excursion route from Portland to Astoria and Ilwaco for many years. (OHS Collections)

Boat-building platforms and repair yards at Portland, about 1900. Notice large mobile winch under trees on right, probably used for raising and lowering boats through the shocks of such drydocking platforms. (OHS)

Governor Grover, built by Willamette Transportation Company and launched early in 1873, shown in the newly-completed locks around Willamette Falls at Oregon City. Note bustled lady standing at side of locks. (OHS Cols.)

The *Multnomah* was built in 1885 for the Oregon City run by the Willamette Steamboat Company. A fast, economical stern-wheeler, she steamed under Capt. W. H. Pope, then transferred to the Cascades run, and later operated on Puget Sound. (OHS)

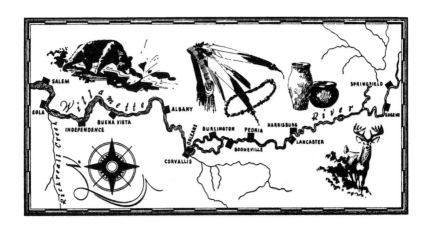

TRADE TOWNS OF YESTERDAY . . .

EOLA, the fragment of a town lying three and a half miles west of Salem, in Polk county, was not always so-called. About the few remaining buildings hangs the aura of a much earlier period of Oregon's history, when the town was known as Cincinnati. Then it fostered the ambitious dream of someday being an important metropolis. Tradition has it that this dream endured briefly, when in the late 'fifties and early 'sixties the place was mentioned as a site for the State capital, but was bypassed, with other valley towns by Salem.

At first Cincinnati was indefinitely located. In 1844, Joshua "Sheep" Shaw and his son, A. C. R. Shaw, settled on the green acres of the Rickreall River—the upper reaches were called La Creole—and the elder Shaw named the locality after the Ohio River town from which he had come. When in 1849 the townsite was platted it was carved, not from the Shaw ranch, but from the land claim of William Duran. The following spring lots were advertised for sale through the columns of the *Spectator*. The advertisement first appearing on June 13, was headed "Cincinnati," and read:

"The town is situated on the west side of the Willamette immediately below the mouth of the La Creole River, in Polk county. The site commands a fine view of the La Creole valley, is well supplied with excellent water from several large springs; timber and rock of excellent quality are plenty in the vicinity, and it has for a back country, as rich and flourishing a section as any in the Willamette valley. Those wishing to locate in the upper country would do well to call and examine the site. Apply to Joshua or A. C. R. Shaw, or to the proprietor, William Duran."

Cincinnati prospered in 1851. J. B. V. Butler arrived and established a store that soon supplied a wide area. The first of the steam riverboats arrived, when Captain A. S. Murray crowded the sidewheeler *Washington* up the narrow Rickreall.

Also in 1851 Cincinnati became sufficiently important to be named a post office. Mail was delivered there twice each week, the first stop on a hazardous seventy-mile route that began at Salem and continued up the Rickreall Valley, to

Nathaniel Ford's, near present-day Rickreall, to Nesmith Mills at Ellendale. Over this frontier trail through the mountains, timber and prairie, the post carrier rode horse-back, the mail in leather saddlebags behind him. Sometimes Indians endangered his going.

Of the town builders, the Shaws were the more aggressive. Already they enjoyed the distinction of being the first immi-grants to drive a flock of sheep over the "Road to Oregon," a feat accomplished in 1844. By 1853 they had set them-selves up as forwarding and commission merchants, and advertised the fact in the *Statesman*. They also announced themselves as "Dealers in Dry Goods, and Groceries and Country Produce." Meanwhile, William Duran's principal interests seem to have been ranching and the disposal of town lots.

A tanyard was one of the town's earliest industries, for J. C. Clarke advertised one for sale or rent as early as September 6, 1853. In the deal was included bark enough to supply the yard for one year. A lot of leather was put up for sale, and a good set of tools "just received from the States." Asa Shreve, blacksmith, purchased for $75 at Salem a bellows to operate his forge.

If credence is to be placed in scattered references, it is more than probable that Cincinnati had both a grist mill and a sawmill as early as 1853. On February 21, 1854, but dated as of January 8, A. C. R. Shaw announced in the *Statesman* that he wished to contract for 10,000 logs, of red, yellow and white fir; also of pine, cedar, oak, ash and maple woods. These were to be delivered at the landing of the sawmills, on the banks of the Rickreall River. He adver-tised also for two good sawyers. Emigrants were coming into the country in greatly increased numbers; lumber was in demand. To the building public, Shaw announced: "sawed lumber of various kinds can be had at the. . . . mills or delivered to Salem dressed or undressed."

Thus established, the community of Cincinnati prospered. Its ambitions grew. At about this time a deposit of coal was discovered in the nearby hills. Keeping its location as secret as possible, its discoverers optimistically prepared in-corporation papers for the Cincinnati Railroad, and proposed to take out the coal. An act, granting such a railroad a charter, passed the Territorial Legislature on June 30, 1854, and called for a capital of $250,000. However, the project lapsed, and the railroad was not built.

After five years of vaguely platted existence, Cincinnati was officially surveyed by T. H. Hutchinson in April, 1855, and recorded on August 31. In that act, Cincinnati was renamed Eola. The town sloped generally south, not quite square with the compass, its forty-five numbered blocks and public square rising from the river margin where stood Shaw's mills. Main, First, Second, Third, Fourth and Fifth Streets ran from east to west, a length of eight blocks; cross streets were Hayden, Riggs, Spring, Mill, Shaw, Duran, Willamette, La Creole, Ingle, Heath, and Walker.

According to one story, the name change was suggested by Lindsay Robbins, a local musician. On the one hand, Robbins disliked the name Cincinnati, and on the other, he was fond of playing the Aeolian harp. From the latter he derived the name Eola, and it was adopted. Another version of the change is that the town name was evolved from Aeolus, Greek God of the winds.

Near the close of the sixth year, on January 17, 1856, Eola was granted a charter of incorporation. The bill requesting such a grant was introduced into the legislature seven days prior to that date, and at the time of reading provoked a ripple of amusement among assembly members. Eola? That was a hamlet of but two houses and one barn, it was whispered around. What need had such a one-horse village for a charter, such as was given commonly only to flourishing centers that had an assured future? But let the hamlet be incorporated, if its residents so desired. And it was so voted. Actually, as some of them well knew, Eola had a store, a tan yard, at least two mills, a school and a church.

The church, of the Campbellite faith, was organized in 1856. It came into being largely through the ministerial efforts of Hugh McNary Waller, its first pastor. Possibly services had been held in private homes for some years before formal organization took place. It should be remembered that the churches were the centers of community life in those early days. Not only Eola's residents welcomed the opportunity to gather in Sunday worship, but pioneer families came from distant points in the valley and from remote claims in the Yamhill mountains. The town of Eola was not only a place of trade, but the social, educational, religious and political focal point of the community.

The first paper at Eola was the *Religious Expositor*, published by the Baptist elder, C. H. Mattoon. The initial issue appeared on May 6, 1856, and was widely circulated. The paper was short-lived; it moved to Corvallis in July, 1856, and suspended publication in October.

Of the political life of the town, little now is known. Two months after it received its charter, the first municipal election was held. The town fathers were then William Hayden, J. B. V. Butler and A. C. R. Shaw, who took charge of balloting.

A school was built in 1853, a one-room structure that stood not far from the present Eola school. The school's first teacher was Miss Abigail Jane Scott, later Abigail Scott Duniway, of more than local fame as a pioneer advocate of equal suffrage for women. After Miss Scott's days at Eola and the burning of the first small structure, a second was erected on February 1, 1858; James and Nancy Clark deeded Lot 4, Block 20, at Second and Mill Streets, as a site. That schoolhouse continued in use until 1937 when it was abandoned for a modern two-room structure financed by a WPA grant. With much of the earlier town long since gone to decay around it, the old wooden building, seven small-paned windows on either side, a single porch-shaded door, and at the front of its peaked roof a pinched cupola, stood facing east. For years, the building was the oldest schoolhouse still in use in the state.

James L. Gwin was the school's first teacher. Thomas W. Brunk, who began his schooling there in 1865, and who still lived on the home place at Brunk's Corner, one and a half miles west of the town, believed in 1937 that he was the oldest living graduate. When interviewed, by Ben Maxwell of Eola, he recalled incidents of his school days, events both vivid and amusing.

"John C. Allen, who later became prominent in county politics, supplied the logs used in sawing the lumber from which the Eola school was built. Allen dragged the logs to the sawmill with two span of oxen—I know, because I've heard John Allen tell about it.

"Dave Holmes was one of my first teachers. In those days the pupils were much older than they are now, and in one or two instances men who were old enough to vote were in the lower grades learning to read. The school term was about three months in the winter period and the pupils paid the teacher's salary. When I started to school in 1865, the fee was $7. Later it was reduced to $5, and a year after I had finished it was reduced to $3, and finally—perhaps in the 1860's—the county paid the teacher's salary entirely.

"The boys were mature and husky, and from the moment school opened in the winter until the closing day in early spring, there was restrained hostility between the teacher and the pupils. Sometimes the teacher couldn't stick it out and had to quit.

"I recall when Ed Ingalls was teacher, in the late 1860's. Billy Hayden was one of Ed's most troublesome pupils. On this particular morning Ed yanked Billy from his seat and hauled him up in front of the class to trounce him for dragging mud into the schoolroom, in defiance of Ed's orders. Billy was pretty much of a boy and there was a struggle. Finally Ed got him where he wanted him, and began to lay it on plenty hot and heavy.

"Estelle Hayden was Billy's sister, and perhaps a bit younger than he. She watched the affray with amused indifference, until it appeared that her brother was in for the whaling of his life. Then with the ferocity of a wildcat, she picked up a heavy slate and sprang from her seat. Perhaps she aimed to hit Ed Ingalls with the edge of the slate and send him spinning. But she missed, and the slate came down flat on Ingalls' head, with an awful clatter. Bits of broken slate flew in every direction and Ed had a ragged edge slate for a collar that cut him however he moved. Taking advantage of the teacher's hapless and helpless condition, other pupils joined the fight in behalf of the battling Haydens, and school and Ingalls were soon out for the day."

During the 'fifties Eola continued to grow. In 1856 the town was placed in the running as a site for the state capital.

Although it is disputed that the pioneer village ever received more than a few votes in the legislative poll for a location, the legend persisted for years that it failed of selection as the seat of government by only a scant margin.

Today the Cincinnati House, pioneer inn, still stands at Eola. During Civil War years, Southern sympathizers, banded together in a secret organization known as the Knights of the Golden Circle, gathered there to plot resistance to the Union. A second hotel was the Boothby House. A newspaper, *The Weekly Times*, was published there. There were three general merchandise stores, a shoe shop, a blacksmith shop, a harness shop, and several saloons. The fiery kilns of S. H. Way turned out bricks and pottery. Wagons were made by D. L. Riggs, and threshing machines by E. T. Lange. Ray's Tannery emitted its strong odors of drying leathers and green hides. The sawmill, at this time jointly owned, spewed its dust and tailings into the Rickreall. Docks and warehouses accommodated the shipping trade, but only when waters were sufficiently high. At such times, river boats from the Willamette splashed their blunt noses through the overhanging brush of the Rickreall, to load wheat and other produce at Eola's waterfront.

In the late 'sixties, Harvey Scott, of the *Weekly Oregonian* at Portland, reported that the town had started to decline. Nevertheless, the *Pacific Coast Business Directory* for 1867 showed that Samuel Beckett then operated the Cincinnati House, and T. G. Waller the Boothby House. A. T. Waller was attorney-at-law, and W. D. Jeffries the local physician. At least a half a dozen others conducted assorted enterprises.

The gravel and sandbars at the mouth of the Rickreall grew with the years until a flat bottomland a thousand feet wide separated the village from the channel of the Willamette.

Old timers of the area recall that Eola languished in the 'seventies and 'eighties. Thomas Pierce's warehouse on the Rickreall received the annual grain harvest of many adjacent farms until 1889, but after that date no more grain was unloaded there.

The raging flood of 1890 reached a crest of 37.1 feet in the Willamette at Salem. The waters that raced through the

Rickreall and the old boat canal, gouged out a new channel for the Willamatte. The old Pierce warehouse toppled into the flood. It finally lodged near the Salem-Polk County bridge, which too was carried away. Only one other Eola warehouse withstood the flood.

THE RED KILNS OF BUENA VISTA

THROUGHOUT its industrial life the village of Buena Vista, twenty-one miles above Salem and on the opposite shore, long a place of red kilns and the principal center of potteries on the Pacific Coast, was served only by Willamette river-boats and a few crude roads. Only in her later industrial years was she aided by the coming of the railroad, in 1879, two and one-half miles to the west. With the decline and abandonment of upper river transportation, Buena Vista lacked any principal artery of transportation. When in 1886 the manufacture of clay products was discontinued, many of the residents either moved away or returned to farming. The numerous Chinamen who had been employed at kiln work, straggled away to other fields. Today only a remnant of this earliest Oregon industrial town remains; none of the early landmarks stand amid the scattered dwellings of the sleepy hamlet.

Reason B. Hall arrived in Oregon in 1846, and at the site of Buena Vista in 1847. He was not the first comer, however, and was greeted by a bachelor whose name was Heck, already living there in a two-room cabin. Heck wished to leave for a time on business and prevailed upon Hall to hold his property as a resident. Hall retained the land since Heck, who had merely a squatter's right, never returned.

Early in the 'fifties, Hall platted a town which he first patriotically called Liberty. Meadows—sometimes called "Meaders"—Vanderpool surveyed the property. In those early years the names of budding municipalities were readily changed. Recalling the Mexican War battle of Buena Vista, in which some of his relatives had fought, Hall renamed his embryonic town—which in scenic attractiveness merited the name—Buena Vista, meaning in Spanish "beautiful view."

In 1851 Messrs. Weill and Sharf started a warehouse and general merchandise business. To boost his fortunes and stimulate the growth of the town, Hall, in 1852 or 1853, commenced operating a ferry across the Willamette.

About this time James A. O'Neal, who had earlier owned the site of Wheatland, thirty-odd miles down-river, moved to Buena Vista and established a mercantile business; soon thereafter a grist mill was erected. With the growth of trade, H. D. Godley established a hotel, E. C. Hall opened a wagon shop, and the red forge glowed in the blacksmith shop built by J. M. Wells.

Two miles to the west of Buena Vista was Bloomington. There in 1847 Harrison Linville had taken a land claim and built a large log house and other buildings, where he engaged in farming, stock raising and store keeping. The movements of incoming settlers were such that he was soon profitably operating a ferry across the Luckiamute River. In the late 'forties the main road between Portland and California, through the Willamette Valley, crossed the Luckiamute at Linville's Ferry. In addition to the emigrant trade, in 1848–50, were many gold-seekers going to and from the mines in California. A few years later, soldiers going and returning from Forts Hoskins and Yamhill crossed by the ferry at Bloomington, which was named as a post office in 1853.

But seemingly it was not Linville's desire to found a town, and with Buena Vista on the Willamette River fast becoming the principal artery of commerce, Bloomington gave way to its rival. Linville continued to ranch and operate his ferry. District elections were held at his house, and there also the first issue of goods and supplies to the Indians was made by General Joel Palmer, Superintendent of Indian Affairs for Oregon. In 1848 Linville was elected to the Provisional Legislature, from Polk County, and was the county's first Judge, serving from September 2, 1850, to July 4, 1853.

Hall, with Buena Vista well established, was inordinately proud of his young town, and in 1856 made a trip to Oregon City and there inserted an advertisement in the *Oregon Spectator*, to the effect that Buena Vista was in the race with other towns as a location for the new State Capital. His lengthy announcement cited the community's advantages:

"NOTICE TO THE PEOPLE OF OREGON

"It has been a matter of dispute where the Capital of Oregon shall be placed.

"The center of the territory you will find as near Buena Vista as any other suitable place for the Capital.

"Buena Vista is about half way between Salem and Corvallis, near the corner of the four counties of Polk, Benton, Marion and Linn, in Polk county, on Wallamet.

"The ground is high and dry, ascending from the river bank, and a more healthful situation cannot be found in the country—no swamp or low wet land about the place, and is backed by as beautiful and as rich a country as there is in Oregon.

"There are plenty of the best building timber handy to the place and thousands of cords of cordwood.

"Such a place as above described we offer to the people for the Capital, together with as much ground as will be wanted to set the State House on, also as available a stone quarry is donated as fine as I have ever seen in Oregon.

"The people in the surrounding neighborhood propose to donate in land and money, about $15,000; besides these numbers of other donations that will be made—should the Capital be moved to the above mentioned place, there is a good mill privilege for either a steam or water mill, also a good steamboat landing as there is on the Wallamet river.

"Such a place as above mentioned, we offer to the people for the capital. Come forward and pole your votes for Buena Vista.

Buena Vista   April 21, 1856"

But Buena Vista's ambition to become the center of State government received the recognition of a mere handful of voters.

Nevertheless the residents believed in the town's future. The number of new settlers increased from year to year. As a shipping point, Buena Vista grew in importance. Riverboats, providing a trade outlet for every bankside hamlet, nosed upstream with accommodating frequency. A school was started in 1859; the building was also used for religious services. A post office was granted the town in 1862.

Among new homeseekers coming from the East, via the Isthmus of Panama in 1865, was Freeman Smith, and his sons. About this time a bed of superior fire clay was discovered at Buena Vista, and Smith, learning of the fact, went there to investigate the possibilities of utilizing it commercially. Finding the clay of a high burning quality, Smith and his sons built kilns and started a stoneware or pottery plant. A deposit of "slip clay" needed for glazing the ware under intense heat, was found at Corvallis, seventeen miles distant.

The Smith and Company pottery was the first such estabment in the Pacific Northwest. Despite the fact that most of the settlers were but meagerly supplied with vessels and containers of durable ware, Smith found that a market for his products had to be cultivated. He hauled his first wagon load of earthenware to Albany, where he found the merchants skeptical of being able to dispose of it. After repeated attempts to make a deal, Smith in discouragement was about to haul his unsold load back to Buena Vista, when a hardware merchant, John Conner, motioned to him to take the entire lot of stoneware to the store's back door. Impulsively, Conner had decided to buy the lot and take a chance on selling or trading it away.

This sale, made at the moment of seeming defeat, heartened Smith and he decided to continue the manufacture of clay products. Eventually Conner paid him at the rate of fifty cents per gallon capacity. In this deal Conner bought and disposed of three hundred gallons of crockery, paying Smith for it in gold. Thus encouraged, Smith improved his business, which grew steadily. With this new source of income Buena Vista expanded into a busy industrial center.

Soon a drugstore was established by March and Woods; two physicians, J. C. Woods and W. C. Lee, opened offices; A. J. Richardson opened a carpenter shop, A. Kintz a cobbler's shop, and Jacob Nash did general teaming. John Wade dispensed "red-eye" and "blue ruin" in a saloon which he later sold to Charlie Henry. At this time a grist mill was owned by H. N. George and Robert Beech, and a sawmill was operated by R. P. Bonzey. There were two large warehouses and a blacksmith shop. Harrison Linville—who had disposed of his farm in 1864 and moved to Eola where he engaged briefly in the milling business—moved to Buena Vista in the fall of 1865. There he carried on a general merchandising business and operated a hotel until early in the 1880's.

In 1870, Amedee M. Smith bought the rights of his father

and brothers in the pottery business. At that time, it was said, the plant employed four "turners" at the wheel, and ten Chinese to mix clay. Amedee Smith enlarged the business, adding to the facilities, and in 1872 began the making of drain pipe. So successful was he that in 1873 the plant manufactured the fifteen-inch sewer-pipe for Portland's Stark Street sewer. From that time on, for many years, Smith furnished most of the pipe for the sewer mains of Portland and other Oregon towns.

In 1880 Buena Vista by census count numbered but one hundred eighty-three persons. In that year Polk's *Pacific Coast Directory*, in speaking of the "very extensive pottery works" located there, declared that their "productions find their way to every market of importance on the Pacific Coast." Smith's Buena Vista pottery, then referred to as the only pottery in Oregon, had a branch store in Portland.

By this date, there had been many changes of ownership in the town's business houses. The Cliff House competed with the Union House, kept by Mrs. D. C. Baldwin. Harrison Linville had become postmaster. General merchants were Bettman & Rosenblatt, Estab & Rive, and S. Freedman. Dealers in boots and shoes were Jefferson Miller and F. A. White, with groceries dispensed by C. D. Lee. The two town blacksmiths were W. E. Wilcox and L. Southworth, the latter recently proprietor of the livery stable. Lumber was purchased from Joseph Smith, keeper of the sawmill. The town had at least one contractor and builder, William St. John. The prescriptions of Dr. J. M. Smith were filled at the drug store of D. M. Calbreath, which also sold nostrums only a little less potent than the liquors dispensed at the saloon of E. Merwin & Company. The local butcher, A. Munzell, also ran a ferry across the river. The large I.O.O.F. Hall housed two stores on its first floor, with lodge quarters above.

In commenting on the educational life of the community, Polk's *Directory* reported that the Buena Vista school house was two stories high, well finished and would accommodate the one hundred forty-seven scholars then in the district. It housed both grade school and excellent academy, with Prof. George Beeler as principal, and his wife as assistant teacher.

A Methodist Church, well attended and capable of seating one hundred fifty persons, ministered to the town's religious needs. Hung in the spire belfry was a good bell.

There were then at Buena Vista two large wheat ware-houses, with a combined storage capacity of 100,000 bushels of grain. Nearby was a large sawmill, with a feed and chopping mill attached, still owned by Joseph Smith. This mill cut from 10,000 to 15,000 feet of lumber daily and employed from fifteen to twenty "hands."

"The great future of the place," the *Directory* of 1881 said, "is the vast beds of potters clay, of a kind that makes the best of stoneware. . . . All of the steamboat lines which run above Salem, stop at this place; in fact, this is the head of steamboat navigation in low water times. Boats can come here whenever they can come to Salem, but can go no higher up at low stages of water. This is the only means of public transportation yet furnished to the people; the O. & C. RR being located about 2 ½ miles west of town."

The Commerce and Industries of the Pacific Coast, published in 1882, stated: "The kilns, which differ from those in use elsewhere, and most of the machines, were designed by the proprietor, and have proved successful. About fifty men are employed, who turn out sewer-pipe, stoneware, flower-pots, vases, fire-brick, etc., which are sold in Oregon and Washington, the factory being the largest one in the industry in Oregon. The wholesale depot is at 269 Front Street, Portland. Mr. Smith has been uniformly successful, although several other parties have attempted to establish potteries in his neighborhood and failed."

Amedee Smith continued to conduct his Buena Vista plant until 1886, shipping thousands of tons of pottery and clay products. Then, after a score of years of local operation, he left his kilns idle and opened a larger and better plant at Portland. But this move did not at first affect the town, for throughout the 1890's some two hundred people lived there. But with transportation facilities improving, and greater business opportunities offered elsewhere, more and more residents seemed disinclined to remain.

By 1915 the population had dwindled to one hundred twenty-one persons. The smoke had long ceased to hang over the red kilns of Amedee Smith's pottery. Without railroad facilities and with river transportation fallen almost into disuse, Buena Vista drifted into a somnolence that some lamented but none openly protested.

ORLEANS IN INDIAN COUNTRY

IN the autumn of 1846 a handful of landseekers—John and William McCoy, Dr. W. B. Maley, a Scotch-Irish physician, and their families—crossing the prairies of the upper Willamette Valley, rolled to a standstill among the scattered oaks, maples and alders fringing the low east shore of the river. There in a region that was still Indian country they found rich bottom land awaiting the plow, and staked out claims.

That single point of settlement in a wide radius of unclaimed country lay approximately one mile above and opposite the homesite chosen the year previous by Joseph C. Avery.

In 1848 Avery laid out a part of his land as Marysville. Isaac Moore, in the same year staked a 322 acre claim just north of the clustered homesteads of the McCoy and Maley families. Casting an eye across the river at Avery's newly platted town, Moore ambitiously chained off the river front levels of his own property in 1851 and called the place Orleans. A ferry that he ran to the Marysville shore was licensed in that year, and the precinct of Orleans was organized. That brought all eligible citizens residing within a wide area to Orleans to cast their votes. Precinct political caucuses, too, were held there. All Oregon pioneers were ardently and frequently violently concerned with politics and it is recorded that the Orleans precinct lifted its voice lustily in the press concerning political affairs of the 'fifties. As early as 1849, the precinct, as yet unnamed, polled twenty-seven votes in the June election.

When the Rev. George H. Atkinson, missionary of the Congregational Church, arrived in Oregon in 1848, he made his headquarters at Oregon City. From there he traveled into wilderness Oregon, preaching to the scattered settlements and stimulating religious organizations. But he also had an eye on the land, its agricultural future and commercial development. In a *Diary* jotting made in the Mary's River country in 1848 he noted:

"The farmer needs only to break the sod, sow wheat or plant corn and vegetables and the harvest will appear like those in the old fields of New Eng. The farmers raise voluntary wheat. While gathering a crop, the seed drops out. This sows the land for the next year. A harrow is drawn over the field and it is left until the next harvest. Fifteen and twenty bushels per acre are raised in this way. Some continue this practice two years & more, & some plow every year, which is the best method. The land as yet is poorly cultivated. The whole valley may be made like a garden. The hills may be turned into orchards of apple and peach and pear as well as of oak. This is indeed a fine country and at this season it is a delightful one. . . . It is thought that the Willamette river is navigable for steamboats of light draft to the forks. . . ."

Few facts are available about Orleans' early history and none at all for some three years after its establishment. In a letter dated July 20, 1854, written from Corvallis by Edward Shiel to General Joseph Lane, then Territorial delegate to the United States House of Representatives, it is stated that the village of Orleans, "as near as maybe in the center of the Territory" proposed "many facilities for the public . . ." For those reasons Shiel wished to be stationed there as Register and Receiver for Oregon, under a recently-passed Congressional land act. In that communication, he referred to the village not as Orleans but as New Orleans. It is not known if the office-seeker secured the appointment or ever lived at Orleans.

Though there are few records of status in the early 'fifties, Moore seems to have done enough business to buy a safe to make secure his financial rating in the community. With land-seekers crowding into the fertile open country, the Orleans precinct was growing in numbers and power.

During that period, Indians—chiefly Calapooyas, but occasionally wandering Klickitats, roamed at will over the verdant, mid-Willamette Valley. Although they did little actual harm, in a country long theirs, their insatiable curiosity and passion for trading made them a nuisance to the settlers. So bad did their depredations become that many homesteaders sawed their cabin doors in half, keeping the lower portion shut and latched, thus defeating the customary unannounced entrance of some begging Indian. Fortunately, doors left half-open in this way admitted needful light, otherwise meagerly supplied by the cabins' few small windows.

On one occasion, a band of twenty-five Indians, traipsing across the William McCoy ranch, killed a calf and were about to feast on its carcass. McCoy, companioned by a neighbor, James M. Smith, surprised them and while Smith held the gun over the cowering natives, McCoy whipped each one of them. The whipping of Indians was a common practice with the pioneers.

At another time, about fifty Indians gathered around the log house of Dr. Maley, remaining all day and making the air hideous with a howling din, protesting that the Doctor had taken, without payment, property rightfully theirs. At last Dr. Maley gave them a young steer as payment for their interest in the land. The gratified Indians managed their new property with difficulty; the animal they found, was not accustomed to being led by the tail. They never held another pow-wow on the Maley place, for they had sold their land for a last full feasting.

Not all of the pioneers were so generous with their lingering red neighbors. Years later, in 1880, it was recalled that an old chief was "gone through" by the wife of a white settler, while the other tribesmen watched in evident humor. The story, as related by Wallis Nash, followed the form of a dialogue between two men who didn't "go much on broadcloth and 'biled shirts'," but preferred "stout flannel shirts and knee-high boots," tobacco, and a frequent session around the stove.

" 'So the ole man came into Benton County in 1845, did he?'

" 'Yes, he and his wife and two young children and took up a claim. . .'

" 'Had the old man any stock?'

" 'He had just brought a few with him from Missouri over

the Plains, and a fine store he set by them. You see the Indians used to come and beg for flour and sugar, and a beef now and then. Some of the neighbors would give them a beef at times, but the old man used to say he hadn't bought no cattle to give to them varmints.'

" 'How did they manage to live at first?'

" 'Well, the old man used to go off for a week at a time to Oregon City to work on the boats there at his trade of a ship carpenter. He had to foot it there and back, and pack flour and bacon on his back for his folks, and a tramp of sixty miles at that.'

" 'Did the Indians bother any while he was gone?'

" 'One time a pack of them came around the cabin and got saucy, finding only the old woman at home. They crowded into the house and began to help themselves, but the old lady she took the axe and soon made them clear out. When the old man came back she told him about it. "Well," says he, "I reckon I shall have to stop at home a day or two and fix these varmints." So three or four days afterward they came back.'

" 'The old man he kept out of sight, and the buck they called the chief came in and began to lay hold of anything he fancied.'

" 'Then the old man showed himself in the doorway with his old rifle on his arm. He looked the chief up and down, and then he says to his wife: "Do you see that bunch of twigs over the fireplace? You take them down, and go through that fellow while the twigs hold together!" And he says to the Indian, "You raise a finger against that woman, I'll blow the top of your head off!" So the old lady takes down the willow twigs and goes for the Indian for all there was in it, and beats him round and round the house till there wasn't a whole twig in the bunch. Lord! you should have seen the whole crowd of twenty or thirty Indians splitting with laughter to see the white squaw go for the chief. I tell you, sir, that Indian made the quickest time on record back to the camp as soon as she let him go, and that crowd never bothered that cabin any more. Now, wasn't that much better than shooting and fighting, and kicking up the worst kind of a muss?"

In 1856–57 several deeds were recorded from Isaac Moore for lots he sold in Orleans, indicating that the town was laid out in at least fifteen blocks, and had a Main Street, so named. But no plat was ever registered at the County Courthouse at Albany. By that date Orleans seems to have progressed to the status of a neighborhood trading center, with riverboats stopping regularly at its low wharves. Widely patronized, it even aspired to outrival Corvallis.

Among the town's best known residents in the late 'fifties were Isaac Moore, Philip Phile, Joseph Gerhard, John Summer, David Milhollen, William Lewis, and Morgan Lilliard, with their wives and families, and Charles Mulkey, the father-in-law of Lilliard.

Then came the great flood of December, 1861. Those living here were to speak with awe for years of those dread-filled days. All that Sunday night of December 1, with the rain drenching down and the Willamette's boiling waters swelling and spreading over the lowlands, there was shouting of men, cries of distress from women, and firing of guns for help. Bobbing lanterns gleamed fitfully. Stock of every description struggled for life in the deepening flood.

In the obscuring darkness, the earliest rush of waters came suddenly and unexpectedly; none had taken any precaution to guard against such a danger. "The first alarm was given by parties who were awakened by drift logs striking against their houses," the *Corvallis Times* recalled, recapitulating the story forty years later. "Those in the greatest danger were moved to safer places in the village. Joseph Gerhard and John Summer conveyed their wives, each with two small children, to the former's hayloft where they remained until the next day. In the meantime these two gentlemen, Philip Phile, and others kept busy with boats rescuing others.

"William Lewis and wife were young persons who occupied a small dwelling in the village, and they were determined to remain in their little house as long as possible, hoping and praying that the waters would recede. Before they took leave of the house, however, the wife was taken violently ill and, as the rising waters dampened the straw mattress on which she lay, a baby girl was born to the family. The necessity of her removal was imperative and the mother and child and the bed were placed in the skiff. They were then rowed to the residence of Mr. Moore and placed on the second floor through an upper story window. When day finally dawned, mother and child were brought to Corvallis where they were able to secure proper attention. As soon as possible after daylight, all the women and children of Orleans were conveyed to the west side of the river.

"During the night and following morning, several houses were washed away on the east side, among which was the one owned by Mr. Summer, whose family took refuge in the hayloft with Mrs. Gerhard; one belonging to Philip Phile which was afterward hauled back. . . . A building which had been built for a brewery was also carried away."

Newspapers in the lower valley at first reported that Orleans had been completely swept away. While this was not the case, the devastation was so extensive and so disheartening that the town struggled only feebly to survive.

Its losses were too great for a pioneer age when even the most meagre assets were almost irreplaceable. Orleans losses were reported in the *Oregon Argus:*

"F. Lewis $600, W. Splaun $150, R. T. Baldwin $600, Sage $600, Philip Phile 1,000, Gearhart $400, Wm. Lewis $200, Mr. (Isaac) Moore $3,000 . . . Mr. Moore . . . lost his safe. The Stage Company lost a coach and one horse."

At Corvallis, across the river, the damage was not great; a warehouse was carried away and another "started from its foundations." A small amount of stored wheat and oats was dampened, low-standing barns were tumbled into the waters; and there, as elsewhere, many head of stock were drowned. Although refuted as fact by some, one huge log, a flood-mark which remained for years, was deposited in the vicinity of what later became the Oregon State College campus, more than a mile to the west.

A few Indians, lingering on in the valley of the Willamette, later told stories of this and other "great" floods they had known. But these Indians were "exceedingly unreliable," Johnson Porter, who lived near Orleans from boyhood, recalled in 1937. "They would tell any kind of a tall tale to impress a listener. We boys used frequently to lead them on by questions just to hear their fantastic stories." Of Orleans itself, Mr. Porter said: "I remember when I visited the site as a small boy there were still several ruined buildings standing, indicating a considerable town."

THE FERRY HAMLET OF BURLINGTON

THE Willamette River, meandering generally northward down its broad valley, between Eugene and Corvallis breaks into a series of waterways that interlace the bottomlands. Certain of these intersecting courses run full the year around, but others, in rainless seasons, are muddy sloughs or dry, mud-caked hollows. Scattered among the channels and sloughs are islands, brush-grown along the margins, which through the years have not maintained a fixed shoreline. More than once, in pioneer days and since, flood waters, plunging down the valley, have altered the river's channels. As a consequence, settlement within that area has been maintained with difficulty, sometimes with tragedy. Communities beside those temperamental waters have, without exception, seen their town-building hopes dashed and the sites of their enterprise abandoned.

Beginning at a point opposite Corvallis and spreading southward, are four islands: Fisher Island (on its west shore stood Orleans), Stahlbusch Island, Kiger Island (the largest), and John Smith Island. Probably none of those was so-named in the 'fifties, during pioneer settlement. Then the main channel of the Willamette River swept by the islands, on the west, while along their eastern edges, in wide curves and half-loops, coursed the sluggish East Channel of the river; connecting sloughs divided the islands, one from another. In later years the main channel was somewhat altered.

Across Stahlbusch Island in 1850, a crude roadway ran west to Smith's Ferry, its rough plank and log landing lying beneath the trees of the island's west shore. There Smith—perhaps the John Smith who, according to the records, staked a 275 acre claim a few hundred feet to the south of the ferry site—built a cabin of the customary pioneer type. There, too, at least as early as 1852, John Donald established a store to serve the movers and land-seeking settlers who crossed the river at that point, *en route* to the upper valley. James Martin also built a house amid the scattered alders and oaks heavily hung with mistletoe. At the river's edge Thomas Cannon blazed a 320 acre donation land claim. The small trade center that sprang up around his home as early as 1850, for a reason now undetermined, was called Burlington. The Burlington precinct was immediately organized.

In those years claim records lying to the east in Linn County, as well as to the west in Benton County, were entered at the Government Land Office at Marysville (now Corvallis). In the original survey map of Township 12 South, Range 4 West, drawn by deputy surveyor George W. Hyde in 1853, a "Road to Burlington" descends from the Orleans area for about three and one-half miles. Burlington's location may be assumed to lay at its southern terminus, which is in sections 19 and 20, though this is not so defined on the map. A few clustered habitations are evident, however, within vague rectangular boundaries. Field notes made at the time but not now found (see 1947 edition of this book) read: "The town of Burlington is situated on the right bank of the Willamette and contains two dwellings, two stores, a blacksmith shop and a schoolhouse; has a good landing and ferry."

Surely this was as promising a beginning as many another hopeful town of that day. Incidentally, this places Burlington just south of the claims taken in the late forties by John McCoy and Wm. B. Maley, mentioned in the Orleans story.

In 1854 Burlington was named as terminus of the territorial road that wallowed through the valley mud to Corvallis, crossing the river at Orleans and laboring the several more miles to Burlington. Later the road continued south, bisecting Kiger Island, in a nearly straight course to Peoria, four miles distant.

A congregation known as Willamette Church, organized in July 1850, held its meetings during the fifties sometimes at the Muddy Schoolhouse, on Muddy Creek just to the east, and sometimes at Burlington. Later, on December 10, 1860, at Oakville, about one mile to the northeast, a "meeting house" was completed by this same congregation at a cost of $1,000, a heroic sum for that day. Its membership, which included the McCoys and Maleys, was fifty-two; in three years it added only three new members. But by 1880 its rolls increased to one hundred twenty-nine. It is recalled that from that Oakville congregation, in the passage of time, came two moderators of the United Presbyterian Church of North America, a denomination that originated at nearby Union Point. These were Dr. T. S. Kendall and Dr. S. G. Irvine.

Although several times menaced by flooding waters, Burlington survived for a time,—later to be stranded by the ever-shifting channel. It last appeared on a map of 1874, but the formation of the Centennial Chute two years later left it on an unnavigable side channel and it soon slipped into oblivion. Some wheat and farm produce were shipped from the Burlington wharf through the years, but there was no warehouse and the part the town played in Willamette River transportation was small. As the homeseekers scattered over the broad prairies of Linn and Benton counties, other roads, traversing higher and drier land, pushed through—shorter and more easily traveled routes than the one by way of Smith's Ferry.

BOONEVILLE ON THE OLD CHANNEL

PRIOR to 1875, the main channel of the Willamette River, sweeping northward, rounded to the west of John Smith and Kiger islands. But the high waters of that year, rushing by these low marshy islands, for the first time in history poured their greater volume down the Willamette's East Channel, broadening its course. These heaped waters then cut through the shallow slough lying between Kiger Island and Stahlbusch Island, rejoining the age-old main channel on the west. By that act the small riverside hamlet of Booneville was stranded at the head of John Smith Island. Thereafter, the former main channel, its waters flowing sluggishly northward, became known as Booneville Channel. An arm of the "old channel" still hugged the wharf of Booneville, but it carried less water and only those boats with freight bound to or from the pioneer landing point navigated its still waters.

The great volume of river traffic used the new main channel, to the eastward.

The history of Booneville—as derived from existing fragmentary records—began in 1853, when Thomas Norris platted a townsite on his donation land claim where its southeast corner touched the west shore of the Willamette River. The plat, a copy of which is still on record at the Benton County courthouse at Corvallis, named Norris as proprietor, thus acknowledging private ownership. The site was situated in the Southwest ¼ of Section 26, Township 12 South, Range 5 West. The surveyor's record observed at the time of platting that "The Town of Boonville [subsequently spelled Booneville], is situated on the west channel of the Willamette River in sections 26 and 35. The town as yet does not amount to much, but the location is a good one. Steamboats have been up to it in high water."

At that date the village claimed as its sole business structures a "storehouse and blacksmith shop, at present unoccupied." There must have been at least one dwelling, the home of Thomas Norris. The site was scattered over with alders, oaks and balm trees. In the tallest of these, cranes nested, or were startled into flight, uttering weird notes; the river shallows were their fishing grounds.

It is reasonable to believe that commercial activity soon came to give life to the village of Booneville. Undoubtedly it became a shipping point of more than local convenience, since it was then and throughout its vague fifty-year existence the only other waterside landing point, other than the infrequent ranch wharf poorly served by any road, between Corvallis, nearly six miles to the north, and Lancaster, about twenty miles to the south. It seems to have been one of the few accessible shipping points in a wide area of moist bottomlands.

The great flood of 1861 may have lapped over the lower street-ends at Booneville, for the inundation spread abroad over the lowlands of the area, but there is no record that Booneville suffered any damage. The name rarely appeared in the news of the day, and while the place must have been a voting point, it seems not to have been a precinct center, as were other more prominent settlements.

It may be assumed that Booneville's life was largely one of river shipping: out-going wheat and incoming commodities. However, the particulars of that activity have been largely obscured by time.

In 1875 a minor flood caused a re-routing of the main channel of the Willamette, driving the river's greater volume northward through the East Channel, and turning its course back to the main waterway above Kiger Island and to the west of Stallbusch Island. Booneville was left with lessened waters, on a portion of the old main channel, which crooked half-around a small, newly-formed islet taking the name of Baker Island. The capricious river, shortcutting across a corner of John Smith Island, had grooved a new channel, connecting with the old riverbed below and above this surrounded land. That new channel, because it thereafter afforded the only water artery to Booneville's wharves, became known, as it still is, as Booneville Channel.

An article on "Early Steamboating," appearing in the Corvallis *Gazette*, February 12, 1894, stated that at that date Booneville was still a shipping point. But that circumstance could not have continued for many years longer, for at the time few boats traversed the stream's upper waters. With a much diminished river traffic, due to the heavy encroachments of railroad transportation, with rail lines running both east and west of the Willamette, less effort was made to keep the channel clear and passable. Also, shipments awaited the favorable seasons of high water—the winter and spring months—an unbrookable delay for impatient shippers in an era of growing competition.

Today very few of the residents of the community that once acknowledged Booneville as its center so much as recognize that a village by that name ever existed on the river's shore. If there were any eventful episodes in the hamlet's history, they have, in colloquial expression, "gone down the river." Only the name lingers on in the channel that for many years remained as Booneville's one waterexit to the outer world. But today that too is cut off from the portion of the old main waterway that curves like a bow past the deserted townsite; the old streambed is now a dead-water slough.

THE EARLY TRADE CENTER OF PEORIA

ALTHOUGH Peoria is still a small community trading point, well marked on Oregon maps, its commercial prominence declined more than half a century ago. In its halcyon days it gave promise of becoming one of the upper valley's most important centers of trade and river shipping. But any hope its residents held, waned during the 1870's, when the new railroad stations of Shedd and Halsey, a few miles to the east, drew off much of Peoria's freight hauling and consequently many of its business concerns. In succeeding years, Peoria, like so many of its sister river towns, watched the meagerly loaded boats pass downstream from their final visits to the town's low wharves. Only the fact that the hamlet was conveniently situated in a rich agricultural area gave it security against time. Its present belongs to the highway that passes through it, but its past belongs to the river.

Into the region in 1851, came H. A. McCartney, staking a government donation claim of 320 acres that bordered on the Willamette River. It lay on the east bank, just below the mouth of Salt Creek, in the southwest corner of Linn County. There the open prairie extended to the water's edge, and the riverbank was sufficiently high and bold to resist flood waters of even abnormal depth. The site was well-chosen, both for security and pleasant view; the soil was rich.

Ranchers who had settled on the broad, oak-scattered prairies to the eastward customarily drove their loaded harvest wagons across McCartney's land to the Willamette. There, from a bankside landing, they shipped their produce downriver—or awaited their incoming supplies from the north. Among those settlers were James M. Coon, Owen Bear and James N. Smith, all of whom had arrived in the late 1840's or soon thereafter.

In 1857, Arthur and John G. North built the first store on the high ground above the boat landing. The location, the ranchers of the prairie believed, had riverport possibilities. With boats then serving the region and the land yet to yield its maximum of crops, golden days seemed ahead.

It is not known when the Peoria townsite was surveyed and platted. It had sixteen blocks, normally of eight lots each, separated into halves by alleys. The meander line of the river broke this pattern on the west, where the lots, all of varied length, ran to the water's edge. Pike Street, on the north, descended to a ferry that crossed the usually sluggish current of the river. Running the length of the town from south to north, and squared between the three tiers of blocks, were the principal thoroughfares, Main and Pearl. All early day maps of the town presented auspicious lures to urban settlement.

It is probable—and so tradition has it—that certain of the settlers instrumental in the town's founding had come west with the Peoria Party of 1839–40. Remembering the Illinois town of their earlier years, they revived all that was unforgettable and still promising in the name, and called the new Willamette River town Peoria.

Because, until the late 'fifties, there was no newspaper town nearer than Salem, fifty-six miles by water and forty-seven miles by land to the north, there is no record of occurrences and exceptional events that may have befallen Peoria and the surrounding countryside in early years. In the few available copies of papers published at Albany, Corvallis and Eugene during the late 'fifties, 'sixties and 'seventies, there are only occasional reference to Peoria and neighboring communities.

In a business directory for Oregon, published in 1873, Peoria appears listed as a place "prettily situated," with "all the usual adjuncts of a well regulated interior village or town." There was a school in the district and the benevolent and church societies typical of the day exerted their influence. In the business roster the names of four blacksmiths were listed: E. Goodwin, William C. Miller, J. R. Strong and William Shepherd. The local wagon-maker was one E. Marshall. From the hides tanned by J. H. Wilson, M. Bond cut and sewed harness and saddles, and Joseph Elliot cobbled boots and shoes. There were two dealers in stoves and tinware, J. W. Bowman and George W. Parker. The town, this directory stated, was "a trading point for quite a large area," and was in a "prosperous condition." There was no mention of the four grain storage houses, of which the town had boasted for a decade or longer.

But warehouses are mentioned in an account of the region issued in 1875, by A. S. Mercer, under title of *Material Resources of Linn County:* "There are four grain warehouses on the river bank, with a capacity of 60,000 bushels. They received this year 30,000 bushels of grain." Mercer continues:

"Peoria . . . before the coming of the Oregon and California Railroad gave promise of making considerable of a town. Since that time its decline has been rapid, and now there are not to exceed twenty residents in the place. . . A very considerable business was done until the building of the railroad, when Halsey [eight miles to the southeast] and Shedd station [five miles to the east] drew off most of the business firms, and the bulk of the trade that formerly centered in Peoria. There is good steamboat navigation on the Willamette to this point during the stages of high, and ordinary high water, but during low stages goods are hauled from Shedd. . . Davis Bros. have a country store of general merchandise, and are doing a fair business. There is a blacksmith shop but at this time no one has it rented. There is a pretty good school with an attendance of about sixty pupils. Peoria Grange No. 116 has its headquarters in the village and is a strong grange. United States mails are received Tuesdays and Saturdays from Shedd."

In 1880 the village had one general merchandise store, one warehouse, and one blacksmith shop. At that time, W. T. Cooke was the town druggist, and I. N. Smith, Jr., attorney.

During the 'seventies and 'eighties there were "many flocks of high grade sheep" grazing on the Linn prairies eastward of Peoria, and the wool clip was a "considerable source of revenue." There was "an abundance of fruit in the township," and the orchards, says Mercer, were "very productive." Although the face of the country was agreeably varied by woodland and prairies, with here and there a scattering of oaks, the entire valley, this observer stated, was "one vast grain field." But in the course of years, with land wearing thin through successive wheat croppings, a diversity of production, with sheep and cattle raising, gradually broke up and diminished the wheat areas. Thus was the over-cropped soil somewhat restored. Small farmers ran their rail fences through the larger holdings, that in 1875 were priced at from fifteen to thirty dollars an acre.

With river transportation becoming a thing of the past, Peoria's life merged with that of the community of which it had once been the heart. Farmers in the immediate locality still traded with the hamlet's few establishments, but in time these came less and less frequently. Roads, almost impassible in wet seasons, none the less grew in number and accessibility to distant centers of greater purchasing advantage. The becalmed community of Peoria dwindled, but lingered. Today, more than half a century after its heyday, the inhabitants have almost forgotten that the town once boasted commercial leadership in a wide area.

LANCASTER, THE FIGHTIN'EST TOWN ON THE RIVER

In 1852 or 1853 a man named Woody started a "house of entertainment," more realistically a saloon, among the tall evergreens of the Willamette's low west bank, about two and one-half miles north of present day Junction City. Whatever the actual date, Woody's establishment—its habitues coming by road and by river—soon gathered about it the nucleus of a town called Woodyville, but more commonly referred to as Woody's Landing. Reputedly the toughest of the Willamette ports, Woodyville, before the close of the 'fifties, had declared itself the head of navigation—a distinction for which it was ready and willing to fight, and for a period actually did so.

Woody seems early to have acquired his reputation for toughness. In his log saloon he dispensed a local distillation commonly known as "blue ruin," and a quality of food which could hardly have been less palatable than that served on some of the flatboats which passed up and down the river.

In the early days of Woody's Landing a blacksmith set up his anvil and bellows, to shoe the horses and oxen of the wagoners and farmers, who meanwhile warmed themselves externally at the stove in the one local store or internally at the bar in Woody's candle-lighted saloon. For half the year, Woody's crude wharves were stacked with wheat and varied stuffs in transit. Houses sprang up among the firs and cedars, felled one by one to make way for the encroachments of a dubious civilization.

At an unknown date—possibly toward 1865—the California & Oregon Stage Company, referred to by valley residents as the "through trace stage," moved its "stand" from Millirons, one and one-half miles west of Woody's, to Woodyville. That portion of the "big road" known as Chase's line, ran from Marysville (Corvallis), to Eugene and Oakland. The regional post office, formerly at Freedom, a place now forgotten in all but name, was likewise moved to Woodyville.

Woody had a large and rowdy family, which became widely and not favorably known as the "Woody tribe." But his sons were nonetheless industrious, building a log jetty into the Willamette's current to deepen its scouring force and provide an area of still water for the flatboats that put in at the docks. Meanwhile the stage line brought revenue to Woody, as swaying coaches halted at his tavern.

The power and influence of the "Woody tribe" grew, matched by an increasing dislike and distrust by persons who were obliged to deal with them. Stocks of merchandise left upon Woody's wharves were frequently looted; and since nearly all of its town's residents were henchmen of the founder, shippers believed that Woody or some of his numerous brood committed the thefts. Any attempt, however, to fix responsibility was met by massed opposition upon the part of the Woodyville boys, who were rough and tumble, and ran largely to size and muscle.

The steamer *James Clinton*, first of the squat riverboats to venture above Corvallis, on March 12, 1856, churned an upriver passage as far as the mud wallow where Eugene Skinner, founder of Eugene, first camped in the shadow of the butte that bears his name. Thereafter, when water was of sufficient depth, Woodyville, Harrisburg, and other scattered bankside landings of the upper river enjoyed an augmented and fairly regular steam transportation service.

These river packets bore upstream such essentials as calico, mill stones and plowshares, and returning downstream loaded the wheat and fatted stock the ranchers sent Portlandward to market. Unfortunately, the upriver steamboat season was a limited one, determined by the water-depth and hindered by frequent obstructions in the shallow steambed. As a consequence Woody's Landing, claimed by its owners to be the "head of navigation," soon became the principal shipping point for a wide area.

The economic life of the river grew, and the destructive vitality of the Woody gang grew also. In 1858, desperate shippers proposed to build a landing above the Woody wharves, at a point where cargoes would be safe from the marauders. A rancher named Coffman owned a parcel of land which drained into a slough running through a small portion of the Woody claim and thence into the Willamette River. Coffman offered to build a warehouse on his property, if the shippers would route their boats through the slough to his landing. They agreed, and the warehouse and docks were built.

Ranchers and shippers, however, had reckoned without the Woody tribe. As related in a rambling communication to the *Oregonian*, May 5, 1859, the Woodys "set themselves to work to obstruct the slough by falling trees across that part of the slough that is on their land, thus fulfilling a part of the threats they made before. The steamer *James Clinton* had the occasion to go up this slough to Coffman's warehouse, and found a great many trees across it. The neighbors 'turned to' and assisted. . . . in clearing out the obstruction."

But the Woodys were undeterred and obstructed the slough as often as it was cleared out. Finally, however, they gave up and river service continued without interruption for the remainder of the 1858 spring season.

"Finally the Woody set sold out to Messrs. Mulky & Co. [correctly spelled Mulkey]," according to the *Oregonian*, "who finished a warehouse that the Woodys had begun and it was hoped by most persons that business would be done up in a proper manner."

But that was a deceptive hope, for the Mulkey crowd

(who changed the town's named to Lancaster) "soon had as hard a name as the Woody tribe," and were forthwith named the "Woody tribe No. 2." As a consequence, merchants in Eugene and elsewhere ordered their freight landed at Coffman's warehouse. Mulkey & Company interpreted this as a waving of the red battle flag and announced with no uncertain vehemence that "no boat should go into that slough, that their town should be the head of navigation, and as to going up that slough, they would sue for trespass, and intended to blockade that slough; and if any boat attempted to go in there, that they would fall trees across her, and smash her up, and if she did get in she would never get out alive, &c, &c. . . ." It almost looked as though the slough and the Mulkey ruffians had the situation in hand.

The steamer *James Clinton* arrived at Lancaster on a Friday night, about dark. After unloading at the Mulkey docks, her captain announced that she had freight on board for Coffman's warehouse, where a load was waiting to "go down." A participant in the events that followed, later related:

"It being dark, we waited for the moon to rise, till about 10 o'clock at night. In the meantime we had heard chopping up the slough, which we found to be persons falling a lot of small trees across the slough, and upon close examination they were recognized as John A. Porter (Mulkey's son-in-law), Charley Hand, and Doc Campbell, who do business there, and another man, sometimes known as the man who borrowed the maul without the owner's leave. . . ."

"The *Clinton* forced her way over the brush with the assistance of a line, which took us some two hours to accomplish. While we were working our way through the drift, the Mulkey tribe were busily engaged in chopping a large tree which stood on the bank ahead of the boat, to have it ready for her when she came along, but the tree fell prematurely, its top reaching across the channel. They then commenced upon another fifty yards above. They cut it nearly off and waited for our approach; we had some trouble crossing over the top of the first tree; we could see the men plainly standing by the tree, as they had their lanterns with them. As soon as the steamer got disengaged from the tree top, they commenced chopping the tree as fast as they could, but we narrowly escaped destruction by shooting by before the tree fell—the tree falling in a few seconds after the boat passed. . . ."

Completing their imperiled run up the darkened slough, the crew of the *Clinton* anchored before the Coffman warehouse. Almost immediately an attachment was put on the boat for trespass and damages, while Captain Cochran was summoned to appear in Justice Court for civil cause, on charges made by Mulkey & Company.

Undaunted by such complex action, the *James Clinton* loaded the waiting cargo destined for down-river points and made its way slowly out of the tree-cluttered slough waters.

Presumably, with that incident the record of conflict ended. It was the expressed intention of the *Clinton's* captain to make the Coffman Landing whenever he had occasion to do so; and it may be assumed that he did, for there is no record to contradict the statement.

During those years there were stores at Lancaster operated by Westley Briggs and Dr. Aubrey, and by Joseph Sternberg and Isaac Sanders. But probably the most prominent of the local "emporiums of merchandise" was Hand and Campbell, which advertised itself as the "Empire Store! Pre-Eminent."

Floods of the early 'sixties hastened the disintegration of Lancaster. In his old age Cassius Crow, early settler in the region, related to his descendants stories of the flood of 1861, which spread devastation through the valley. That deluge of snow and rain choked every watercourse sweeping into the Willamette, which rose with an incessant roar, overlapping its wooded banks and spreading across valley, farm and town. Water was climbing at the rate of one foot an hour when the Crow family, clambering into the farm wagon, fled from house to barn, with swirling water splashing over the wagon-boards as the frightened horses floundered belly-deep in the flood. Climbing into the barn loft, the family remained there terrified for two nights, warming themselves by turns at a fire built on the flat sides of a split-open oak block, which the father of the family cut amidst the swirling waters and lugged up to the loft floor. The children were posted about the stored hay, to stamp out any sparks which might fall into it.

Rail fences that sprawled their zig-zag curves and angles across the uneven valley floor, went to pieces as the flood boiled higher. Young Cass Crow, peering from the left, saw a whole house hurtling downstream, with a rooster crowing on the roof. Amos Hyland, son of Benjamin Hyland, who is remembered as another of Lancaster's storekeepers, after assisting his wife and family into the barn loft, pitched down hay upon which his hogs climbed to the upper security shared by the family. But everywhere cattle, horses and hogs were drowned. Thousands of rails lodged high-up in brush and timber; and after the waters had receded the ranchers about generally helped themselves to them, as no one knew to which farms they belonged.

Of the damage suffered by the business section of Lancaster no record remains, although the *Statesman* of the day, in an early report, announced that "all but two houses are reported gone, and those about to go." While this statement may have been hastily made, Lancaster's losses must have been considerable. But whatever its structural losses were, a greater and irreparable calamity lay in the Willamette's altered course: the river had been swept out of its former shallow bed into a newly grooved channel some distance to the east. Its waters no longer washed against Lancaster's docks or Coffman's Landing.

Through succeeding summers and winters, Lancaster's remaining residents watched the river withdraw still farther from its former course. Tracing new channels over the spreading land to the eastward, it left the town's plank wharves and supporting piles well beyond reach of boats. Lancaster's one main street was flanked by two stores, a blacksmith shop, and a handful of houses, some of them partly of logs. But the once prosperous days were gone. Farmers in the area were now compelled to take their produce to Harrisburg on the east bank for shipment down-river.

With the coming of the O & C Railroad in 1871, Lancaster faced extinction. To the south, not far distant, Junction City sprang up where the steel rails went through, with bluff Ben Holladay boasting that he would make of the new town a second Chicago. In that boast lay a glimmer of hope for Lancaster's businessmen, who for years optimistically believed in the prophecy.

In time, Sternberg and Sanders moved their stock of merchandise to Junction City, followed later by a merchant now remembered only as Solomon. The town of Lancaster stood bleak and deserted. Later, someone stocked a grocery store in one of the few remaining buildings, vaguely reviving the town's identity. When finally the state's great north-and-south artery, the Pacific Highway, came up the valley well after the turn of the century, it swept through what was once the busy center of Lancaster and just west of the dry, willow-grown channel where, more than a half century before, the flat-bottomed riverboats had tied up and the sweating roustabouts, the river in their blood, had wrestled the produce of the countryside.

Today, were it not for the white highway marker identifying the location, the speeding motorist would peer in vain for the site of the town that was once the "fightin'est town on the river."

Interior of Eola School classroom, used into early years of present century. Location of old town was four and one-half miles west of Salem. (Ben Maxwell photo.)

At right is 1851-1852 official survey of T 7 S, R 4 W, showing Cincinnati, later Eola, as it appears left below from 1878 Linn and Marion County Atlas. At right below, 1852-1853 survey shows area of old town site of Burlington, south of claims of McCoy and Maley, on east side of Willamette.

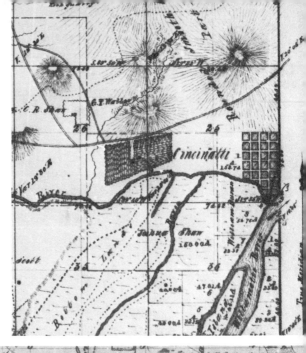

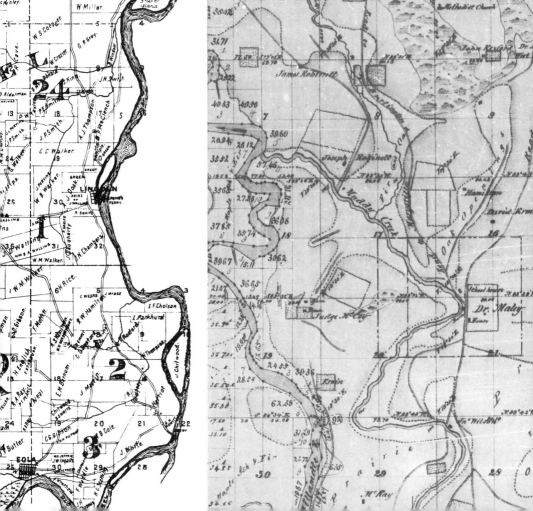

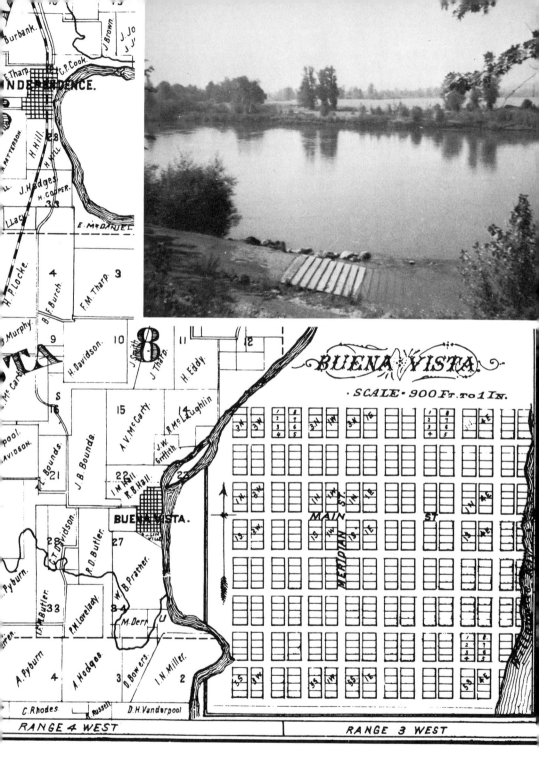

Buena Vista's location on the river, as well as a plat of the streets
appears in the Polk County Atlas of 1882. (Note the claim of R. B.
Hall.) Above, right is a 1971 photo looking at the present Peoria
boat ramp. (H. Corning photo.)

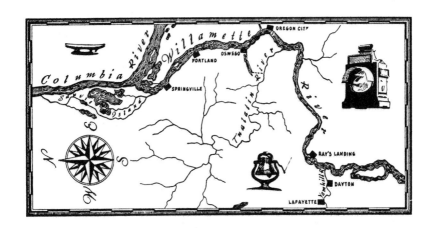

OTHER LANDINGS OF A BYGONE DAY ...

PROMINENT among Oregon's earliest deep-water ports was Springville. At a point near where today the Portland-Astoria highway passes under the west end of graceful St. Johns Bridge, there sprung up in the early 1850s a town whose landmarks vanished long ago. Drawing to her wharves the vast stores of wheat produced each year on the north Tualatin Plains, beyond the green hills at her rear door, Springville within a few years became an important wheat-loading center.

Situated about six miles northwest of pioneer Portland and one mile east of Linnton, it was first called Cazeno, for the Multnomah Indian chief whose property had become the donation land claim of W. H. Baker, sometime prior to 1852. In that year a territorial road was projected through the area. Theoretically the road began at Vancouver, on the far Columbia shore, and crossed that expansive stream to the length of land that extends fist-like between the Columbia and the lower estuary of the Willamette. Traversing these bottomlands, it passed through James John's Town, later St. Johns. The way was then by boat or ferry over the Willamette River to Cazeno on the wooded west bank.

For a short time at least the Baker holdings continued to be known by its Indian designation, for a petition calling for the continuation of the road across the hills and into the valley of the Tuality, to Hillsboro, carried the original place name. That paper, filed with the clerk of Washington County (Multnomah County was not created until December 22, 1854, when its area was carved from the parent county), was signed by forty-eight citizens, including Joseph L. Meek, then a prominent rancher of the north Tualatin Plains area. Other well-known signers were G. W. (Squire) Ebbert, E. H. Lenox, living near Joe Meek, and Levi Linkham.

The records show that the Cazeno-Hillsboro Road was surveyed by Reuben W. Ford. Stephen A. Holcomb was axman and marker, and John Mauzy and Archibald Bull acted as chainmen. These latter two, with James W.

Chambers and John Bonser, served also as "viewers," inspecting the thoroughness of the completed job, which was little more than the "slashing out" of a roadway. The report began: "We the viewers find the rout as Surveyed by R. W. Ford to be a good and practtibel rout as per plot and field notes of Said rout. ..."

When the road was finished in the fall of 1852, Baker built on his land at Cazeno a wharf, calling it Baker's Landing. It functioned as a ferry point for those wishing to cross the river, and as a flag-stop for steamboats. Passengers for Portland, Fort Vancouver, St. Helens, or Astoria had but to wave an arm, a flag, or a lantern to attract the desired transportation or to halt a ship to load their most important product, wheat.

Another stimulus to the growth of the small port was a second wagon road that in 1852 came down the west bank of the Willamette from Portland. This passed Cazeno, or Baker's Landing, and continued to a point opposite the Sauvie Island ranch of a settler named James Miller. Cabin homes passed en route were those of Peter Guild, not far outside Portland; of a Mr. Polk, living a distance north and near to the river; of a Mr. Doan, who lived near Cazeno; of Mr. Baker and Solomon Richards. The petition creating this road, and likewise addressed to the Washington County court, carried such well-known names as H. D. O'Bryant, first mayor of Portland, Peter Guild, W. W. Chapman, John Couch, Stephen Coffin, and A. R. Skidmore. Many signers were Portland residents. The Portland-Sauvie Island Road was likewise surveyed by Reuben Ford. It was "viewed out" in May, 1852, by William Mauzy, Stephen A. Holcomb, and John L. White, with the assistance of George Kittredge and L. C. Potter, chainmen; Richards acted as marker.

Baker's Landing remained a convenient but hardly important loading wharf until 1859. In that year Baker sold to Creesus B. Comstock and LaFayette Scoggins sites for certain business buildings and dwellings. The sites the two buyers immediately improved. Under the name of Comstock & Company a commodious warehouse was erected and used for the storage of wheat hauled down to the landing by the farmers of the fertile valley plains beyond the hills. A general store supplied the family needs of the settlers; and the grower who came to the warehouse laden with wheat and other produce, returned to his home with such necessities as brown island sugar, coffee, denim for work clothing, and calico and muslin for the "women folks." Here too a few houses were erected to shelter the families and extra help who tended trade or roustabouted on the wharf.

With the growth of trade came an improvement of the wagon road over which the farm produce flowed in. This work the farmers themselves did under the stimulation of Comstock and Scoggins. In the midst of prosperous conditions Baker's Landing changed its name to the more impressive one of Springville, and the road from over the hills came to be known as the Springville Road. Over it many thousand bushels of wheat were hauled by oxen, mules, and horses. Even improved, it was a happy-go-lucky, if sometimes arduous, road. It meandered over the hills the easiest way, had no ballast, and, compared to present-day roads was a mere trail curving around stumps and boulders. It was rutty and dusty in summer and hub-deep in mud during the rainy season, but it was the only market road for the northside Tualatin country farmers and they used it gladly. For nearly a decade, until the Canyon Road was improved, it was favored by many travelers as the best road to the Portland area. From Springville, the route continued over the road that crept along the Willamette's west bank to the Oregon metropolis.

It is not known just how large Springville grew to be. About 1860 it was made a post office point. Some estimate of its importance at that time may be gathered from the fact that it was then the only postal center, other than Portland, in Multnomah County. One may imagine, lacking the actual facts, that these two places must have enjoyed a nip-and-tuck competition as to which should ship the most wheat. There seems to have been as deep water for boats at the Springville wharf as at Portland. However, Portland stood at the head of deep-sea navigation and was more centrally situated for the majority of growers in the interior. She was favored, too, by the up-river traffic, bringing to her docks the heavy harvests of upper valley production.

Springville, in its heyday, was probably a lively little hamlet. Possibly—as at most other prominent shipping points—there was an over-night house or hotel, where haulers and shippers might obtain meals and lodging. Possibly there was a tavern that dispensed the "ardent spirits" sought by many of the wagoners after the long, often chill and rain-drenched ride. There must have been shelter-sheds where the weary stock were fed and cared for and a wagon and blacksmith shop, since those establishments were standard for almost all frontier points of trade.

Springville's trade kept growing through the years, so that in 1868 more than 20,000 bushels of wheat were received for storage in the Comstock & Company warehouse; not a large amount as produce is now measured, but indicative of an enviable business for its day in Oregon. In that year, on November 21, the brig *Sally Brown*, the first ship to leave the Willamette with a cargo exclusively of wheat and flour for New York City, dropped down from Portland to complete her loading there.

That, and the following year, were undoubtedly banner years for Springville. In 1867 the road from the Tualatin Plains had again been improved. But Springville, from its beginning, had been in constant competition with Portland, which also had a much-used wagon road tapping the Tualatin wheatfields. Begun in 1848, this road had at several times been improved, with the same opposing conditions of no bridges, few ferries, freshets, a miry and only partly planked roadbed, and the consequent disadvantage of mud in winter and dust in summer. Yet it carried much of the trade that might otherwise have gone to Springville. There remained the business carried on with the settlers of Sauvie Island; but this, apparently, was hardly enough to assure prosperity.

When in 1870 it became evident to Lafayette Scoggins that his career as a wheat shipper and storekeeper was declining, he sold his interests in his various holdings to some less skeptical spirit—perhaps his partner, perhaps another whose name has faded from the records. Clambering aboard one of the boats that in years past he had laden to the gunnels with the products of his warehouse, he journeyed up the Columbia River; he settled in eastern Oregon, and, thereafter engaged in the stock raising business.

Springville was doomed when in 1871 the arteries of steel crept from Portland into the Tualatin Valley. In 1872 final catastrophe struck Springville; the warehouse burned to the water's edge, and with its burning the whole reason for the town's existence crumbled into ash. Already the small town of Linnton, through the years growing to a size that made it a neighborhood competitor, attracted most of the trade and the shipping.

So the babble of the wharves ceased and Springville faded from public mention. It disappeared from the postal route. Occasionally a boat put in at the landing, whenever hailed by some local shipper or prospective passenger. But local boats customarily did as much for any riverside settler. Only the Springville Road remained to become a permanent traffic route in the Oregon network of roads.

OLD OSWEGO AND THE LOWER TUALATIN

Although the community of Oswego had its beginning in 1850 when Albert Alonzo Durham, a York Stater, settled on Sucker Creek and built a sawmill, the town's significant story began in the middle 'sixties. Its history concerns transportation more than lumbering, and more than either of these the smelting of iron ore and the manufacture of iron products. Much of this story belongs to that epoch of the river's life following the flood of 1861, whose tumultuous waters did not reach to the high levels of Oswego.

Ancient Oswego, or "Old Town," as the inhabitants of the present community call the former site, was situated about eight miles south of Portland, on the banks of Sucker Creek later Oswego Creek—where that tiny stream spills down the sloping benchland which there forms the west shore of the Willamette. Something over a hundred feet above water level, the bench, slanting unevenly downward, is rocky and swampy. Today it is overgrown with scattered evergreens and thickets of wild brush which cluster around the ruins of the iron works that once stood here. Farther back from the river extend the business and residential sections of modern Oswego.

When Durham built his small water-power sawmill on Sucker Creek, which was fed by the overflow from nearby Sucker Lake, the first thread of a road was being cut through the dense timber from Portland to the young settlements at Willamette Falls. At that time travel within the area, with the exception of that using the Barlow Road over the Cascade Range and a road through the west hills behind Portland, was almost wholly by water. Retarding road construction was the heavy forest growth, which so completely shut out the sun that the earth beneath was dry only in mid-summer. Consequently, the sooner the land was cleared of timber the better. Any able bodied rancher could cut it into shakes, fence-posts, or cordwood; but only a few were equipped for the roughest of lumber sawing. As a result, the most rudimentary sawmills were welcomed by the settlers and were almost sure to prove commercially profitable. Sucker Creek—so named for the common fish that swarmed in its waters—offered an advantageous site for such a mill, since the stream had a fall of almost a hundred feet in a third of a mile.

When Durham—who was born in 1814—settled here he christened the place Oswego, for a town in his native state. To acquaint the public with his lumbering enterprise, he carried an advertisement in the *Weekly Oregonian* throughout much of 1851. New settlers came to widen the clearings in the nearby timber. Some of his raw product Durham loaded aboard the steam-propelled riverboats. He operated his sawmill until 1865, when he sold out to John Corse Trullinger.

Trullinger—shrewd, energetic, and restlessly ambitious— was wide awake to Oswego's possibilities. Born in Indiana, July 29, 1828, he came to Oregon in September, 1848. Before investing in Oswego property, he had engaged in several mill and warehouse enterprises elsewhere. In addition to the sawmill, he bought Durham's Oswego townsite and secured the waterpower privileges of the lake and its outlet. He grouped the whole under the title Oswego Milling Company, naming himself general superintendent. Besides the manufacture of lumber, he "aimed" to engage in railroading and general transportation.

The sawmill, situated so that the foot of the lake served as log-pond with the creek furnishing power, was 150 feet long and 42 feet wide. The machinery consisted of two double circular saws; a large Woodsworth's planer for dressing, tonguing and grooving planks; and a complete set of saws for laths and pickets. Lumber sold readily in the Portland market and adjacent territory for twenty dollars to thirty-five dollars per thousand feet.

Power for the machinery was furnished by a massive overshot waterwheel, thirty-six feet in diameter, with a ten-foot breast; and by a much smaller wheel invented by Trullinger. This wheel, only ten inches in diameter, furnished approximately twelve horse-power by means of a twelve-inch stream of water dropping on it from a height of thirty feet. Trullinger later went east to exhibit the wheel and to make arrangements for its manufacture.

In 1865, the same year in which Trullinger established his sawmill, Messrs. Jones, Vinson and Wyatt built the Sucker Lake and Tualatin River Railroad, to supply the mill with logs from the most available timber. It ran along the swale between the head of the lake and the north bank of the Tualatin, a distance of about one and three-quarters miles. The rails were of wood and the rolling equipment consisted of small cars; the motive power was a span of horses and the trip took twenty to twenty-five minutes. Each car was capable of hauling from eight to ten tons, so that it readily kept Trullinger's mill supplied with logs, then being sawed principally into sidewalk lumber. The railroad began operating on May 29, 1865.

Encouraged by its successes, the railroad's proprietors laid plans for a general transportation service from Portland to Hillsboro. The route then in use was around the Willamette Falls by portage; then along the north bank of the Tualatin, also by portage, to steamers loading upriver freight at James Moore's flouring mill above the river's un-navigable mouth. The proposed route would proceed from Portland by boat, to the landing below Oswego; from the bank of the Willamette to Sucker Lake by portage; along the lake shore, about three miles, to the railroad; over this to the Tualatin River; thence up the Tualatin by boat to Hillsboro. It was thought that, operated in reverse, freight might be brought to Portland at a cost of about $6 per ton. The facilities of the People's Transportation Company were to be employed over the Willamette stretch of the journey. The plan seemed especially feasible since at that time the river road out of Portland, along the west bank of the Willamette, had fallen into general disuse about three miles south of town, due to the preference for transit by water.

Gambling on the prospect, the Oswego Milling Company and the People's Transportation Company ordered machinery for two steamboats to be built for use on the Tualatin River. The steamer *Minnehaha*, constructed during the summer of 1866 for use on Sucker Lake, was built by the milling company at a point just back of the sawmill. It was seventy feet long, with a beam of sixteen feet, and drew only three feet of water. Its engine was of the single cylinder variety, with a ten-inch head and an eighteen-inch stroke. The steam-scow *Yamhill*, Captain Edward Kellogg commanding, was already running on the Tualatin, having replaced the earlier *Hoosier*. The point at which the *Yamhill* stopped—the terminus of the wooden railroad—was at first called the Depot. The editor of the *Oregonian*, on a visit to the site on August 25, 1866, christened it Colfax—a name it thereafter kept.

The Tualatin Valley transportation problem was an old one. The area embraced some 460,000 acres, a good deal of it flat or gently rolling and all of it very fertile. Some of it was heavily timbered with fir, hemlock, and cedar. As early as 1856 the Oregon Territorial Legislature had tried its hand at solving the question of how the Tualatin farmers could get their crops to Portland while they were in prime condition, since grain sometimes lay in barns for several years before it was possible to market it. Optimistically the Tualatin River Transportation and Navigation Company was chartered in 1858 by the Territorial Legislature to dredge and straighten that extremely crooked stream. A campaign to finance the undertaking raised some money, and several months work was done by the crew of the steamer *Hoosier*. But the legislature's plan was abandoned in 1859; the *Hoosier* had then been removed from the river.

The *Yamhill*, owned by some of the principal stockholders in the People's Transportation Company, began to operate in the mid-'sixties. Joseph Kellogg and his brother Edward, skipper of the *Yamhill*, were men of bulldog tenacity; and Edward, by a fund of patient good humor, made at least semi-regular trips with his boat as far as Hillsboro throughout the winter of 1865 and the spring of 1866. There was plenty of freight available from the head of navigation to the portage railroad depot, and way-landings were built at frequent intervals along the river.

As Captain Kellogg became familiar with the stream, his boat trips grew more and more regular and were suspended only when the water was low. He used to relate that toward summer the mosquitoes grew so large and ferocious and attacked him so viciously that he had to leave the wheel; whereupon the boat would ram into one of the brushy banks. At other times, he claimed, the creatures bore down on him in such dense swarms that they obscured his vision. Whenever the crew of the *Yamhill* had time and opportunity they cleared away some of the snags and sinker-logs with which the Tualatin River was filled. The job was almost endless, and special windlass machinery was rigged for the work.

Despite such handicaps, the transportation program proposed by the Oswego interests was working—not with glowing results, but nonetheless profitably.

During the low-water summers of 1867 and 1868, much time was devoted to stream clearing; so that when the fall rains began, the steamer *Onward*—built at Oswego by Joseph Kellogg—was put on the Hillsboro run. The *Onward* was a stern-wheeler of one hundred tons, a better boat for the narrow Tualatin than the wider side-wheeler. It was easier to navigate around bends, of which the river had so many that it seemed all turns. It was also so shallow in places that at frequent intervals the boats slid along the muddy bottom on their keels.

By the beginning of 1869 the *Onward* ran from the Depot —now Colfax—to Emerick's Landing, sixty miles upriver. Throughout the shipping season the boat left Colfax on its up-stream trip every Thursday morning, bound as far as Forest Grove and Centerville Landing; touching, wherever flagged, at intermediate points. Returning, it left Forest Grove and Centerville Landing each Monday at 6 A.M. Portland passengers wishing to connect with the weekly up-river schedule of the *Onward* had to take the steamer *Senator* at the foot of what is now Ash Street. On Wednesday evening, the first night out, passengers stopped at Shade's Hotel, in Oswego. Early the next morning the steamer *Minnehaha* was boarded for the trip across Sucker Lake, passing *en route* the cliffs called Lover's Leap and Disaster Rock. From the dock at the head of the lake the portage railroad took the travelers to Colfax and the *Onward*.

Beside the many farmside landings there were a number of scheduled stops. Two miles from Colfax was Bridgeport; while Taylor's Bridge, formerly Taylor's Ferry, was six miles away. From there on, upriver, distances became vague. The first bend of note was Edward's Bend, a few miles above Taylor's Bridge. Then the stream became a succession of loops, the better known being called Panther, Scholl's, Tulip, Kellogg's, Foster's, Bowlby's, Jackson's Horse Shoe, Goose Egg, and Grecian Bend. Some of the more prominent landing points were Taylor's, Scholl's, Farmington, Harris, Hillsboro, Centerville, and Forest Grove.

The number of passengers and the amount of freight varied. A February trip taken in 1869 may be cited as an average one. On this upstream journey there were nine passengers and an unrecorded amount of mixed freight; returning, there were seventeen passengers and twenty tons of freight.

T. S. Wilkes, writing in the *Hillsboro Argus* in 1927, recalled the days of early navigation on the Tualatin River. "It must have been sometime around 1865," he wrote, "when Joseph Kellogg started the Tualatin River boat line, and one of the red letter days of my boyhood was when I stood on the bank at the Jackson Warehouse and watched the column of steam and smoke curling up among the tree-tops as the *Onward* wound in and out of the bends between the Minter and the Jackson bridges."

It is probable that Trullinger was influenced toward investing in Oswego property because of the iron ore deposits in the nearby hills. That iron existed there had been known for years; but the deposits had not attracted much attention until 1861, when interested parties visited the site. The following year a local blacksmith smelted twelve pounds of the product, making from it a miner's pick and some horseshoe nails. From then on the ore deposit caused much comment, and plans for its extraction and use were made in various quarters. However, nothing definite resulted until 1864, when the deposits were thoroughly examined.

On February 24, 1865, the Oswego Iron Company was ambitiously incorporated and was at once hailed as representing what was sure to become the most important industry of the state; it would not only furnish iron for local use but would supply the whole coast.

On August 24, 1867, the company began operating the first unit of its plant. Expenditures for building the works, for opening the mines, for machinery and other materials, and for the construction of a dam, ran between $124,000 and $125,000. The dam—for operation of the works—was built across Sucker Creek, just below the foot of the lake.

The iron works, for its day on the Coast, was considered an achievement in construction, with the chimney stack— a massive pile of masonry—thirty-four feet square at the base and rising to a height of thirty-two feet. Although numerous buildings stood about it, this stack alone was destined to endure, a landmark through the years.

When the plant was in full operation, eighty men were employed—miners, charcoal burners, heavers, teamsters, and artisans. Charcoal, needed in smelting, was burned in the surrounding woods, much of it on nearby Iron Mountain.

On March 28, 1869, the Tualatin River Navigation & Manufacturing Company was organized to exploit the resources in and about Oswego and the Tualatin River. Capital stock was $100,000.

During the year, the company purchased Trullinger's sawmill and that portion of his land claim embracing the Oswego townsite, paying $26,000 for the latter. As a first job the company proposed to dig a canal to connect the Tualatin with Lake Oswego—as it was now called—and to build some kind of a manufacturing plant to use the water-power that would be created. The canal would be navigable and would make of the Tualatin a highway of commerce. A second canal would connect the lake with the Willamette River, with an added freight chute on the riverbank for receiving and sending down freight.

Not until November 1871, was the upper canal completed and opened. But the flow of water from the Tualatin was disappointing; and cold weather soon lowered the river where the *Onward's* crew were engaged in their usual pastime of clearing away snags. Meanwhile, the state had entered an ambitious railroad-building era. Confronted with opposition, the Lake Oswego-Tualatin River enterprise lagged.

Nevertheless, boat service on the Tualatin River was maintained. Finally, in 1873 the *Onward* successfully negotiated the narrow passage cut between the Tualatin and Lake Oswego.

Meanwhile, clouds had appeared in the otherwise serene sky of the Oswego Iron Company. The local ore was low-grade limonite, giving only one ton of pig from two and one-half tons of rock. Consequently production costs were excessive. What was worse, Scotch pig could be bought by the ton in San Francisco and laid down in Portland for nearly five dollars less than the Oswego plant could deliver it. It was these differences in quality and price that were to spell eventual doom for the Oswego works. To cope with such problems, and to speed production if possible and thereby lower costs, the company was reorganized several times; in the end, to little avail, as time proved.

It is said that in the spring of 1888, with a reconstruction program at its height, about 175 white men and 150 Chinese were employed; the monthly payroll was $11,000.

For this anticipated new epoch, a wharf had been built where a derrick hoisted ashore the machinery and lumber arriving daily by Willamette riverboats. Wagons conveyed the materials to the works.

For a time Oswego became an industrial center to be reckoned with. The water commissioners of Portland ordered two thousand tons of cast-iron pipe for city mains. New ore mines were opened and twenty charcoal-burning

kilns were put to work. Four miles of side-track connected
the works with the Portland & Willamette Valley Railroad,
which ran close by.

So powerful was the new furnace that within a few weeks
after it was put into operation the stack was blown through.

For nearly five years the reconstructed works produced
at a profit; the biggest year was 1890, when 12,305 tons of
pig iron were made. Then the hard times of 1893–94 struck
the Northwest. Iron prices slumped sharply and the Oswego
plant was forced to close. Later all of the plant except the
pipe foundry, which was under contract to the Portland
Water Commission, was leased to Eastern interests for two
years.

But the plans of the new concern did not mature; the
Oregon Iron & Steel Company kept its doors closed. Finally,
in the summer of 1895, with national business beginning to
show improvement, a fifty-man crew was put to work.

From 1895 till well past the turn of the century, the iron
works ran at random intervals, whenever markets and orders
warranted. In 1910 the plant was virtually abandoned.
Then during the first World War, when prices of iron sky-
rocketed, efforts were made to operate the plant, to sell or
lease it; but nothing came of these endeavors. It was then
planned to dismantle the works that had been such a long-
lived enterprise of little profit. But quite unexpectedly the
plant was acquired by a Seattle concern with some hope of
rehabilitating it. Work was begun but soon discontinued.
The works were cold forever.

In 1929 the furnace and foundry were dismantled and the
machine parts removed—some for use elsewhere, others for
the scrap heap. Only the heavy masonry walls of the plant
remained; and these were so weakened by the wrenching
out of the parts and the attrition of the elements that they
were soon leveled to earth. The great stack had fallen earlier.

To the casual eye of today little remains to mark the site
where between 1867 and 1894 some 83,400 gross tons of pig
iron were produced; where hundreds of men labored in the
heat of the great fires; and where heavy sums were spent on
plans that were never realized.

Of the pioneer sawmills and the simple frame dwellings

of the old town, no evidence remains. With the abandonment of the iron works many persons moved away. There
had never been steady employment at the foundry, in the
mines, or at the mill; and consequently the town had not
grown substantially. The warehouse at the docks had shut
its doors, the lumber mill was dead; the wooden railroad had
gone to decay, and the canal was growing over with weeds
and willows.

As far back as 1895, United States government engineers,
after a brief survey, declared the Tualatin River unsuited
to navigation. But their report was, in effect, an obituary,
for shipping on the Tualatin was already dead.

LAFAYETTE AND THE TOWNS OF THE YAMHILL

TWENTY-NINE miles above Oregon City, the saffron-colored
waters of the Yamhill River empty into the Willamette.
This stream, for half a century an important transportation
artery for pioneer westside ranchers and town builders, has
its source in the Coast Range. It is a winding, usually placid
stream, coursing to the northeast between the Yamhill and
Chehalem Mountains, and with its tributaries drains an
expansive and fertile region of oak-dotted prairies and red
clay hills. Reasonably navigable, its waters, neither very
wide nor very deep, afforded definite hindrances to early day
navigation at two points. These were Yamhill Falls—a mile
below the pioneer village of Lafayette; and a sandbar at the
river's mouth. For decades these obstructions were tenaci-
ously overcome by hardy voyagers who maintained a commercially profitable and at times eventful river life.

Because of the Yamhill, two towns came into being:
Dayton, five miles upstream; and two miles farther west,
the pioneer town of Lafayette. Eleven miles distant,
McMinnville marked the head of navigation for a time.
Originally, all of these towns faced the river and stood among
sheltering trees. Today rebuilt towns replace the old, but
the river has ceased to be their motivating force. Only an
occasional raft of logs move over the waters which in former
years bore the throb and burden of steam-driven boats.

The earliest known settler on the fertile soil about Yamhill Falls was Absalom Hembree, who arrived with his family in 1843, from Tennessee. Far-spreading Yamhill County was organized in that year. Another resident was Daniel Johnson, who came from Massachusetts in 1844. Yamhill Falls became Lafayette—until recent years spelled La Fayette—in 1847, when Joel Perkins platted on his land claim the townsite which he named for his former Indiana home.

Topographically, Lafayette was ideally situated on the north bank of the stream; the business district lay on the open flat, while the residential portion mounted the gentle slope to the northwest. Lacking a suitable building, the first court of Yamhill County was held under a large oak near the river, afterwards called the "council oak." By 1849 Lafayette had a half-dozen houses, and ferry service was in operation.

In 1848–49, a second river town, Dayton, was founded a few miles downstream by Joel Palmer and Andrew Smith, who built a sawmill on the south bank.

By 1850 many settlers had established themselves in the Yamhill country. Their only way of reaching the lower Willamette River markets was by raft or small boat down the Yamhill and thence into the Willamette, or by wagon over the single road that wound tediously across the uneven terrain of the Tualatin Plains and the west hills to Portland's back door. The land journey could be made at the rate of only ten or twelve miles a day, conditions being favorable. Not uncommonly the loaded vehicle became mired several times *en route*.

It was a welcome development when, in the spring of 1850, James D. Miller of Linn City, then in his early twenties, inaugurated water transportation on the Willamette above the falls, ascending as far as the mouth of the Yamhill River. Arriving there in a flatboat sixty-five feet long, capable of carrying 350 bushels of wheat, and manned by four Klickitat Indian oarsmen, he looked for freight which he might carry to Canemah for portage to Oregon City and lower river points. He found a part of a cargo a short distance up the Yamhill, where Louis LaBonte, a French-Canadian settler of 1836, had built a landing. From this point Miller proceeded to Dayton and Lafayette, procuring a full load of wheat and taking fifty cents a bushel for carriage.

Throughout 1850 Miller made many profitable trips by flatboat between Canemah and the towns of the Yamhill, taking two days for the up-journey and one for return. His up-trip cargoes were miscellaneous merchandise, for which he collected at the rate of thirty-five dollars a ton. Much of this freight consisted of consignments from lower Willamette River merchants to others opening stores in the new and growing Yamhill County towns. The strength of his red oarsmen and the shallow draft of his boat, ideally suited for skimming the sandbars and the rapids, enabled him to traverse his trade route in a speedy manner. Miller himself steered, with an oar at the stern. He paid each Indian sixteen dollars a round trip.

A friend of Miller's, Captain George A. Pease, commenced boating on the upper Willamette shortly after the former initiated his venture, using an old Hudson's Bay Company batteau. He employed six Spokane Indians for motive power. Races between the two craft were frequent.

For a year Miller and Pease operated without competition. Then on May 19, 1851, the *Hoosier* appeared as the first steam-propelled boat on the upper Willamette. A reconstructed long-boat built below the falls by Captain Swain and Engineer John Kruse, she was portaged to the upper river and launched at Canemah. Though small and crude in construction, she could carry wheat much faster and cheaper than any flatboat; and she soon put Miller and Pease out of business.

The first appearance of the *Hoosier* at LaBonte's Landing, Dayton, and Lafayette was a great event in Yamhill County life; and farmers flocked to see the boat. But the paying freight business which she inherited from her forerunners rapidly drew competitors. On June 6, 1851, the small *Washington* churned up the Yamhill for her share of the great grain wealth bound for lower Willamette flouring mills.

After some months of competition with the *Hoosier*, the *Washington* withdrew from the Yamhill trade and was sent down to the lower Willamette. Her place was soon taken by the side-wheeler *Multnomah*.

The *Multnomah* was followed by the *Canemah*. Like her predecessor, she did not confine her journeys to the Yamhill artery, but voyaged farther up the Willamette as well. That extended itinerary was followed also by the succession of steam-driven boats which joined upper-river traffic in the years immediately following: the *Oregon, Shoalwater, Portland,* and *Wallamet.* Only when low water exposed the sandbar at the mouth of the Yamhill were steamers prevented from ascending.

Meanwhile, the "shire town" of Lafayette had been growing slowly but consistently. The first bridge of its kind, and almost the first bridge in the whole Oregon Country, was thrown across the Yamhill there in 1851. It was a double-track structure placed on abutments of hewn timber, bolted and filled with earth and raised fifty feet above low water. On July 30 of that year the Portland & Valley Plank Road Company was organized at Lafayette and soon thereafter received a charter from the Territorial government. In the summer of 1853, Scott & Abbott inaugurated stage service between Lafayette and Portland. Amos Cook, who in the late 'forties drove portage around the falls at Oregon City, came from his Yamhill Valley farm, recently acquired, to "enter the mercantile business," and put up various buildings, among them the hotel known as "the Oregon Temperance House," conducted in 1853 by John T. Scott, the father of Harvey Scott. Among early merchants was Sidney Smith.

The first Yamhill County fair was held at Lafayette on October 7, 1854, "where at two o'clock P.M. at Marquam's corral cattle, sheep, hogs, and farm implements" were shown.

The pioneer prominence of Lafayette was described by Joseph Gaston: "Old Lafayette once figured as the 'Athens' of Oregon, and in the classic halls of its court house reverberated the thunderous eloquence of Deady, Logan, Pratt, Williams, Burnett, Chapman, Dryer, Nesmith and others. And in commercial importance it was scarcely less important than in politics. At one time Lafayette had far more business than Portland, and more than thirty stores of all kinds flourished and sent away pack trains to the mines of southern Oregon and northern California." The courthouse, costing $14,000—a goodly expenditure for that day—was erected in 1858 by Rush Mendenhall, who burned the brick nearby. As early as 1850 a railroad from Lafayette to St. Helens, through Cornelius Pass, was proposed by the *Oregon Spectator*, but enlisted no investors. The first telegraph line reached Lafayette in 1856.

Throughout the early decades of its existence, Lafayette belonged almost equally to the river and the growing network of roads. Much travel came overland from the Tualatin Plains country to the north, and some from Corvallis to the south; but freight moved chiefly by the more expeditious river route.

In 1857 the steamer *Elk* was launched at Canemah to compete with the *Hoosier No. 3* on the Yamhill run.

The *Elk*, according to Lewis and Dryden's *Marine History of the Northwest*, "has always been remembered by steamboat men because of the terrific explosion which sent most of the craft skyward at Davidson's Landing, one mile below the mouth of the Yamhill. Capt. George Jerome was in command; William Smith, engineer; and Sebastian Miller, pilot. Dr. J. R. Cardwell of Portland and Berryman Jennings were directly over the boiler, and, although the stove by which they were sitting was shattered, neither of the men was hurt." But Captain Jerome was blown up in the air to such a height that it was averred that he looked through the top of the smokestack on his way down and saw "Bas" Miller sitting on the bank. He alighted in the top of a cottonwood, and for twenty years afterward pilots and captains on the Willamette took especial pains to point out this remarkable tree to tourists on the river.

After the flood of 1861, interest in river traffic slackened somewhat; but trade remained good on the Yamhill route, which had suffered least from the ravages of the waters. Captain John T. Apperson, with a heavy interest in the burned *James Clinton*—which had operated on the Yamhill— used its machinery to build a boat which he cautiously named the *Unio*. Uncertain about the outcome of the Civil War he was reluctant to add the final "n" in view of the intense sympathy of many Oregon residents for the Southern cause.

Soon afterward he sold this boat to Captain Miller, who immediately took her up the Yamhill River. Miller did not favor the half-implied sentiments of the name *Unio*, and in the spring of 1862, while lying at the Lafayette landing, replaced the former name-board with one fully spelling *Union*. This was done under cover of darkness and the following morning those who viewed it rubbed their eyes in astonishment at the sudden transformation of name.

Hitherto, steamboating on the Yamhill had been by individual effort or by associations not too strong to prevent farmers from securing fair freight tariffs. Then in 1862, following the organization of the powerful People's Transportation Company, new and finer steamers touched Dayton and Lafayette. Consequently, freight rates went up.

A decade passed. In 1871 Ben Holladay, of Oregon railroad history, absorbed the People's line, taking over all of its boats. To buck these boats, the Willamette River Transportation Company put the *Governor Grover* on the upper river in 1873, and the *Shoshone* on the Yamhill. A rate war ensued; and, while it lasted, the farmers benefited.

As early as 1866 a special committee had reported to the Oregon Legislative Assembly that in 1864, while wheat was selling in San Francisco for two dollars a bushel, it brought the Willamette country farmers only seventy-four cents. This low price to producers was blamed on the steamboat companies. When in 1872 agitation brought the westside Oregon Central Railroad from Portland to a point about a mile north of the Yamhill River and two miles below Lafayette, the cry for lower rates still went up; but now it was the railroad that was charged with extortion, for railroad rates were higher than water-route rates.

Equally discouraging to Yamhill County farmers was the uncertainty of transportation by river during low-water periods, especially over the rapids below Lafayette and from there up to McMinnville. For years individuals and associations had advocated improvements for this stretch of the river, with little response. Then finally in December, 1869, the Yamhill Locks and Transportation Company was incorporated, with a capital stock of $75,000. Their objective was to construct two locks, one near the river mouth and one at the falls below Lafayette.

In its early years Lafayette's progress was slow, both in

population increase and business growth. By 1880 its residents numbered four hundred. It then had two dry-goods stores, several drugstores, saloons, hotels, meat markets; a wagon and blacksmith shop, a harness store, paint shop, furniture store, restaurant, and millinery establishment; there were tin and hardware stores, a flouring mill and sawmill, and a livery stable. Among its citizens were lawyers and doctors. A tumble-down, twenty-year-old Evangelical Church admonished toward well-doing. The courthouse and jail recorded and reproved the life of the town and the community.

At that date Dayton's population was 375 and many believed it had a better future than any of its neighbors. Its business life was less extensive but more industrial in nature, with three dry-goods stores, a drug store, a hardware store, two large warehouses and two blacksmith shops, a large sawmill, and—most calculated to keep the payroll up—an implement factory and wagon-making shops.

In 1888, as outgrowth of a heated contest, McMinnville became the new county seat of Yamhill. In the fray Dayton, included in the contest as a possible choice, had actually circulated petitions to prevent herself from being chosen. Local merchants feared the trade competition of new concerns that would result from the town's added importance.

Lafayette, in losing, suffered a setback from which she was never to recover. The abandoned courthouse was deeded to the city for use as a school house, then redeeded to the Lafayette Institute with the understanding that, should this institution fail, the property would revert to the city.

Not until the late 'nineties did the Yamhill farmers obtain the resources needed for construction of a locks system at the falls. In November, 1897, a letter from Brigadier-General John M. Wilson, chief of engineers, United States Army, Washington, D. C., informed the Commissioners of Yamhill County that, by act of Congress of June 4, 1897, there had been appropriated $160,000 to supplement the $40,000 appropriation of June 3, 1896, thus creating a fund sufficiently large to undertake the project.

In that year, work began about a mile below Lafayette and was carried on during the periods when low water per-

mitted. The locks were 275 feet long, with two gates to
secure the needed sixteen-foot raise of water, which also
would maintain sufficient depth to float any Yamhill steamboat as far up-stream as McMinnville. The finished locks
were opened on September 21, 1900.

As an aid to water transportation, the Yamhill Locks
came much too late. Railroad rates were cheaper than
formerly; the water route was too slow. Lafayette experienced no eleventh-hour recovery. Lafayette Institute failed,
and the property was sold for a mere $400.

As late as 1915, a few boats still traversed the Yamhill;
a few riverside farmers still chose to ship by water. But
Lafayette's period of glory was gone, leaving few traces;
and Dayton was a drowsing country village grouped around
its large public square.

RAY'S AND FULQUARTZ LANDINGS

THREE quarters of a century ago a few miles below the
mouth of the Yamhill there clung to the muddy shores of
the Willamette two landings that have long since been
washed away by the freshets. Known as Ray's Landing
and Fulquartz Landing, names now scarcely recalled by the
reminiscent, they had brief prominence as terminal points
on the narrow gauge railroad that threaded the valley
between Portland and upriver points. Two attempts were
made to join the landings by a bridge, but both were
abortive.

To a riverside claim on the east Willamette shore, came
Charles Ray in the fall of 1869. In 1850 he had purchased
the first mail route in Oregon Territory on which wheeled
vehicles were used, a line that ran between Oregon City and
Salem. This he afterward extended to Corvallis, and inaugurated the first Concord stagecoach service in the Pacific
Northwest. Still later he operated the first livery stable in
Salem, a business of no mean distinction in that day.
Finally, he took up farming, the occupation followed by a
majority of Oregonians in the early decades of settlement,
and bought a property on the Willamette not far north of

St. Paul. There he built a boat landing and established a ferry.

Like all ferry landings along the river, Ray's served as a shipping point for nearby farmers. There is no evidence that trade there exceeded the average volume of other farm landings, although it was soon marked on contemporary maps. Ray seems not to have had the town-founding ambitions that stirred some early Oregon settlers. He quietly tended his farm and operated his ferry on call. Then in 1880 came news that put a new zest into the calm sylvan atmosphere of Ray's Landing.

For Ray's Landing site, it was announced, was to become the bridge-head for a cross-state railroad which was to begin construction at Silverton, in the east Willamette Valley, in April. Already on the opposite side of the valley, in Yamhill County, the Oregonian Railroad Company had built a narrow-gauge railroad which ran from the small town of Dayton to Sheridan, on the west. Continuation of the Yamhill line southwest was in prospect, also a section from Dayton to Fulquartz Landing, on the west Willamette shore. There, spanning the river, a bridge was to be built.

Ray's Landing soon became a bustling construction center. Much of the material for the east-side Willamette link that would connect with the new bridge, was shipped by boat to Ray's wharves. There rails and equipment were unloaded and construction proceeded toward Woodburn, then toward Silverton. Grading of the right of way was of the most rudimentary nature, yet at one time in August, 1880, some twelve hundred men, including many Chinese, were at work. A half-mile of track was laid each day, the rails weighing about twenty-eight pounds to the yard. The line was opened to Silverton on October 4, 1880—a fast job. Further railroad building was under way west of the river.

Work on the Willamette River bridge at Ray's Landing began in November, 1880. But it was barely under way when early in 1881, Henry Villard strode into the Oregon railroad picture and in the name of the Oregon Railway & Navigation Company leased from its holders the entire narrow-gauge system. Curtailment of services over a portion of the system followed almost at once. Service was stopped over the ten-mile run from Ray's Landing to Wood-burn, and from Fulquartz Landing to White's junction, a distance of sixteen miles.

Not until 1886, with Villard out of the story, was service on these lines partially restored. Some restoration of disused tracks and bridges then followed.

Meanwhile, life at Ray's and Fulquartz Landings had resumed its former drowsy pace. No trains crossed overhead at Ray's ferry; the bridge, only well begun, stood unfinished.

But this drowsy order was changed—temporarily. Construction work on the bridge was resumed, train service was restored to and from Woodburn, and life at Ray's Landing was revitalized.

Then in 1887 the reorganized Portland and Willamette Valley Railway, holders of the line, passed into control of the Southern Pacific interests. Almost at once the bridge project was again abandoned. The section of road between Ray's Landing and Woodburn was discontinued from operation.

So was Ray's Landing eclipsed as a bridge-head and a railroad terminal point.

With the passage of time Fulquartz Landing was all but forgotten. In 1911, Charles Ray, eighty years of age and in good health, still lived on his farm on the Willamette's wooded shore. Season and water-depth permitting, a few steamboats passed along the tranquil river. Now and again one blew for a landing. Sometimes one stopped for grain or other produce at the site where Ray, for so many years, had plied his ferry and where once a bridge had almost been built. But the sound of iron wheels on rails had long ago ceased. Those narrow steel bands, lying three feet apart, which for several decades streamed southeastward through the evergreens and cottonwoods and over the rising land into the rich farm country of the east Willamette Valley, had been removed, while the ties on which they rested were crumbling into decay.

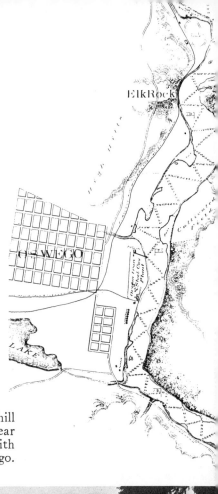

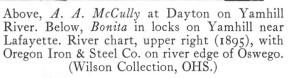

Above, *A. A. McCully* at Dayton on Yamhill
River. Below, *Bonita* in locks on Yamhill near
Lafayette. River chart, upper right (1895), with
Oregon Iron & Steel Co. on river edge of Oswego.
(Wilson Collection, OHS.)

Left is water gate at Tualatin River in 1930s. (Verne Bright photo.) View of Oswego Iron Works below was taken in 1867 by Watkins. (OHS.)

AROUND 1890 the Willamette Falls was re-surfaced and crested with concrete five feet in thickness. In the sixty years since the first white settlement, the rocks of this barrier, under the abrasive force of the waters, had worn down several feet. By that date the stream's flood was increasingly utilized by paper and woolen mills and by an electric plant, the building groups of which stood partly on the rocks, partly on the mainland of either shore, and on Abernethy Island in midstream at the fall's head. Into their giant turbine pipes the river waters were sucked, so that at times little or none spilled over the rocks. The river, under the control of man, lost some of its beauty but none of its power.

Meanwhile, other floods swept the Willamette out of its banks in 1874, 1890 and 1894. Some said the latter surpassed, by three feet, the flood of 1861. The water rose to a depth of 51.3 feet below the falls. The damage, however, was far less severe; a well-learned lesson had caused the surviving municipalities of that earlier devastation to rebuild on higher levels.

Less and less wheat was raised now in the overworked soil of the middle and upper valley, where instead sheep multiplied and pasturage widened. Much of the valley's produce went to market by rail; little traveled the river route. Inability of the government to keep the channel open as far as Corvallis for more than seven months of the year, was an added factor in the decline of river commerce. Only boats of the lightest draft could clear the upper shallows. Moreover, each winter's high waters altered portions of the irregular channel; a captain returning downstream on the heels of flood, no matter how moderate, could expect to encounter some part of the way that he had not seen or navigated before, and must alter his charts accordingly. The waters invaded the wide lowlands with unpredictable restlessness, and the stream grew broader and shallower.

Among the last of the upper river boats was the *Gray Eagle*, which ascended as far as Junction City landing in 1903, with Captain Arthur Riggs at the wheel. Fifteen years earlier, while serving his apprenticeship, Riggs had wrestled a huge stone aboard the steamer *Multnomah*, at Fisher's Landing, just below Camas on the north Columbia shore and above Vancouver. This stone was put off at a Portland dock, where Riggs reloaded it onto the *Three Sisters*. The great rock was then carried to Corvallis and in 1888 became the cornerstone of the Benton County courthouse. Now the captain, who as a youth had brought this stone upriver, took the last steamer over the extreme upper river waters; thereafter no boats journeyed above Corvallis. The descending *Gray Eagle* left behind a slowly fading past and overhead a dwindling streamer of white smoke.

After that day the bankside fuelyards no longer stood neatly stacked with cordwood. Silence deepened over the stream and gradually a semblance of the original wilderness returned to its shores. Trees interlaced deeply their branches; new growth stemmed from the old wood; small tributary streams of former canoe and flatboat commerce were screened away with precluding finality. Sandbars grew and snags piled up where no snagboats came to remove them. Only the infrequent tugboat climbed the river to tow down some raft of logs. The upper river had seen its "great day" and that day was over.

Frank J. Smith, river captain and a local historian, commented in detail on this metamorphosis in an article published in 1910 in the *Portland Telegram:*

"The river above Eugene has not been navigated for many years and from Eugene to Harrisburg only in very high stages of water. At times, years have passed without the citizens of that city ever hearing a steamboat whistle. From Harrisburg down to Corvallis, some thirty-five miles, is a winding turbulent channel that has had no regular service for years.

"After leaving Harrisburg, instead of finding warehouses filled with grain, as in the earlier days, one will see old weather-beaten, abandoned structures with roofs caved in, marking the spot where it was a time-honored custom for the farmer to meet the wheat buyer and receive the reward of his labor, making sometimes the occasion for a gala day. Many of the country maidens, now grandmothers, have danced with the ever-ready steamboatmen on the warehouse floor after the boat has been loaded.

"In some cases the river has cut these landmarks off from the mainland, and others have been left a mile or so away by the ever-changing channel. More particularly is this the case of Daw's warehouse, once a noted shipping point. Now the river has left it away inland. Immense deposits of gravel grown over with balm trees and willows intervene between the present channel and the old house. There it stands, a mute reminder of bygone days, the old weather-beaten sign still bearing the name of Sam Daw.

"The Long Tom River, once a navigable stream, which is known far and wide as the Posey County section of Oregon, has succumbed to the inevitable and has retrograded so far that it would take an experienced riverman to ascend it in a skiff . . .

"A few miles below Peoria, in what was termed Centennial Chute, a cutoff opened during the year 1876. Here the river had branched off in many different channels . . ."

In the two decades following 1910 an occasional boat ran between Oregon City and Salem, carrying freight, towing log rafts—a casual business in a speedy age. Then on August 1, 1928, Captain G. M. Walker, Portland resident, for thirty years a "steamboater" on the Willamette, and before that on the Ohio River, announced that he was working steadily on a steamer, partly new, partly rebuilt, then unnamed; she would, upon completion, he said, ply between Portland and Salem. "River boats are coming back," he announced. "They did on the Ohio, and they will here." When asked what christening the boat would have, he said: "Don't need any fancy trimmings—she's just for work. But I'm building her right. I guess you might call it a christening when we slid her off the blocks last week—an old crow sailed over just then and said 'Ha-ha!' " He thought, however, lacking a better cognomen, he would call her *Stranger*.

And so Walker's boat was named a few months later; a craft one hundred and thirty feet long with a twenty-eight-foot beam, capable of carrying one hundred and fifty tons of freight. But she found little enough to haul and her months of cruising on the Willamette were few. She was soon taken down the Columbia where she operated out of St. Helens.

Save for the small boats used for log-raft and barge towing, the days of Willamette riverboat shipping were gone and the aging captains knew it. The sounds they heard cutting through their dreams were the shrill whistles of trains and the sharp horns of transport trucks, not the deep-throated whistles of the boats, foggy with steam. Now that this was the order of their days, it was time to sit in the sun and recall a way of life that was no more, and the stories of the vanished towns.

Below the falls at Oregon City, probably in the 1920s, the *Claire* dodges log rafts perhaps waiting use in paper mills.

Portland harbor in 1937, above, reflects a different use of river, with barges and tugs, than the 1912 scene below, with Battleship *Oregon*, sailing ships, steamboats, ferry, etc. The plane is a wonder. Broadway Bridge pier in foreground. (OHS postcard collection.)

Until about 1907 the *Elmore* ran up the Willamette as far as Corvallis, then was shifted to the tourist run on the lower Columbia. "Our Jubilee" (the Fourth?) features a cannon on the lower deck, as well as holiday dress, and the location is Oregon City.

⚅ AS THE YEARS TURN: A LATER LOOK

AFTER A THIRD of a century the Willamette is curiously very much the river it was. Its course of flow, generally south to north as the land falls, with its now largely man-controlled margins, defines closely a river long familiar to sojourning life and notable to Oregon history. But in the minds of many present valley residents, historically it grows yearly more and more dimly defined. For the Willamette's world is changing, continually, gradually over the years, while the past is fading from vision and even more rapidly from the common memory.

Largely these changes are earth changes, scene changes. Particularly is this true in such sizable cities as Eugene, Corvallis, Albany, Salem, Oregon City and Portland. Annually within these corporate municipalities and their considerable environs—residential, commercial and industrial growth thickens—multiplying the turbulence of human endeavor to a degree never before known or anticipated. In such city centers of steel and concrete, massive structures standing shoulder to shoulder or sprawling in block-widths, overlay and obscure the long-familiar realities of simpler days. Likewise, concrete arteries intersect and overlay the formerly well-recognized outlines of the historic past. Megalopolis grows. Only in favored residential areas, in the occasional park and stubbornly reserved field, is verdant growth still the superior claimant of the good earth.

On the lower Willamette, at Portland in particular, there are specific aspects to this picture. Portland is the region's only fresh-water deep sea port and the second largest city in the Pacific Northwest. Here eleven bridges span the river (1973). This is the center of a web of railways and highways covering much of Oregon and southern Washington, bringing into Portland the considerable harvests of extensive farmland acreage and the manufactured products of numerous industries located throughout the region. From Portland also, similar products and produce move by air and sea to distant markets, or travel east by train and truck widely over America. Concurrently, a large human force labors, while continually throughout the region, man's desires and imperative needs

multiply and are met. Whatever all this adds up to—the
good life, as we may choose to call it—it is the life we have
made and as we celebrate it, it celebrates us.

Meanwhile the Willamette River, central in Portland's
life as in the valley's life, serves its extensive land and life
coverage without protest or applause, steadfastly maintaining its flow down the long length of its beautiful valley that
accommodates almost two-thirds of Oregon's population.

Yet there is another story that is the Willamette's and it
is as old as time. Upriver, in largely undisturbed and forested
regions—though here in logged-over portions the wilderness
has been cut away and the land denuded—all is very different. Or rather, all is very much the same. Here in a clime
of narrow and secluded watercourses, of steep tree-green,
shrub-thicketed and meadow-pocketed wilderness, human
life is scant and the seeker after primeval realities finds much
to his regard. For it is in this wild land that the Willamette-
shaping tributaries, the Coast Fork, the Middle Fork and
the more turbulent McKenzie River, gather their beginnings.

Along these developing streams long-native wildlife, afoot
or on wing, moves almost at will. Blue herons, singly and in
pairs, rise clumsily from the waters, yet with massively-
spread wings move deftly through a maze of trees. Mallard
ducks explode suddenly from behind leafy blinds. A belted
kingfisher screams angrily at any disturbance. Overhead, sometimes an osprey climbs, diving swiftly riverward to snare his
dinner. Perhaps on a sun-filled gravel bar or under an overhanging cliff, a black bear may emerge, blinking at the light.
More frequently, deer with fawns, their nostrils twitching,
lift through dense greenery and trustfully walk across a
sunny glade. The traverse of these creatures is through
dense-growth evergreens, salal, big-leaf and vine maple,
balm, alder, dogwood and willow. Their movements are over
thicketed terrain, along tortuous streams, and by turbulent
rapids-churned waters that a short distance below may be as
tranquil as the wilderness silence itself.

One can only imagine the numberless secluded springs
welling out of secret earth, gathering minutely and continually the Willamette's great waters. To this steady slow ac-
cretion are added, too, the saturating seasonal rains and the

winter's melting snows, in their time overrunning the slanted earth, congesting and overflowing contributing waterways and lowland marshes, coalescing finally into the river's central flood. So the greater stream grows out of many gradual beginnings. Magical waters evolving out of magical lands! In a region where in seasons of spring and renewal the voices of many small creatures are raised, where birds call and sing. Where later, summers fatten to their fullness. Yes, and where the abundant year, glory-crowned, terminates in seasonal rains and the ermine snows again heap the wild country. And because of this and out of this nature bestows her benevolent and considerable bounty, all to the shaping of the Willamette's 188-mile length of life-supporting river. The very waters known to Portland residents, as to middle-stream communities, large or small, as indeed throughout the valley's entire farmland and city-centered length.

Not that the Willamette is all-beneficent and blameless; far from it. For out of this primitive naturalness, as the record well shows, great havoc has come. In years of excessive precipitation, with heavy snow-melt in the mountains, floods have plunged down to valley levels, crashing destructively into cities and towns, pouring over fields, sweeping away the results of man's endeavors. And because of this continuing condition, in the later 1930s there developed such public concern that considerable measures were undertaken to control the Willamette's wild strength. Major flood-control projects were undertaken by agencies of the Oregon and federal governments, and a series of dams, reservoirs and lakes were planned and built, largely in the lower Cascade mountains, most of these on Willamette River tributaries. These projects were Detroit, Dexter, Dorena, Fern Ridge, Green Peter, others. Gradually, flooding along the Willamette has been brought under control and a desirable seasonal river-volume maintained. Consequently, too, river navigation has benefitted. And to a degree at some locations, water quality has freshened and fish life is renewed. But most of all and primary in the intent, a vastly more favorable economic security for riverside residence and occupation has been developed; and this will continue to be so.

It is in the Willamette's greater story also to observe that a renewed interest in recreational boating on Northwest waters gained headway as Oregon's second half-century dawned. In an age seeking recovery of spirit following a major world war, many recreationists took to the gently-tidal waters of the lower Willamette for marine sport. Especially of weekends they appeared, a few with large but many with small craft, motor and sail propelled. By the hundreds they shuttled over the river's cool and spacious waters. Whole families went picnicking. Designed for the service of all, waterside marinas, some with boat-launching facilities and ready gasoline, appeared at convenient locations.

This gasoline flotilla moved upriver and by the summer of 1960, in the Salem area alone, some 2,000 boaters swept gleefully over the Willamette's inviting waters. Still farther upstream on the currentless waters of the reservoirs the Corps of Engineers had created, more craft appeared. And the high-pitched clamor of their motors dispelled the formerly prevalent silence of remote places. All this has added a continuing activity to the river's life though perhaps not a vital one.

Meanwhile over the years the Willamette was generating a controversy of problems, mostly people caused. What with the damming of tributary streams, the generation of hydro-electric power, the increase of industry, the spread of settlement, and the spiralling of pollution, shouldn't we also be concerned with what we are doing to our resources? What is to become of our ecological balance if all our zeal is directed toward production and economic prosperity? Here and there still at our doorstep, as in the green adjacent mountains surrounding the Willamette Valley, are the living bounties of a generous nature. But not long to remain ours unless we utilize and direct those resources in ways not to destroy them. Yet haven't we, in many instances, been eroding our bounty? True, for some time now we have been restricting the dumping of pollutants into our rivers. And as a result, the Willamette fishery is again renewing its life, yet still too gradually. And why shouldn't the river itself be preserved, naturally and for full public enjoyment, before our materialistic prosperity has grabbed its green shores forever out of our hands?

And so, in 1967 Oregon's citizens proposed a program for

the establishment of a greenway that would extend the length of the river. Soon, by legislative action, the task of developing this plan was placed in the hands of the State Park System. As projected, lengthy portions of the Willamette's main streamway were named for acquisition. Some of these stretches included facing shores while some are intended to include old pioneer townsites and abandoned landings of another age. But the undertaking is a long-range one, with a continuous greenbelt at present impracticable, and perhaps undesirable. For instance, there are intractable bottomland stretches that seemingly defy human entry. Very well; part of the intent is to preserve the river's ecological and biological balance, for wild habitation as well as for man's popular enjoyment.

Are you a local history buff? You are a rarity among thousands. And do you sometimes wonder where the old landmarks stood, the man-made achievements of a former, more rudimentary age. The exact sites where history was made? For today most of these landmarks have faded, with all evidences gone. Old locations, even, are forgotten. What remains? Pages such as these, the few old and yellowing and not always accurate maps, scant and scattered references. Scarcely any physical facts. Time then to be asking, what now can we do to define what formerly we were, what our early lives actually were at this location and that, what our endeavors, great or small, have meant. And perhaps to ask for a last time: what have we lost?

Looking first at Eugene, head of early-day navigation on the Willamette, we already find established a green parkway closely following long portions of the river's course through town. Yet there is none of the really old of man's endeavors noticably adjacent to the river, though certain aging aspects of later times still linger. Of course one can point to the original stream-crossing location used by pioneers, beneath the present Ferry Street Bridge. Today on either shore there are serviceable boat-launching aprons and parks—no longer Skinner's Mudhole. Other adjacent downtown waterside levels are hard-surfaced or overspread by warehouses or industrial activities. Only the occasional barge, tug-propelled, and local sportcraft, move over the Willamette's calm surface. Indeed the old river makes little more than a refreshing ripple in metropolitan Eugene's daily life.

From here on downriver for eighteen miles by any road the traveler takes, he finds little to identify the historic past with the restless present. Only in scattered open-water areas is the river used for sport or for floating the occasional log boom. For a brushy stretch Goodpasture Island divides the stream. East of Junction City, the inrushing McKenzie joins the growing river. While here and there some riverside resident may thoughtfully tell you where such and such an old boat-landing lay, only the rare traveler would ask and few would look. For long sections the river is brush-grown and difficult of passage by any craft, though sometimes its bright waters come into view from the near-passing highway. On the river itself, canoe travel is favored.

So it is not until the traveler passes the two locations of Lancaster—the one lost in the altered channel and the present but hardly notable site on US 99W—and actually enters Harrisburg over the tall old bridge looking down on the Willamette, that he noticeably touches the past. But today in this agricultural trade town of former times, the past, long here, is now rapidly fading. Many of the tall, leafy trees, cottonwoods and locusts that for long decades cooled the town's hot summers, have been cut in the wake of a plan to modernize the town to contemporary needs. The railroad that came a century ago, draining off the river's scant seasonal commerce, still hurtles through the town. Two sun-drenched riverside parks greet the visitor by road or by river.

Northward from Harrisburg for the next twenty-five miles the Willamette is a generally shallow and meandering stream, variable in width and with sometimes difficult areas that provide unpredictable navigation for any craft. Gravel bars and drifting snags are encountered, and log-drifts pile up. Normal stream flow is ten to fifteen miles an hour, and all movements are casual. Through its sprawling watery domain the river divides around numerous islands, large and small, making this world a wilderness wonderland of infrequent transit. Bird and animal life are multiple, with beaver common. Rustling balm trees, black ash and alder wade in and out of the sloughs and overshadow the mingling waters.

Mistletoe-endowed oaks stand firmly footed on dry land nearby. Surrounding river-bordering cultivation makes this some of the valley's richest farm country. The Long Tom River, passing Monroe community to the west, lapses almost unnoticeably into the major stream.

Of the few early-day communities located along this east-side margin, only small Peoria lingers on. Lying close beside the river and skirted on the east by the road coursing between Harrisburg and Corvallis, its few businesses now supply only primary needs. As the years pass, a few new houses come to join the fading old, renewing the town's life. A small streamside park where steamer docks formerly lay, is county-maintained. A boat ramp provides river access.

It is in the area downriver from here and south of Corvallis, that the old townsites of Booneville and Burlington were platted, the former at the head of John Smith Island and the latter on Stahlbush Island. Kiger Island, the largest of the three land masses that here break the Willamette in its downriver movement, is best accessible from the west, by modern concrete bridge over Booneville Channel. In recent years tree growth in portions of this area has become so heavy and slough channels so filled with silt, that it is far from easy knowing just where one actually is amid the inter-lacing waters, roads and islands. The sites of both Burlington and Booneville today seem lost to precise location.

And should you be looking for the former location of Orleans, north of here, the nameboard you see today, a half-mile east of Corvallis beside the highway and far removed from the river, does not mark the town's original site at the head of Fisher Island and just north of the Marys River entrance into the Willamette. That site is now a willow-grown gravel bar, opposite and just below Corvallis at the south end of its downtown district. Here the river's many-channelled waters draw together at last.

Standing on the Willamette's west shore at Corvallis, one can readily see how favored from the start this townsite location actually was. Not that flooding waters, in years past, never encroached here—they did. But the land-shelf north of the Marys River estuary mounts so promptly higher, with hills above and beyond these the Coast Range, that the invitation to favorable settlement must have seemed obvious from the start.

Because of the difficult upper-river conditions, Corvallis early became actual head of river navigation. Here through many years the smoking stacks of steamers stood just visible above the bankside, amid many trees. Cottonwoods and maples still flourish here. But today the wharves and loading platforms, once approachable from the town's lower south end, where grain mills stood, retain only vague earth-markings of former identities. A narrow bankside parking area and walkway follows the old riverfront northward. Modern Corvallis is a prosperous university city, facing westward, rather more than toward the river. Perhaps its one most distinguishing identification with the river as a navigable stream is the occasional presence on its waters of the racing shells of Oregon State University's crew classes.

Between Corvallis and Albany, the meandering Willamette—now a single-channel stream—flows generally northward through bordering nearly level lands. On the north along progressing miles, the hills rise. Waters are calm and, as everywhere, their marginal verdure is tall and dense.

So the river follower reaches Albany. Here in a changing age much of the old and characterizing downtown riverfront structuring has gone the way of the wrecker; no vestiges of early steamer landings remain. In place new construction advances while a second long bridge crosses the Willamette's wide waters. Still, one finds the wooded shore as beautiful as ever, but for how much longer, one wonders? In sunny autumns the crowding balm trees stand tall and golden. At the town's foot, Bryant Park, equally wooded, occupies still its ample space where the cool Calapooya spills into the Willamette from the southeast. Even today, viewing this river-juncturing location, it seems easy to accept the early though hardly favorable designation of "Hole in the Ground," enchanting as the site has remained. And what a sizable and vigorous modern city Albany is, spreading away eastward and southward, inviting new growth and life!

A few miles below Albany the twin mouths of the Santiam River enter the Willamette, while the Luckiamute from the west flows in just below these. Control of the Santiam's waters at Detroit Reservoir, thirty-five miles eastward, greatly affects the water-level stability of the Willamette, particularly in seasons of much or little precipitation.

The small town of Buena Vista, thirteen miles below Albany on the west shore, survives as one of the river's most picturesque communities. It is still one of the important mid-valley river crossings and ferry service continues in regular operation. But the pioneer brick and tile works that for twenty years prior to the turn of the century, supplied the town's industrial hardihood, no longer displays the decaying kilns and work sheds it still retained a third of a century ago. Instead, this riverside area is levelled and parked and a modern boat ramp tilts down to the waters that in former times floated the cargo vessels that carried local products to downtown river markets. Here and there in banksides, fragments of burnt clay may still be found.

Travelers continuing downstream can expect to pass some of the middle valley's more important landing sites, some of these once industrious "fuel yards" for operation of the steam boilers that propelled the ships. Named among these are Judkin's, Ankeny's, Whitman's, Murphy's, with the landing at Ankeny Bottoms the great fuel yard of the upper river. Few are recognizable today, however, without local reminder, and none are of consequence in the river's present life.

It is at this point, either way up and down the river for some ten miles, that the river traveler most becomes conscious of the prevailing stillness. This is unlike other river portions, where well-traveled roads or freeways closely parallel the stream, and the roar of traffic is constant or frequent. But here only the infrequent motor of small private boat or side road vehicle troubles the stillness.

Further downriver, at Independence, the old and the new jostle elbows, with much of yesterday's architecture still characterizing the town. Indeed Independence would seem to be the one river-related community least altered by the hand of time. The Willamette, here almost at ankle level, continues calmly past the city's center, on its east margin, little concerned with the activities of prosperity. And one must believe the unhurried populace likes it that way. Northward the bottomlands spread shallowly and broadly, particularly along the river's western margins. Eastward the Salem hills climb, though Salem itself is still eight miles below. Through marshy, low country Rickreall Creek, pride of local fishermen, enters from the west. Waterfowl make this section a favored haunt and birds an avian paradise. Gradually the river widens, breaking into divergent sloughs, one of which brushes the pioneer site of Eola, or old Cincinnati. But today much of that location is overspread by the expressway coursing between Dallas and Salem while the river in this widening area has altered its margins at several locations. Likewise, the small cluster of habitations that was old Eola, long ago moved to higher levels, climbing northward into the Eola Hills.

It is in these widening waters that the Willamette becomes a recreational playground for Salem-area boating enthusiasts. Over these waters moves an occasional log raft, bound for Salem mills. And here too, the hum of industry and harsher traffic begins to be heard in heightening volume.

At Salem, Oregon's capital city, the Willamette turns abruptly northward, flowing under twin highway bridges where little more than a decade ago only one such bridge crossed. The railroad bridge long in service is close by on the north. An inviting marine park lies just beneath these, on the west shore. But the traveler, intent on acquainting himself with the living river and the lingering aspects of history, does not tarry at Salem's undeveloped waterfront, glimpsing however the extensive and busy city above. Rather he keeps asking himself what time has done to the old river, and where now is the fading past? Recalling that from here on downstream much of Oregon's early and significant history was enacted at scattered riverfront locations. Also growing aware that, if following the river itself, he must pass many abandoned and crumbling landings and old dock sites, washed clean by the flooding years. Reference tells him too that some of these are still enumerated by their early names: Savage, Kaiser or Kizer, Rice Bar, Doak's, Spong's, Labish, Simmon's, Garrison's—with little regard that over the years, in common parlance, some names have lost their possessive apostrophe. Just as some are lost to actual location and memory, even to the reminiscent few. Doak's Ferry lives on as Lincoln.

In visiting Lincoln, the history seeker traveling by the river's west side highway, drops down to near water-level acreage that brings him through open meadow—not orchard today—to the cluster of well-kept houses that is the modern community. But no commerce moves through here today, and no one would want such renewal. Great maples arch overhead. Other maples and alders and brush-thicketed growth—save where cultivation has cleared it—bower the Willamette's bankside, with the shadowy river moving discernably below. Examination reveals still some of the gradings down which wheat-laden wagons once moved to loading platforms for downriver shipment. Great days those, a century ago! But today in this idyllic pocket of retreat, no such activity hums. Yesterday, all time, any time, seems far away. The one anachronism linking this place with the feverish age we all share, is the fabricated steel tower that lofts the region's electric power lines overhead.

After passing the highway marking of the first brick residence west of the Rocky Mountains—not a brick remains in the cultivated field where the George Gay house stood as late as the 1940s—the traveler continues northward several more miles to the road-turning that brings him to the riverside community of Wheatland. For the Willamette has once again turned away from him, to the east.

Wheatland is today a community of "little landers," and their modest frame houses stand amid small, flourishing gardens where flowers bloom profusely in season. About them wide orchards and open, sunny fields convey a feeling of contented security. Wheatland is the second and middle ferry-crossing of the Willamette, now operated by the State and at the exact location maintained for decades by the pioneer settler Daniel Matheny and later by his descendents. A granite marker of recent placement stands at the entrance to the estate property.

At Wheatland the history-minded traveler crosses the Willamette, here sizable in width and popular with small boaters. And here, just south of the eastshore ferry apron and a short half mile through the trees but buried and inaccessible in the brush, is the site of the Jason Lee Mission, notable in earliest Protestant church annals. It continues to give name to the broad brushy lowlands, some cultivated, some still in "the bush," long known as Mission Bottom. Today this area is central in the State Parks program of greenway development.

Two miles farther east, the exiting ferry road junction with the Salem-St. Paul highway over which one continues northward, soon junctioning again to the left, where the traveler passes the location of old Fairfield, the once prosperous wheat-shipping port. But the community characteristics of Fairfield, so evident on the river's high east shore in the 1930s, are now missing. The river road has pulled away from the bluff and the few commercial structures formerly here, have been moved to lower locations or torn down. Below, at river-edge, the long wharf which for so many years was charged with activity, is gone also. Entrance to the lower site of Fairfield is by private road, and on foot only.

Today's frequenters of the waters, coursing through these wild stretches, report sighting ducks, geese, blue herons, rail-tailed hawk, and the occasional golden eagle. From this point northward for some five miles, large and agriculturally productive Grand Island divides the central stream. The river draws together again at Lambert Bar above St. Paul. Vine maple, willow and salmonberry multiply. Areas of good fishing abound.

San Salvador Park and Beach (never so named on early maps), accessible by road from nearby St. Paul, offers attractive entry to the Willamette's sandy east shore. Here the river is broad and on the offshore bar Carnelian agates, agatized wood and jasper are found. Picnickers come here. The area affords a serviceable boat-launching apron. Just below and on the same shore though today difficult of access by any road, lies historic Mission Landing, point of river entry to early day Catholic church activities on French Prairie. Almost directly opposite and across the river, at a point closely below the old town of Dayton, enters the narrow, now scarcely navigable Yamhill River. Largely log rafts use its waters. A short distance upstream and long unused, Yamhill Locks is a blackened hulk of concrete.

While there is no chapter in this study of the river on the
St. Paul or Mission Landing, the location near St. Paul came
into use as a convenient site for arrival and departure of
dignitaries and servants of the Catholic church in Oregon—
individuals whose ecclesiastical activities were first centered
at St. Paul, among the French Canadian residents of the
Prairie. A considerable responsibility, surely. And maintain-
able by river passage only, and over the crude bankside
footings of Mission Landing.

Outside mission supplies also came in at this point. But
commercial activities and the shipping of crops seem to have
been handled largely through Champoeg and Butteville,
nearby to the northeast, or at Fairfield farther south. Access to the river at Mission Landing, though direct, was
steep. Principally—as the records show—this St. Paul community port was the Mission's most immediate travel link
with the northern Oregon settlements, and with ocean passage to the outer world. But there were numerous other
similar convenience landings along the Willamette in those
early times. Today this landing lies at the foot of Mission
Road, on private property.

Of interest to the railroad-minded historian should be the
locations of Ray's and Fulquartz Landings, the one a few
miles below Mission Landing, and the other, Fulquartz,
directly across the river and near Dundee. Both of these
sites are now almost forgotten. The writer and his son shared
several inquiring occasions meandering both river shores,
seeking with some bewilderment these long-abandoned landings, certain only of their approximate locations, again on
private property.

Downriver from Ash Island, where the Willamette curves
directly eastward for an ensuing fifteen miles, the river's
course is invitingly broad and beautiful and is much favored
by boaters. In journeying, one passes the old and substantially prosperous community of Newberg, spreading northward over its gently rising land level. But the steel bridge
that for many years marked the crossing from the expansive
French Prairie on the south and east, to the equally historic
Chehalem country of American settlement, is gone, replaced
by a larger and more modern bridge several miles below. It

is of interest that this new route passes closely the near-river location of Willamette Post, oldest fur storage station of white settlement in the Willamette country.

A few miles farther east, the traveler by whichever route, road or river, comes to historic Champoeg, acclaimed and honored (though not without some controversy among historians) as the center of Oregon's earliest endeavors toward self-government.

How forested the shore-cresting banks have grown! So much more so today than even a third of a century ago. For peer as the viewer will, the broadly placid waters below can scarcely be seen through the dense foliage. Likewise the meadow to the south, where Champoeg's pioneer streets once spread openly to the sun, is today yielding its airy freedom to innumerable trees, great Oregon maples, fir and ash. Everywhere the wilderness is growing back. In former times red natives annually burned over the great Willamette Prairie, thereby rounding up the wild game for killing and winter food, consuming also some of the region's constantly multiplying growth, but today this green proliferation continues unrestrained, save as modern development moves in to alter the patterns of settlement. Leaving one to wonder whether man's present ardent concern for total preservation of his natural habitat, may not, with the years, prove too excessive a bounty.

The Willamette at Champoeg is a sense-pleasing stream, certainly. Sun-filled or rain-wrinkled, as weather dictates, it is a stream of many moods; its waters reflect the green of its forested shores. And the river, as in the park above, is a sporting area. Boaters gather here, their gasoline-driven engines confounding with noisy glee the otherwise prevelant stillness. And where formerly steam-propelled sternwheelers of pioneer commerce drew up for bankside landing, now only the small pleasure craft nose in. Swimmers, water skiers, the shouting throat of youth, make joyous the weekends of summer. For decades now, by hundreds and by thousands, Oregonians and Oregon's visitors, have made Champoeg State Park the valley's primary center for picnicking. History here? But all that was something that happened long ago.

As a footnote, it may be recalled that the last of the stern-

wheelers, the *Claire*, visited Champoeg from Portland, on
June 29, 1952, bringing more than one hundred celebrants
for one of the last annual picnics of the Veteran Steamboatmen's Association. Later, its last great day ending as it
moved down stream, its melodious three-note whistle blew
a final goodbye to the age of steam on the Willamette.

What more of riverboat history is left to characterize the
river above Willamette Falls as a transportation artery? A
few miles below Champoeg, on the same east-south shore,
the pioneer community of Butteville, once a boisterous
center of French Prairie life, sinks yearly ever more deeply
into the pocket of time; its once commercial features fading
gradually into the common anonymity of the wooded shore.
Plank docks, long known here, are gone, and its few remaining streets are vaguely defined.

From here on downriver one is to be reminded frequently
that residential development is increasing everywhere. Scattered older homes have long stood adjacent to the river, but
now new construction is annually more and more evident.
This is stimulated by the fact that as the traveler enters the
constantly widening Portland metropolitan perimeter, areas
that might have seemed distant once are today convenienced
by an expanding freeway system, making country living
ever more inviting and possible, even for the wage-earning
thousands.

At Wilsonville, site of long-operating and important
Boone's Ferry, the Willamette today flows under twin
bridges, carrying overhead to and from Portland and Salem
the major volume of western Oregon's motorized traffic. A
constant roar of it. Nearby, residential development prolif-
erates. A few miles below, the Molalla River, consuming
into its flow the sluggish and wide-wandering Pudding River,
enters the Willamette from the east. Thereafter the Canby
Ferry landings, among deeply-wooded shores, are approached
and passed. Ferry users today are many, particularly in
summer seasons of holiday travel. Further down, bottomlands spread more openly, some cultivated, some orchard-
covered. But long-neglected river landing sites of variable
early-day name are rarely recognized. Some were important
"fuel-yards" for the boats.

And thus the pilgrim to the past, scantily rewarded in his wandering search, comes to the Rock Island bend where the river makes its final turn northward through a constricting rocky chute, and heads for its plunge over Willamette Falls six-and-a-half miles distant. Just short of this point, however, the river traveler arrives at the mouth of the Tualatin River on the west side, where it dawdles over its shallows to a merging with the greater stream. Here he finds a modern marina, making boat landing or launching convenient. On higher levels to the north the old trade town of Willamette sits quietly beside its one highway, while a massive new freeway plunges by above.

And now by whatever route he takes, the traveler approaches "the falls," the great barrier of Indian and pioneer times. If he approaches by motorcraft he may choose to cross the river and pull his boat ashore at the narrow site of Canemah—as dreamy and little-regarded as ever. Or he may hug the western bluffs and move into the canal and locks that will carry him to navigable lower levels, between Oregon City and West Linn. In this passage he must brush shoulders with the massive structures of the electric generating plant and several paper mills, with their constant, sound-consuming purr always in his ears. Doing this, he moves past the several levels early occupied by Robert Moore's Linn City, before the great flood of '61 swept the town and "the works" away. Barges, some boxcar size, and boats must follow this one channel, its locks skillfully operated and available to all seeking passage, down or up the river.

What now greets the passenger? Upon entering the lower river the boat occupant looks back promptly for the cascading waters of the falls themselves. Instead those waters are largely syphoned off—as they have been for years—through industrial flumes, for operaton of the encumbering mills. Only in seasons of excessive water volume does the creaming flood arch over the rock escarpment that for centuries has made this a strategic location in the history of the region. But what has man done to his heritage of grandeur! The paper mills here provide the economic lifeblood of the greater Oregon City area, and will continue to do so.

Perhaps meaningful history still blows in Oregon City's winds, but to point and say "here" or "right over there," means little more than to recall—after a third of a century so little of the old and recognizable remains. Progressively, much of the older construction lying within local perimeters is undergoing demolition and redevelopment; a new and different age grows. This is true not only of portions of Oregon City, but adjacently as well. For instance, on the low waterfront location that was Multnomah City, and where today a few scattered houses of fifty or so years ago still stand, the massive concrete footings of a new highway bridge are planted, to lift speeding motorists over the wide Willamette. At the site of former Clackamas City, too, a half mile up that stream of Indian name, a commercially-operated earth-and-gravel works hauls away even the footprints of history. Similar earth change is everywhere. The future crowds in.

Always man stands amid his own history; he only engages former realities as facts, recorded or unrecorded. Meanwhile, much of the history he and his thousand fellow-kind progressively make, fades daily into the legend of the unrecorded. It is and always has been thus. Now and again, however, something is recollected and retold, and so passes vaguely into folk expression, colored, perhaps, by reverence or the over-expression of the garrulous of tongue. So altered by these presumptive factors, yet partaking still of actuality, certain of these stories seep back into accepted history, and are further retold. Such aspects of humanized fact, we call folklore.

And perhaps here is the place best to remind ourselves that despite any nostalgic inclination to lament unduly the lost values and beauties of a former era the river knew, that era had also its crude and raw aspects and deportments, had certainly many far from admirable characteristics. That there was in certain instances much cursing and hard-handed treatment, with some skulduggery and duplicity. But hasn't this always been so wherever man has endeavored toward gainful ends? Perhaps better that we little regard this shadow of our ugliness, in favor of the enriching worth of commendable endeavor we can remember with pride and admiration.

Continuing downriver, the history-seeking individual must by now have realized that it is human life, many lives that he has been touching—though often tenuously—at all the old townsites and landings he has visited or groped for. That such places are really lives as much as tangible or intangible realities, or lingering landmarks; and that all nostalgically remembered people once resident there are gone—persons once of high repute in the regard of their fellows, some only locally admired but others of broad personal admiration elsewhere—names only, history now. People who were the simple and priceless substance — with virtues and with faults—of which Oregon has been shaped. That the old towns one visits in passing, existent or vanished, are or were, some measure actually of their lives. All places are people, all places are history.

Consider, for instance, the dozens of old landings, most of them little noted in the records: for residents living above them or nearby these landings in their day, were convenient harbors in a river-dependent and rudimentary age. Residents, some of whom were totally reliant on river transportation for supply of their economic necessities and human concerns. Most at vaguely recalled locations today and lost to identity save in the memories of the aging few, who sometimes recall fondly "the old days at Risley's Landing when everybody came."

One of the lower river's more inviting beaches for boat launching and water sport lies at the foot of Lake Oswego's George Rogers Park, where the furnace chimney of Oswego's old iron smelter still stands. This gaping red brick structure, fenced about for preservation, lifts amid the cultivated luxuriance of seasonal bloom, and is the one historic landmark the old town boasts. Here a footbridge crosses the much-abated flow of Oswego Creek. Today happy crowds gather in the park, applauding their good hours. Also preserved here is the fog-bell of the steamer *Claire*, previously mentioned, which operated on the lower Willamette from 1918 to 1958.

Not all of the Willamette's life through this area is today recreational and of weekends, however. Daily there is a measured amount of commercial activity over these lower

waters. Tugboats pushing scows and barges, some sawdust-
filled, some bearing rolls of newsprint, others bearing mounds
of bright sulphur for the paper mills above, are seen in passage. Log rafts, less numerous than a half-century or even
ten years ago, move down to the few remaining Portland-
harbor sawmills. But few sternwheelers are seen, these operating as tugs.

Understandably, today's river-viewer seeking the historic
past would hardly find reason to stop at modern Milwaukie's
ample harbor, though it was at this eastside river location
that the Willamette's first paddlewheel steamer, the *Lot
Whitcomb*, was built. Modern log-boom accommodations are
large here.

Northward and clinging to eastside shores, lie sizable
houseboat colonies, rocking in the riverswell. Hardtack (originally Hardhack for its wild vegetation) and Ross islands
broaden the divided river as it approaches Sellwood Bridge.
In a changing age when many of Portland's industrial enterprises that for years maintained waterfront locations, are
moving away, there is consequently a freeing of river-facing
stretches for greenway development. This encouraging
restoration of the old stream's natural enchantment is to be
applauded; picnic and recreational advantages, with parklike appeal, will restore something of what once was native.
A few of the old sites, too, are being marked. Indeed, even
today one can stand at specific locations and say, "From
over there the Sellwood Ferry put out, crossing to the Fulton
district. Sometimes people went to Riverview that way. And
up there a-ways was White House Landing—the great sporting center at the turn of the century."

Moving past old South Portland and northward between
the concrete seawalls that fend waterfront Portland from the
Willamette's spring volume, today's traveler can only imagine locations where now none of the old sailing vessel and
riverboat wharves remain. True, one may recall that at the
foot of Stark Street, from earliest settlement times, Portland's busiest ferry crossed and recrossed. Laborers and
merchants, mayors and judges, standing together, face-up
whatever the weather. Whatever would Portland have done
without that ferry? Or for that matter, without the Stephens

Ferry to the south, and the Albina Ferry to the north?

Today no river-serving facilities are operative on either side of the immediate downtown harbor front, though four deep draft vessel berthings are provided. Instead, flanked by paralleling streets and streaming freeways, and in portions on the westside by green parkway with waving trees, the Willamette flows quietly through town. Farther down harbor, at other riverfront levels, however, municipal and privately managed docks, grain elevators and warehouses are operating. But with no wharves for paddlewheel craft, for none now ever come.

On nearby Swan Island, over recent decades, many changes have occurred. This island of wild swans that in the thirties and forties was the city's first airport, became a center of World War II shipbuilding activities, then was converted to drydocking and warehousing, and today continues these latter services. Thus a portion of the island's life still belongs to the river. So also at other surrounding harborside locations. But hardly with the close people-relationship of former times, when cruising craft could put in at any wharf or bankside that hailed it over. All of today's business operations are impersonal and commercial and competition-geared.

Not that we would wish to go back to the hunt-and-find river commerce of an earlier day. A more rudimentary world then, but gone now. And what do we have today, we may ask, that is not greater, though different in kind and perhaps in value? And think again, what do we ask of the past, ever, but something of ourselves; something we have lost, perhaps, regretfully yet half-acceptably? Perhaps therein is the paradox that carries the true answer: something of ourselves we have lost in the turning of the years, and this must be so and must be accepted.

Finally, should the river-viewer peer down from the lofty railings of the beautiful St. Johns Bridge, in lower Portland harbor, with the new Rivergate industrial district close below, let him be reminded that the old St. Johns Ferry operated here until the year 1934, and that at the bridge's west-shore footings once crouched the wheat-shipping hamlet of Springville, loading the rich harvests of the Tualatin Plains for world markets. But all of this is now nearly a century ago, before the coming of the railroads. Today on this same river-fronting site only localized activity is found.

Continuing its flow oceanward, the Willamette passes historic Sauvie Island, and at its tip enters the Great River of the West, the Columbia. This juncture lies some twelve miles below the St. Johns Bridge, and 101.5 miles from the Pacific. But the island's life today is little visible from water-level; at all but a few locations of recreational beachland that life is obscured by the high-rise dikes needed to restrain the combined waters of the two rivers in periods of flood. Largely the island's boat dockings lie on the westside Multnomah Channel, now little used for river traffic, but once the principal artery for paddlewheel commerce.

It is a long journey, physically speaking, that the Willamette makes from the midstate evergreen wilderness of its origins, through time and history and down half the length of western Oregon. But it is one that in some good manner everyone can undertake, as the river flows or as the road runs, or simply by the casual armchair reading of these pages. And this latter may in time be the only way our early simple greatness can be recalled at all—the history and the legend that is Oregon.

View of Wilsonville, above, about 1910, with boat landing right. (SP&S Col. OHS.) In 1973, modern freeway and railroad bridges cross river. Roads are vastly different than in photo below of horse and sulky in Clackamas County. (SP Col., OHS.) Aerial view right includes modern highway and bridge linking mid-valley riversides at Independence, with Eola hills on north horizon. (Aerial photos here and following courtesy Oregon State Parks, Geo. W. Churchill, Director Willamette Riv. Park System.)

Dexter Reservoir, above left, southeast of Eugene, gathers considerable part of Cascade snow-melt. With a near-dozen other dams and reservoirs built for flood control, the Willamette today is a much more negotiable stream in the valley's life. Right is Norwood Island area of Willamette, at mouth of Long Tom River, now a designated State Parks development in Willamette Greenway. (State Parks photos.)

Above left is Skinner's Ferry site at Eugene, marked by covered bridge used in 1880s-1890s. Most of town is out of photo at right. Today river shores here are attractively parked and modern bridge carries heavy traffic. Right view above is of present-day marina at east shore footing of what was Boone's Ferry, while below left is 1903 photo of travelers waiting for that ferry. (Seth Pope Col., OHS.) Crumbling boat locks in 1972 photo below right, are at Yamhill Falls. Adjacent state park makes this pleasant picnic site. (M. Hodge photo.)

In a year of particular Willamette flood rampage, 1894, dapper citizens boated through Goodyear Rubber Co. premises (amid floating invoices) in Portland, on 1st St.

Air view at mouth of Willamette River, head of Sauvie Island. St. Johns district is in upper middle, with Swan Island Airport above and upriver. Linnton lies on right bank at right center, below West Hills, with productive Tualatin Plains spreading westward behind them. Gillihan Landing site was at center on Sauvie Island, across from Columbia Slough. (U.S. Army Engineers photo, OHS.)

Left, well-worn pioneer road descends from River Road toward St. Paul Mission Landing site, half-mile below. Author points back toward mission, one mile to southeast. Former wagon route is probably oldest remaining evidence of kind along Willamette. Right photo is riverboat captain Seth Pope's view of landing, August 1903, with log landing platform well above low water. Growth is scant, where today banks are buried under vegetation. In aerial view, site is on top or east bank (just above Yamhill River entry from west), in Willamette's sharp turn to north. (Oregon State Hwy. Comm. photo.)

T.4S.,R.3 W.,W.M.
T.4S.,R.2 W.

55

MISSION BAR

RIVER

RAY BAR

DUNDEE BAR

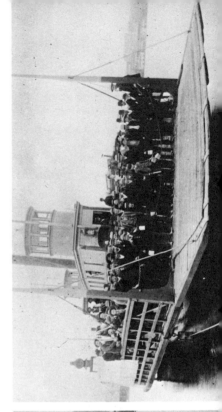

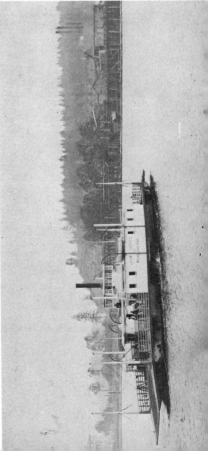

Beyond Wheatland Ferry (once Matheny's), above left, is Jason Lee Mission site, now part of Willamette Greenway development. (Hodge photo, 1972.) Right above is Corvallis ferry, c. 1905. Left below is Sellwood ferry *John F. Caples*, c. 1915; lower right shows full load on *Daisy Andrus* (built 1883), Jefferson St. ferry, Portland. (OHS Cols.)

WILLAMETTE RIVER STEAMBOAT LANDINGS
COMPILED IN 1940 BY
CAPTAIN ARTHUR RIGGS

GILLIHAN's Landing. One mile from the mouth of the river, at its confluence with the Columbia, on the north side of Sauvie Island.

BYBEE's Landing. On the south side, or west shore, just across the river from Gillihan's.

HOWELL's Landing. On the north side of the river, one-fourth mile above Gillihan's on Sauvie Island.

LINNTON. On the west shore.

SPRINGVILLE. On the west side of the river just above Linnton.

ST. JOHNS Landing. On the east side of the river, opposite Springville.

LOVER's Lane. On the east side, one-half mile above St. Johns.

MOCK's Landing. On the east side, at the lower end of Mock's Bottom, and about three-fourths mile above Lover's Lane.

PORTLAND Flour Mills. East side of the river.

OLD PORTLAND Dry Dock. East shore.

SHAVER's Dock, Albina. East side.

Ross Island. On the east shore of the river.

STEVENS Point. On the west side near Fulton.

JOHNS Landing (1973). On west side just south of B. P. John Furniture Co. site on Macadam Ave.

SELLWOOD. On the east bank.

FULTON Landing. On the west side, across the river from Sellwood.

THE OLD O. S. N. Co., Bone Yard. West side, about one mile above Fulton Landing.

LAMBERT's Landing. One-half mile above Sellwood.

THE WHITE HOUSE Landing. On the west shore, just across from Milwaukie.

MILWAUKIE. On the east side.

ELK ROCK. On the west side, just above Elk Rock Landing. This landing was the terminal for the west side narrow gauge railroad, 1886–1889, when the trestle was built around Elk Mountain.

OSWEGO Iron Works Landing. On the west bank.

OLD OSWEGO Landing. On the west side.

WALLING's Landing. Also on the west side, about two miles above Old Oswego.

RISELY's Landing. On the east shore.

STARKWEATHER's Landing. About one mile above Risely's.

JENNING's Landing. Also on the east side, now known as Jenning's Lodge.

MELDRON's Landing. One mile above Starkweather's.

MAGOON's Landing. On the west bank, at the foot of Clackamas River Rapids.

ABERNETHY Creek Landing. At the mouth of Abernethy Creek on the east side, one and one-half miles below Oregon City.

OREGON CITY. Had three landings, namely: The Sand Bank, The O. C. F. Company, and the Imperial Flour Mills Dock.

LINN City. Across from Oregon City on the west side.

OREGON City Basin. On the south side, just above the old Flour Mills, where wheat was often milled in transit.

CANEMAH. About one mile above Oregon City, on the south river bank.

BAKER's or Field Landing. On the north side, or west shore, one mile above Willamette Locks woodyard.

GANNUN's Landing. South side, or east shore, one mile above the Canemah wood-yard.

STRING Town. On the south side, one-half mile above Gannun's.

MOUTH of the Tualatin River. A landing stood on the west Willamette shore.

PULP Siding. On the south side.

PETE's Mountain. On the west side, just above Tualatin River mouth.

CRITESER Landing. West side, between Pete's Mountain and Katie Smith Landing.

KATIE Kamm Smith Landing. On the west bank, at the foot of Rock Island.

DOERNBECHER Landing. East side, just above Rock Island.

DOONEY's Landing. West side, one-half mile above Rock Island.

HOFFMAN's Landing. One-fourth mile above Dooney's, on the west shore.

NEW ERA Landing. Flouring mill, on the east shore.

CHARLIE Hinse Landing. North side, or west shore, near Rockry Reef woodyard.

FROST's Landing. One mile above Rockry Reef on the south side or east shore; a pioneer landing.

TOM Buckman's Landing. On the north side. Mr. Buckman raised hay for the Vancouver Barracks.

SHANK's Landing. South side of the river. About seven miles above Oregon City; wood-yard at this place. Terminus, road to Canby.

NOLAN's Landing. One-half mile above Shank's Landing, on the south side.

OHIO Landing. On the north side opposite Nolan's; owned by Captain John Coulter, an old-time Ohio River steamboatman.

JIM Evan's Landing. On the north side of the river, one mile above Ohio Landing. There was a woodyard at this place.

SOPHIA Evan's Landing. On the south bank, across from Jim Evan's Landing.

ADVANCE Landing. On the north side, one-half mile above Jim Evan's Landing.

MOUTH of the Molalla River or John Tice's Landing. On the south side, across from Advance Landing.

OLD Evan's Landing. On the north side, one-half mile above Advance Landing.

BLACKER's Lower Landing. On the south side, one mile above the mouth of the Molalla River.

JOHN Kruse Landing. On the north side, one mile above old Evan's Landing.

EILER's Landing. On the south side, situated on the west end of the Blacker donation land claim.

JAKE Miley's Landing. On the south side, one mile above Eilers; a wood-yard at this place.

CHAS. Wagner's Landing. On the north side, and one and one-half miles above Kruse Landing.

WAGNER's Landing. (No relation to Charles Wagner.) On the south side one-half mile above Jake Miley's Landing.

HINCE's Woodyard. On the north side, three-fourths of a mile above Chas. Wagner's Landing.

SCHULPIUS or Brobst's Landing. One-half mile above Hence's woodyard on the north side.

STROP's Landing. One-fourth mile below Boone's Ferry, on the south side.

WILSONVILLE, Lower Landing. On the north side.

BOONE's Ferry. On the south side. The ferry was established by Jesse Boone, direct descendent of Daniel Boone. He was murdered at this place.

WILSONVILLE, Upper Landing. On the north side of west shore. There was a woodyard here.

SHAVER's Landing. On the north side, one-fourth mile above Wilsonville, Upper Landing.

TAUGHMAN's Landing. On the north side, one-fourth mile above Shaver's Landing.

McCLINCIE's Landing. On the south side, one and one-half miles above Boone's Ferry.

R. V. SHORT's Landing. On the north side, one mile above Shaver's Landing.

CHRISWOLD's Landing. On the south side, about one-fourth mile above McClincie's.

EPLER's Landing. On the north side, one-half mile above Carrall Creek. This landing is on the southeast quarter of the Jefferson Shaw donation claim.

STEVEN's Landing. On the south side, one mile above Chriswold's Landing.

SHAW's Landing, later Zumwalt's Landing. On the north side of the river.

GRAHAM's Landing. On the south side, across the river from Zumwalt's Landing.

GOLDING's Landing, once Zumwalt's Landing. A ferry established here in 1854 was known as Graham's Ferry.

WALLACE Graham's Ferry. On the north side.

CARTER's or Vaughn's Landing. On the south side, just across the river from Graham's Ferry Landing.

ROLLEN's Landing, now Chris Wilhelmen's Landing. One-half mile above Graham's Ferry on the north side.

CHASE Kingon's Landing. Just across the river from Wilhelmen's Landing.

BARNHARD's Landing. One-fourth mile above Wilhelmen's Landing, on the north side.

CRAWFORD's, now MacIntosh's Landing. One mile above Wilhelmen's Landing, on the north side.

TATMAN's, now Ive's Landing. On the north side, one-fourth mile above MacIntosh's Landing.

BUCHANAN's, now Kenyon's Landing. On the south side one mile below Butteville Landing.

MAYCOCK's, now Struvies' Landing. On the north side, one-half mile above Ive's Landing.

RED Warehouse. One-fourth mile below Butteville on the south side.

BUTTEVILLE. On the south side or east shore of the river.

FRED T. Geer's, now McCully Landing. On the north side opposite Butteville.

THE Joel P. Geer Landing. One-fourth mile above the Fred Geer Landing on the north side.

OSCAR Cone Landing. One-fourth mile above the Fred Geer Landing on the north side.

BEAR's Landing, now Sellwood's Landing. One-half mile above Cone's Landing on the north side.

DAVE Weston's Landing. On the south side, one and one-half miles below Champoeg.

BROWN's Landing. On the north side, across the river from Weston's Landing.

SWAN's Mill Landing. On the south side, one mile below Champoeg.

HOPEWELL, originally Castleman's Landing. On the north side, one mile above Brown's Landing.

THOMAS Hubbard's, now Dan McCann's Landing. On the north side across from Champoeg.

CHAMPOEG Landing. On the south side, or east shore.

JIM Eldridge Landing. On the south side, one-half mile above Champoeg.

ABERNETHY's Landing. On the north side, one and one-half miles above Champoeg.

FRANK Osborne's Landing. On the south side, across the river from Abernethy's Landing.

NEWMAN's Landing. On the north bank, one-fourth mile above Abernethy's Landing.

EVERHART's Landing. On the south side, one-fourth mile above Frank Osborne's Landing.

GEARIN's Landing. On the south side, three miles below Newberg.

WINOOSKIE Landing. This was the old Farmers' Warehouse at one time; one-fourth of a mile below Newberg on the north bank.

NEWBERG Landing. This was originally Rodgers' Landing.

ASH Island Landing. One-half mile above Newberg.

MARKLEY's Landing. On the south side or east shore.

YEAGER's Landing. On the east side, at the head of Ash Island.

FULQUART's or Dundee Landing. On the west side, at the head of Ash Island.

MORGAN's Landing. On the west side, one-half mile above Fulquart's Landing.

RAY's Landing. This landing on the east side, was the original Davidson's Landing. It was here that the steamer *Elk's* boiler exploded in 1875.

CRAWFORD's Landing. On the west shore, opposite Ray's Landing.

MOUTH of the Yamhill River. On the west side.

HELL-ROARING Smith's Landing. On the east side, one-fourth mile below Mission Landing.

ST. PAUL or Mission Landing. On the east bank.

BRANTANA's Landing. On the south side or east shore, one mile above Mission Landing.

DOONEY's Landing. On the north side, two miles above Mission Landing.

CAREY Bend Landing.

CANTIANNA Bar and Landing. On the east side.

WESTON's Landing. On the west shore side, five miles above Mission Landing.

SAGER's Landing. On the west side, two miles above Weston's Landing.

COFFEY'S Landing. On the east bank, across the river from Sager's.

JACKSON Bend Landing and Warehouse. On the east side, about three miles above Coffey's Landing.

PHIESTER'S Rock Landing. On the east bank, at upper end of Jackson Bend.

LAMBERT'S Bend Landing. On the north side, at foot of Grand Island. There was once a warehouse here.

DURETT'S Landing. On the east shore, two miles below Fairfield.

DUKE'S Slough. A landing on the west side of Grand Island, across from Durett's Landing.

FAIRFIELD. On the east shore. An early grain-shipping port.

GRAND Island. A landing on Grand Island, on the east channel.

IMLAW'S Landing. On the east side, about one mile above Fairfield.

ELDRIDGE'S Warehouse Landing. On the east bank.

TOMPKIN'S Landing. On the north side, or west channel, on Grand Island.

LOWER Wheatland. On the west side; an old warehouse site.

UPPER Wheatland. The main Wheatland landing.

EAST Wheatland or Lafollette Landing. On the opposite bank.

MILL'S Woodyard. On the west side, one-fourth mile above Wheatland.

GARRISON'S Landing. One and one-fourth miles above Upper Wheatland, on east shore. This was the Lee Mission site.

JOE Simmons' Landing. On the east side, three and one-half miles above Wheatland.

LABISCHE Landing. On east shore.

SPONG'S Landing. On the east side, across the river from Lincoln.

LINCOLN. A large grain shipping point. Two warehouses, one stood on the west shore.

BEARDSLEY'S Landing. Two miles above Lincoln, on the opposite shore.

RICE'S Bar Landing. Opposite Beardsley's Landing.

KAISER'S Landing. Three miles below Salem, on the east bank.

SAVAGE Landing. On the west side, two and one-half miles below Salem.

SALEM. On the east bank, at the mouth of Mill Creek.

LANDING on Brown's Island. Just above Salem.

EOLA Landing. Also on the north side, just above the Baughman and Du Ran Chutes.

RICKREALL. At the mouth of the Rickreall River on the west shore.

HALL'S Ferry Landing. On the east side, about eight miles above Salem.

ED DOVE'S Landing. On the west shore of Birds Island, about four miles below Independence.

ROCKEY Point. On the east bank, three miles below Independence.

INDEPENDENCE. On the west shore.

KREB'S Hop Yard. Two miles above Independence on the west side.

JUDKIN'S Landing. On the east side, three miles above Independence.

SIDNEY Landing, originally Ankeny's Landing. On the east side.

WHITMAN'S Landing. On the south side, or east shore just above Sidney.

MURPHY'S Landing. Two miles below Buena Vista, on the west bank.

BUENA Vista. Also on the west side.

EAST Buena Vista. Across the river from Buena Vista proper.

MOUTH of the Luckiamute River. On the west side.

MOUTH of the Santiam River. On the east side.

BLACK Dog Landing. On the east bank, two miles above the Santiam River.

WELLS' Landing. About two miles above Black Dog Landing on the west side.

SPRING Hill. On the west side, two miles above Spring Hill proper.

ALBANY or Takenah. On the south side or east shore.

RAINWATER'S Landing. On the north side, about one and one-half miles above Albany.

Calapooya River. Flour mills once stood at the mouth of the Calapooya River, on the south Willamette bank.

BOWERS' Rocks. On the north side, four miles above Albany.

HALF Moon Bend and Landing. On the east side about five miles above Corvallis.

ECKLAND'S Landing. On the north side, half way between Half Moon Bend and Corvallis.

CORVALLIS. On the west side.

ORLEANS. Across the river from Corvallis.

FISHER'S Mill. At the mouth of Mary's River on the west side.

BURLINGTON or Stalbush's Landing. On the east side, four miles above Corvallis.

BOONEVILLE or Booneville Slough. On the west shore.

COON's Landing, Centennial Chute. On the east side.

PEORIA. On the east side, about ten miles above Corvallis.

IRISH Boy's Landing. Mouth of the Long Tom River, on the west side.

HOOVER Slough and Landing. On the south side, four miles above Peoria.

Dow's Landing. On the west shore.

FINLEY's Landing. A large grain warehouse stood on the west bank.

CUMMINGS' Landing. On the east side, about eight miles below Harrisburg.

INGRAM's Island Landing. In midstream.

HARRISBURG. On the east shore of the river.

LANCASTER, or Woody's Landing. An early port town on the marshy west shore.

COFFMAN's Landing. About one-half mile above Lancaster.

JUNCTION City. About five miles above Harrisburg, on the west side.

EUGENE City. On the west side, head of navigation.

SPRINGFIELD. Occasional head of navigation; on the east shore.

ORIGINAL SURVEY LOCATIONS
WILLAMETTE RIVER TOWNSITES
Township, Range and Section Readings
Willamette Meridian

LINNTON—T 1N, R 1W (sec 3)

SPRINGVILLE—T 1N, R 1W (sec 11)

PORTLAND—T 1S, R 1E (sec 3) (foot of Morrison St.)

MILWAUKIE—T 1S, R 1E (sec 35)

OSWEGO—T 2S, R 1E (sec 11)

CLACKAMAS CITY—T 2S, R 2E (sec 20)

MULTNOMAH CITY—T 2S, R 2E (sec 30)

LINN CITY—T 2S, R 2E (sec 31)

OREGON CITY—T 2S, R 2E (sec 31)

CANEMAH—T 2S, R 1E (sec 36)

WILLAMETTE—T 3S, R 1E (sec 2)

BUTTEVILLE—T 3S, R 1W (sec 32)

CHAMPOEG—T 4S, R 2W (sec 2)

RAY's AND FULQUARTZ LANDINGS (opposite)—T 4S, R 3W (sec 1)

LAFAYETTE (via Yamhill River)—T 4S, R 4W (sec 1)

MISSION LANDING (at St. Paul)—T 4S, R 3W (sec 13)

ST. PAUL—T 4S, R 2W (sec 19)

FAIRFIELD—T 5S, R 3W (sec 13)

WHEATLAND—T 5S, R 3W (sec 34)

LINCOLN—T 6S, R 3W (sec 34)

SALEM—T 7S, R 3W (sec 27)

EOLA (Cincinnati)—T 7S, R 4W (sec 13)

INDEPENDENCE—T 8S, R 4W (sec 28)

BUENA VISTA—T 9S, R 4W (sec 23)

ALBANY—T 11S, R 3W (sec 6)

CORVALLIS—T 11S, R 5W (sec 36)

ORLEANS—T 11S, R 5W (sec 1)

BURLINGTON—T 12S, R 4W (sec 19-20?)

BOONEVILLE—T 12S, R 5W (sec 36)

PEORIA—T 13S, R 5W (sec 8)

HARRISBURG—T 15S, R 4W (sec 16)

LANCASTER—T 15S, R 4W (sec 20)

EUGENE—T 17S, R 4W (sec 29) (ferry crossing)

SPRINGFIELD—T 17S, R 3W (sec 35)

Index

Portland's "ship boneyard" and harbor, from traffic, perhaps about 1905. (Captain William Goggins Collection, OHS.)

Boating "on the river" above, near Ross Island, around 1910 (Stout Collection).

Page to left shows Willamette flood of 1894 at windowsill height on Portland's Third Street. Rowboat traffic has taken over in this view of section from Washington Street to Burnside.

Peoria's bucolic character, shown here in late 1930s, has remained little changed over many years. Half a century earlier its riverside docks loaded such upper valley produce as wheat, hides, wool and cured pork. A pottery, located on Muddy Creek to northeast, utilized local clay. (FWP, T. J. Edmonds photo.)

BACK COVER: Steamboat wheel (*Henderson*). Lawrence Barber photo, Bates Collection, OHS.

FACING: Map of Upper Willamette, Sheet No. 14, Tualatin River to Sellwood. Surveyed under direction of Major James C. Post, Corps of Engineers, U.S.A. by J. H. Cunningham, Asst. Eng. Sept. 1895. OHS Collections.